A Portrait of Chen Wangting, founder of Taijiquan

A Portrait of Chen Changxing, Chen Family's 14th generation Taijiquan master

A Portrait of Chen Fake, Chen Family's 17th generation Taijiquan master

A Portrait of Chen Zhaopi, Chen Family's 18th generation Taijiquan master

A Portrait of Chen Zhaokui, Chen Family's 18th generation Taijiquan master

Author's Photo, taken in UK

Family Photo, in front of Chen Zhaopi's Tomb

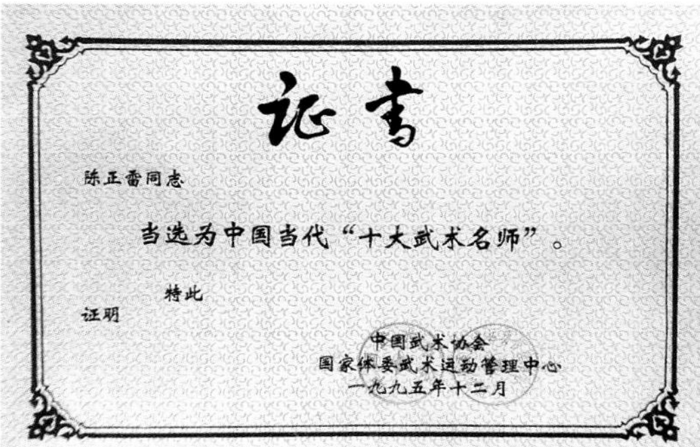

证书

陈正雷同志

当选为中国当代“十大武术名师”。

特此
证明

中国武术协会
国家体委武术运动管理中心
一九九五年十二月

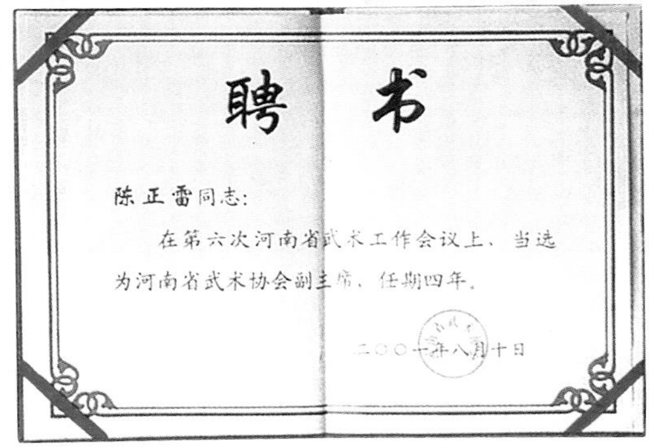

聘书

陈正雷同志：

在第六次河南省武术工作会议上，当选为河南省武术协会副主席，任期四年。

二〇〇一年八月十日

A Certificate of “Top Ten Wushu Masters” of present day China

十大武术名师

中国武术协会
国家体委武术运动管理中心
一九九五年

Board of “Top Ten Wushu Masters” of present day China

Author's Taijiquan Posture Photo

Author's Sword Posture Photo

A Lecture in UK, April 2003

Teaching in UK, April 2003

Teaching in France, April 2003

A Lecture in the USA, July 2001

Chen Style Taijiquan, Sword and Broadsword

by Chen Zhenglei
19th Generation Master

Translated by Zhang XinHu, Chen Bin,
Xu Hailiang, and Gregory Bissell

Table of Contents

Author's Preface

Chinese Wushu or martial arts has a long history and possesses many schools and styles. Taijiquan is one of the exquisite works of Chinese Wushu and is deeply loved by all for its positive effects in health preservation and self-defense. It is becoming more popular with each passing day.

Taijiquan is based on the boxing style handed down within the Chen family, and is in accordance with the theory of *Book of Changes* or *Yi Jing*, the traditional Chinese medical theories and practices of *Jingluo*(the main and collateral channels through which the body's internal energy passes), *Daoyin*(gymnastics for guiding and harmonizing the energy within the body), *TuNa*(literally exhaling the stale air through the mouth and inhaling the fresh air through the nose-breathing exercises or qigong) and also the principles of dynamics.The creators of Taijiquan comprehensively summed up all of the above in creating boxing routines whose movements have the characteristics of alternating Yin with Yang,hard force with soft force,and quick movements with slow ones;having leaping and rapid energy releasing movements,and being possessed of a relaxed,yet resilient and wave-like,vibrational type of energy. This is in accord with human physiology and natural principles,and that is why the art is known as "Taijiquan"(boxing art based on the Chinese cosmological principle of the primordial state of matter possessing the two inherent potential energies of yin and yang).

Chen style Taijiquan is the origin of the other main styles of Taijiquan. Over the course of the last one hundred years,it has been handed down from generation to generation with the same dedication of purpose. It has subsequently developed into the Yang style,the Wu(Jianquan) style,the Wu(Yuxiang) style and the Sun style of Taijiquan.Taijiquan has become well known throughout the world due to each of these style's contribution to the development and popularization of Taijiquan.

At present,the Taijiquan routines still practiced in Chenjiagou (Chen family village)are:First Routine(Old Style),Second Routine or Paochui (Old Style),First Routine(New Style),Second Routine or Paochui(New Style),First Routine(Small Style),Second Routine(Small Style),and,Five Types of Push Hands Practice.

The weapon routines are:Single Taiji Broadsword,Double Taiji Broadsword,Single Taiji(Straight-Edged)Sword,Double Taiji Sword, Taiji Twin Mace(iron rods),Lihua Spear with White Ape Staff, Spring and Autumn Great Broadsword,Three Step Pole(two-man set),Eight Step Pole(two-man set),Thirteen Step Pole(solo set),and Paired Practice with Long Pole versus Long-handled Grain Flail(Shao Gan Dui Lian).(Pole = a long spear without a spearhead). These routines still preserve their original flavor and self defense aspects.I have already systematized and published in Chinese all of the above routines.

From an early age, I studied the Old Style systematized by Chen Chang-Xing of the fourteenth generation; learning the First Routine, the Second Routine, the Taiji Broadsword, Spear, Sword, Staff and other weapons as well as push hands and the theory of Taijiquan from my father's elder brother, Chen

Zhao-Pi. In 1972, after Chen Zhao-Pi passed away, I studied the First Routine and the Second Routine of the New Style (that my great uncle, Chen Fa-Ke, had established in his later years), and also the techniques of push hands and *Qin Na* (arm twisting techniques) all from my father's younger cousin, Chen Zhao-Kui (third son of Chen Fa-Ke). I was very fortunate to have had over twenty years of instruction in the art of Taijiquan by these two masters of the previous generation, and as a result have a good grasp on the basics of the different sets and their training methods. Later, I was also able to learn by practicing and exchanging knowledge with my gongfu brothers. Further researching Taijiquan, I have been able to gradually and continuously raise my level of skill.

Chen Zhaopi

Since 1978, along with the adoption of our country's reform and open policies, international cultural and sports exchange have become much more frequent. Taijiquan has gradually become known throughout the world and more popular. More and more people are coming to Chenjiagou to exchange techniques and learn Taijiquan. "Up till now, Chenjiagou has received over 3000 visitors, students, and over 180 delegates from more than 20 countries and regions, such as Japan, the United States, Singapore, Malaysia, Canada, Hong Kong, Macao, and Taiwan. Some of the Taijiquan masters from Chenjiagou are often invited to teach and give lectures in Japan, Singapore, France, Switzerland, and Italy. Especially noteworthy in the development of Taijiquan, the September 1992 China, Wenxian International Annual Meeting of Taijiquan put the development of Taijiquan on a new upsurge. Thousands of Taijiquan enthusiasts from 24 countries and 40 organizations attended the meeting.

During the meeting, people discussed the development and popularization of Taijiquan, and expressed the view that written materials on Taijiquan, in languages other than Chinese, are urgently needed. Though already published in Japanese, the teaching manual *Chenjiagou Taijiquan* is far from filling the pressing need of international Taijiquan enthusiasts. Thus, I have exchanged views with Mr. Zhang Xin-Hu of China and Mr. Gregory Bissell of the United States on the publication of *Chenjiagou Chen-style Taijiquan* in English. Through our mutual efforts, with the support of Great Circle Publishing Company, and the translating abilities of Mr. Zhang Xin-Hu, Mr. Gregory Bissell, Mr. Clarence Lu, and the graphic design and layout work of Mr. Herbert Rich, the book *Chenjiagou Chen-style Taijiquan* has finally become a reality. This book will not only promote the friendship between countries, but will also promote international cultural exchange and improve the course of mankind's health conditions through helping to spread more information about the health benefiting techniques of Taijiquan. It will have a far-reaching influence on Taijiquan's development.

Chen Zheng-Lei 12/19/92

Chen Wang-Ting and Jiang Fa

Chen Wangting (right) and Jiang Fa

The stories about Chen Wang-Ting (1600-1680) and others within the Chen family tradition serve to inculcate moral standards in the minds of the listeners. They probably began as oral tales, passed on by village elders to the younger generation. There is probably no better example of the didactic purpose they serve than is to be found in the so-called *Xu Huai* of Chen Wang-Ting (see below).

The following biographical anecdote on Chen Wang-Ting is from the *Fu Lu Chen Shi Jia Sheng* or *Appendix of Chen Family Chronicles* written down by Chen Xin at the beginning of the 20th century.

Chen Zou-Ting, otherwise known as Chen Wang-Ting, was a soldier during the last days of the Ming Dynasty. He became a civilian scholar when the Qing Dynasty overthrew the Ming. He was skilled at Taijiquan.

Once, while on his way to visit a friend in Shanxi Province, he came upon two youths wrestling each other and two old men nearby watching. Chen Wang-Ting stopped to watch the contest. One of the old men said to him, "would our guest like to try his hand at a wrestling match?" Chen Wang-Ting said, "yes". The old man ordered one of the youths to wrestle with Chen Wang-Ting. The youth grabbed him by the waist and lifted him up off the ground. The youth then proceeded to bounce Chen Wang-Ting's stomach with his knee three times and throw him to the ground. Suddenly, it was as if the two old men and the two youths had vanished into the twilight, they were nowhere to be seen. Chen Wang-Ting was crestfallen so he just returned home.

Li Ji-Yu, a military licentiate of Dengfeng County, was a friend of Chen Wang-Ting. The people of Dengfeng had rebelled because of the local officials' intolerable exactions. Li Ji-Yu became the leader of the rebellion. Chen Wang-Ting went to dissuade him. When he ascended the mountain where the rebels were, the arrows fell like rain but he was not wounded. He came upon one of the rebels and chased him three times around the top of the mountain without catching up to him. After Li Ji-Yu had been defeated, Chen Wang-Ting had a servant named Jiang. He was the one that Chen Wang-Ting had chased on that day; he could catch a hare in one hundred paces and was skilled in the martial arts. Chen Wang-Ting lived in troubled times. He took part in countless battles, but with the fall of the Ming Dynasty, all was lost in the ensuing chaos. The only written work that he left behind was a song in "long and short" verse. It goes like this:

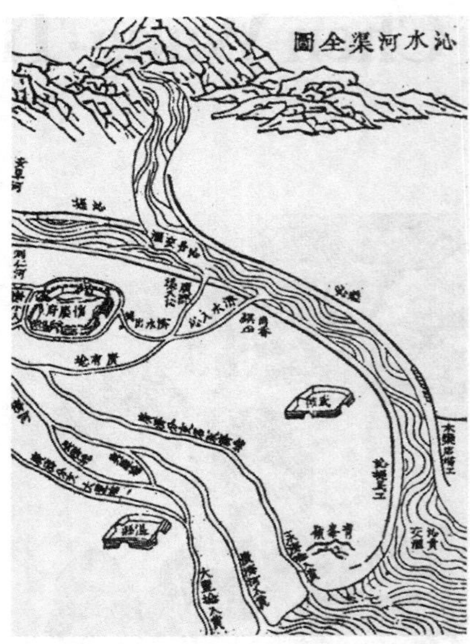

Detail of a Ching dynasty era map showing Chenjiagou (lower left) and its environs

Xu Huai (A Song of Remembrance)

I sigh to think of those years, wearing armor with a lance in my hand.

We swept away countless enemies, several times in mortal danger.

I was rewarded with honors, all to no avail.

Now that I am old and short of breath, my only constant companion is the book (Huang Ting).

When I am depressed I practice

boxing routines, during the busy times I plough the fields.

In my spare time I teach my sons and grandsons, it is up to them whether or not they succeed.

It is advantageous to pay the grain tax early, it is important to pay back personal debts immediately.

Don't be prideful and don't flatter others, be patient and always make the first concession.

People say that I am foolish and that I am seedy, I hear this but I don't take it to heart.

I laugh at the people and nobles fussing about anxiously, not like me keeping in good spirits and staying calm.

I don't covet fame or profit, having been involved in affairs I understand trickery.

I understand the illusory nature of life.

Happiness is to fish and to wander in the countryside, without a care for prosperity or ruin.

Suppose there was a world where peace and health prevailed, tranquility and simplicity would be commonplace.

There would be no hatred and no want.

I don't care that others look down on poverty, I am not concerned about success or failure.

If I am not already an immortal then who is?

In the year 1645, the leader of a popular uprising of miners and peasants in Henan Province (in the region between Songshan and Luoyang) was executed in Beijing and his entire family was also wiped out, his name was Li Ji-Yu. With one of their strongholds on top of the Shaoshi Mountain (on the slope of which is located the Shaolin Monastery) Li Ji-Yu had on one occasion led several hundred rebels in an attack on the Shaolin Monastery killing all of the monks. (see Zhao Bao-Jun *Shaolin Si,* Shanghai 1982p.105-107).

It is from the "Fu Lu Chen Shi Jia Sheng" or "Appendix of the Chen Family Chronicles" (see Chen Xin *Chen Shi Taijiquan Tu Shuo,* published in 1933, written from 1908 to 1919, and incorporating material that is based on the oral tradition and written records of Chenjiagou) that we know that Jiang Fa was one of the rebels under Li Ji-Yu. It is mentioned in the passage that Jiang was skilled in martial arts and was so fleet of foot that Chen Wang-Ting was unable to catch him when he tried to do so. When Li Ji-Yu was defeated, Jiang became Chen Wang-Ting's servant.

A recent book out of Wenxian has the following to say about Jiang Fa: "Li Ji-Yu was defeated and suffered the extermination of his entire family. One of his officers, Jiang Fa, surrendered to Chen Wang-Ting and became his servant.

In order to conceal his real identity, everyone in the Chen family called Jiang Fa "Jiang Bashi" (skilled workman Jiang). Although Chen Wang-Ting and Jiang Fa were master and servant, in actuality they were bosom friends. Every day they learned martial arts from each other by exchanging ideas; tilling the fields together and teaching the next generation.

Up to the present day there are the following well-liked stories (oral traditions) handed down in Chenjiagou, "Yudaishan Yingxiong Jie Yi", "Chen Wang-Ting Yi Shou Jiang Fa", "Mu Men Zhai Shi Tu Tao Niu", and "Yanghaiwa Jiang Fa Zhen Xie" among others. Once again, according to the recent book: "It is worth mentioning that, the Jiang Fa who was mentioned earlier, because of his contribution during the time that Chen Wang-Ting created Taijiquan, and because he was a good friend of Chen Wang-Ting and his disciple, was included by later writers (such as Chen Xin) in the Boxing Manuals of Chen style Taijiquan. In the Chen family shrine, to this day is a portrait of Chen Wang-Ting, with Jiang Fa standing in back holding a halberd."

The Main Lines of Transmission of Chen Family Taijiquan

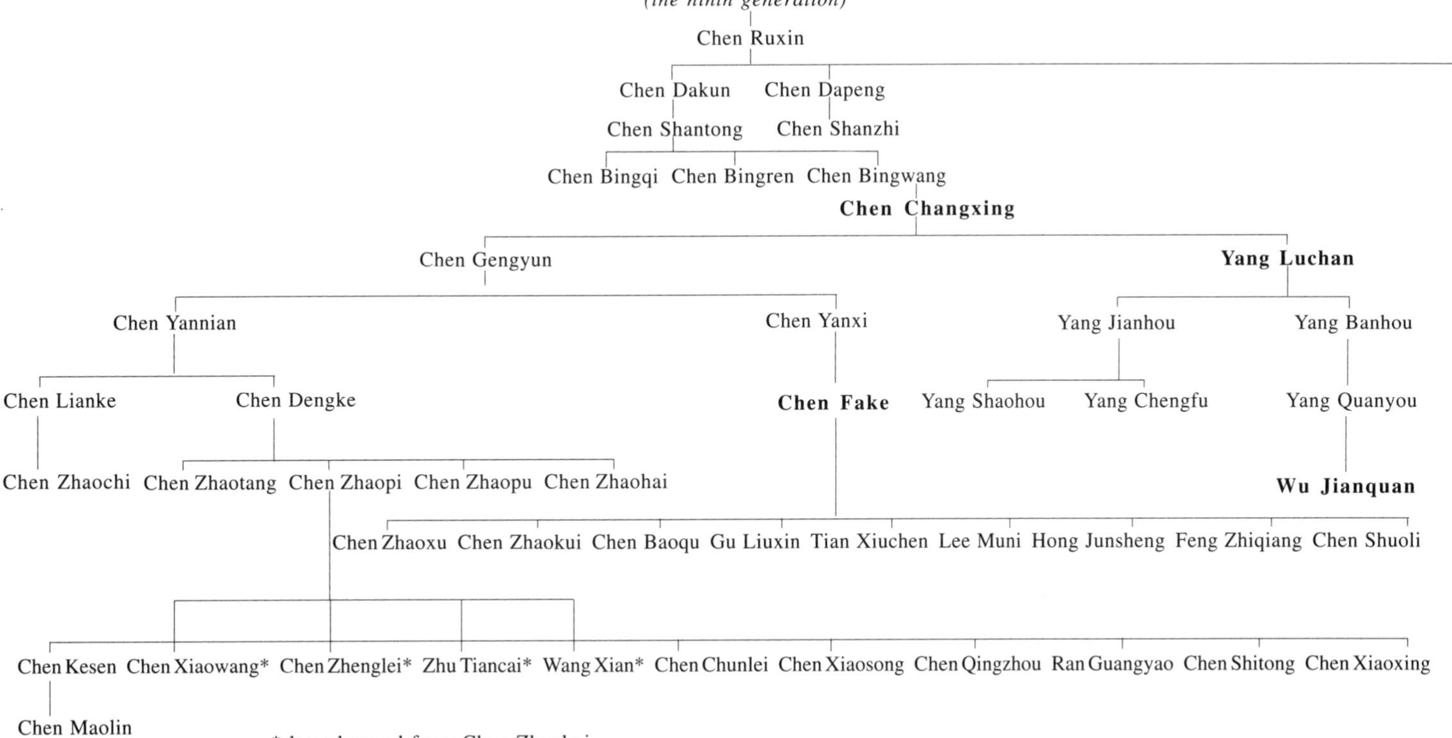

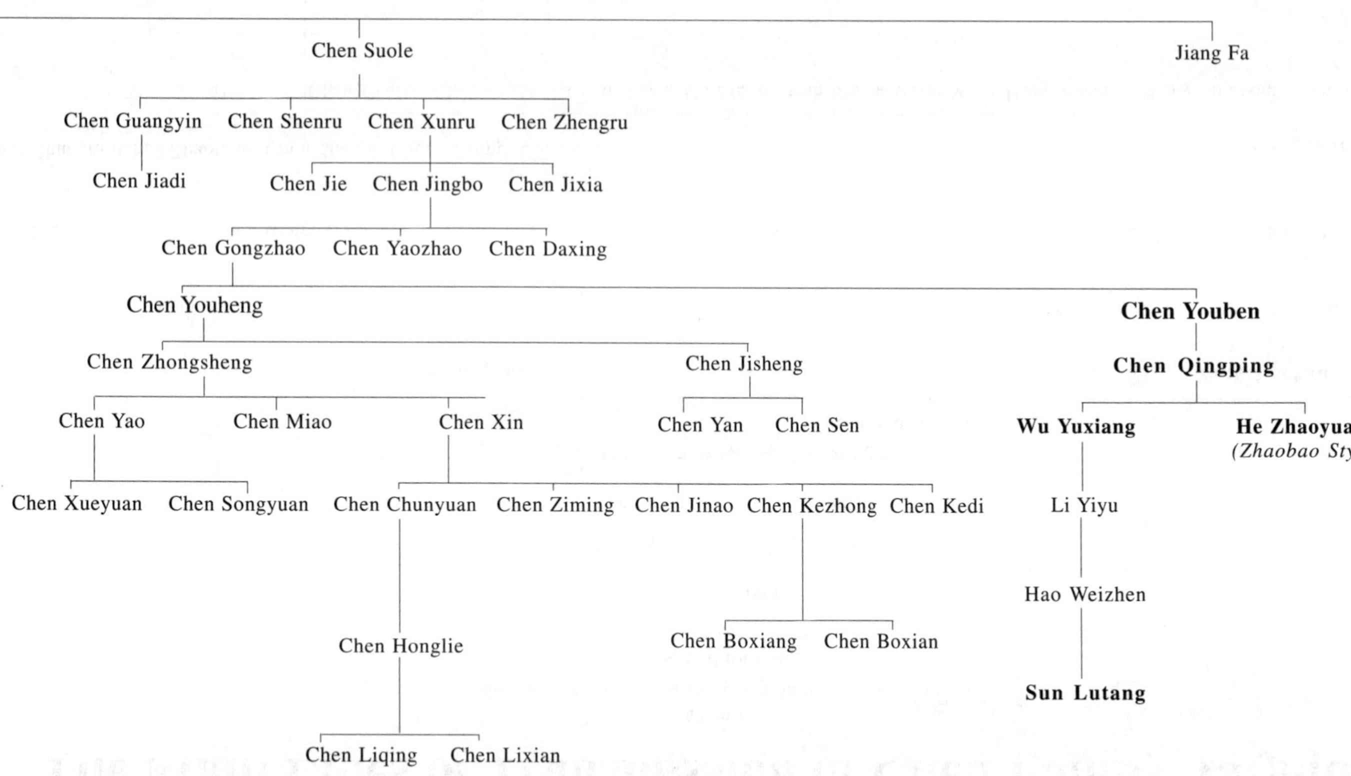
Chen Suole
Jiang Fa
Chen Guangyin
Chen Shenru
Chen Xunru
Chen Zhengru
Chen Jiadi
Chen Jie
Chen Jingbo
Chen Jixia
Chen Gongzhao
Chen Yaozhao
Chen Daxing
Chen Youheng
Chen Youben
Chen Zhongsheng
Chen Jisheng
Chen Qingping
Chen Yao
Chen Miao
Chen Xin
Chen Yan
Chen Sen
Wu Yuxiang
He Zhaoyuan
(Zhaobao Style)
Chen Xueyuan
Chen Songyuan
Chen Chunyuan
Chen Ziming
Chen Jinao
Chen Kezhong
Chen Kedi
Li Yiyu
Hao Weizhen
Chen Honglie
Chen Boxiang
Chen Boxian
Sun Lutang
Chen Liqing
Chen Lixian

The Chen Family Code of Ethics

The Rules and Prohibitions of the Elders of the Chen Family

1. The Chen-style School Strictly Requires 12 Qualities of Character

Propriety (Duan) *dignity of bearing*

Fairness (Gong) *impartiality*

Kindness (Ren) *benevolence*

Nobility (Hao) *broad-mindedness*

Loyalty (Zhong) *faithfulness*

Honesty (Cheng) *sincerity*

Respect (Jing) *esteem for ones' teachers and elders*

Integrity (Zheng) *decency*

Righteousness (Yi) *what is right*

Bravery (Yong) *ready to fight for a just cause*

Trustworthiness (Xin) *good faith*

Morality (De) *ethical conduct*

2. 20 Prohibitions (Precautionary Rules) of the Chen Family

1. Don't rely on a position of authority to bully others.

2. Don't defer to the strong (out of

fear) or insult the weak.
3. Don't fear for oneself, come to the aid of others in danger.
4. Don't commit crimes.
5. Don't rely on your Gongfu skills to fight with others.
6. Don't take advantage of a superior position to become arrogant.
7. Don't sell your art on the street.
8. Don't travel here and there to set up a clique.
9. Don't wallow in luxury, or live a paupers' existence.
10. Don't be prideful or self-satisfied.
11. Don't get into arguements with a crazy or violent person.
12. Don't contend with the ignorant.
13. Don't be proud toward the poor or fawn on the rich.
14. Don't hanker after ill-gotten gains.
15. Don't have anything to do with drinking or prostitution.
16. Don't refuse to pay any public or private obligations.
17. Don't use public office for personal ends.
18. Don't pursue the trappings of high office or a handsome salary.
19. Don't betray your country or be a rotter.
20. Don't slack off and waste your time by not practicing.

3. 12 Prohibited Negative Character Traits

1. Inappropriate affairs (Xie) *immoral practices*
2. Comitting crimes (Fan) *bad people, bad deeds*
3. Creating difficulty *(Diao) artfulness*
4. Cunning (Hua) *trickiness*
5. Excessive luxury (She) *free-spending ways*
6. Cheating and swindling (Zha) *hoaxing others*
7. Inappropriate words/deeds (Feng) *violent behavior*
8. Baseness (Bei) *inferior character*
9. Fraudulence (Jian) *hypocrisy*
10. Dishonesty (Huang) *untruthfulness*
11. Extremely self-willed (Kuang) *arrogant*
12. Viciousness (E) *fierceness and maliciousness*

4. Two Standards of Conduct

1. A good, morally upright person who practices Taijiquan does so for the purpose of obtaining good health and strengthening his body, promoting the basis of life.This is advocated.

2. A bad, evil person who becomes involved in martial arts uses his skill to take from others, creating harm and suffering.This is forbidden.

5. Essential Knowledge

In studying Taijiquan you cannot neglect respect (jing). Without respect you will be hindered in making friends and acquiring a teacher. If your mind is undisciplined, how can you study martial arts?

In studying Taijiquan, you cannot be arrogant or overbearing. Arrogance leads to trouble. Not only should your actions be free from arrogance, but you also cannot be arrogant in your speech. In your movement and demeanor you must carry yourself in the refined manner of a Confucian. If not, and your outward actions are arrogant, then you will lose your inner composure as well.

In studying Taijiquan, you should carefully try to figure out each and every form. If you don't figure out a form, then this form will be without any inner substance. You must connect what comes before with what follows after, paying special attention to every detail (this may also be taken as an admonition to follow faithfully the teachings of ones' master). If you don't pay attention to this one point, then your energy pathways won't be correct and you won't be able to move with facility. Your movements will be separate and distinct, without being able to perform from start to finish in one continuous flow, then you won't be able to discover the ways of the one "great harmonizing primordial energy" (tai he yuan qi)

In studying Taijiquan, you should first make a study of its' writings. Once you understand the theories of the writings, then learning Taijiquan will naturally become easier.

Special Characteristics of Chen-style Taijiquan

1. Appearing outwardly soft like a maiden, yet inwardly strong like a Buddha's warrior attendant (Jingang).

There are numerous schools and sects of Chinese martial arts. There are several hundred barehanded boxing styles alone. Each school has its own unique characteristics, but, summing everything up, they can all be separated into either internal or external schools. External martial arts put more emphasis on striking with the fists and kicking with the feet, with vigorous jumping and leaping, rapid shifting to the side, with its attacking and defending maneuvers easy to distinguish. With one look, you can tell that it is a martial art.

Chen-style Taijiquan has different special characteristics: it uses thought to guide energy, and uses energy to move the body. If the internal energy is still, then the body doesn't move and is still. The internal energy just has to move, and the body follows the internal energy in moving. It uses internal energy to drive the movement of the external form, with the upper and lower parts of the body leading and following each other, continuously without stopping. It uses the waist as an axis,with movements strung together in succession, from start to finish and within each form, with no breaking off or resisting. Your body turns lightly and stops silently.

The attack and defense meaning of its forms is mostly hidden within and not displayed on the surface. This frequently brings about the misconception that this style of boxing more resembles fishing than it does martial arts. Especially the first routine of the "old frame" (lao jia) style which is mainly soft and requires that the body relax and not use stiff force. It mainly trains the gongfu of the legs, causing the feet to put down "roots", the hips to turn freely, and the circulation to flow unimpeded. Practice brings internal energy to a state of overflowing. When your thought arrives on its mark your internal energy arrives together with it on target. The posture is upright, the stances sturdy and stable (literally supported against eight directions of attack), causing both the internal and external parts of your body to put up strong lines of defense. There are "five bows" formed within your body that can store and release energy. In this way, you hold back before you make contact with the opponent. If the opponent is strong, then you can abruptly issue your internal energy (thus catching him unawares), like a clap of thunder or a sudden, violent gust of wind. Therefore, outwardly you seem soft like a maiden, yet inwardly are strong like a Buddha's warrior attendant. This is one of the main characteristics of Chen-style Taijiquan.

2. A Spiraling, Circular Way of Moving Internal Energy

Everyone has seen performers breaking bricks with their heads and wrapping iron reinforcing bars around their necks, this is how practitioners of "hard" style qigong (qigong = specialised internal energy training exercises) move their internal energy. They move their internal energy to the tops of their heads, and their heads can just smash the bricks to pieces; moving their internal energy to their necks, they can just wrap iron bars around their necks.

Chen-style Taijiquan combines the study of dynamics (force, energy, motion, and the relationship between them) with the theories of the traditional Chinese medical theory of "jingluo" (which holds that there are internal energy channels and collateral channels within the body). It makes use of a spiraling method for moving internal energy, using a small amount of force to overcome a large amount of force, and using a weak force to overcome a strong force. It's just like a very small screw jack, which can raise a truck carrying several tons of cargo. The so-described "Taijiquan changes back and forth between storing up and releasing of energy" (xu fa xiang bian), "leading the opponent's energy harmlessly into a pitfall" (yin jing luo kong), "using the opponent's own strength to strike back at him" (jie li da ren), and "using four ounces to deflect a thousand pounds" (yi si liang bo qian jin), are all uses to which spiraling strength can be applied. Therefore, the *Boxing Theory* states: "springing a surprise or leading in the opponent, is only the turning of a circle."

In regard to jingluo theory, jingluo indicates the circulatory system for blood and internal energy that fills the human body and which originates in the visceral cavity and circulates into the limbs. When the system loses its stasis or balance then the whole system functions abnormally and illness arises. When the system is in harmony, then the blood and internal energy circulate freely and the body is thereby strengthened and longevity is enhanced.

Taijiquan, which is combined with the theories of jingluo, includes using its barehanded boxing art with "daoyin" and "tuna" together as external and internal components. The boxing postures and movements make use of a spiraling, silk-twining (chansi) style of expanding and contracting, rotating movements. It has the requirement of: "using your thought to guide your internal energy, using your internal energy to move your body" (yi yi dao qi, yi qi yun shen); and "internal energy should be mobilized (qi yi gu dang), spreading throughout your body".

Internal energy (nei qi) starts out from the acupuncture point below your navel (dantian), uses the waist as its hub,and penetrates successively throughout your body, part by part. It rotates lightly, and causes your two kidneys to expand and contract alternately. Through rotating your waist and turning your spine, with circular and twining movements, it is spread throughout your body.

Passing through the ren and du channels [the ren and du channels form a circuit that starts from the dantian, goes up the center of the back (du channel), over the top of the head, and down the front (ren channel), along the centerline of the body, returning to the dantian - or "small circuit of heaven] it moves upward with the rotating of your wrists and turning of your arms and moves downward with rotating of your ankles and turning of your knees. The internal energy thus reaches to your four extremities and then returns again to your dantian (i.e. "large circuit of heaven"). It moves in arcs, turning freely and linking up together, move by move, connecting what comes before with what follows, all at one go, resulting in the circulation of internal energy and blood. This is moving energy (moving internal energy) which is different from the application of energy. This systematic method for moving internal energy is in accord with the principles of Chinese medical theory (jingluo) and is seldom seen in other styles of boxing or other athletic activities.

3. Combining both Daoyin and Tu Na with Martial Arts

Daoyin and Tui Na are ancient Chinese health nourishing arts that have been around for ages. As early as a few hundred years B.C. there were already references in the Laozi and the Mengzi. In the early Han dynasty, Huainanzi or Liu An compiled the "Six Animal Play". In the later years of the Han dynasty, the famous medical specialist Hua Tuo revised it into "Five Animal Play". He imitated the movements of animals—waving, drawing in and stretching out, raising up and lowering, turning one way and then the next, and leaping into the air—also combining breathing techniques. It was used both as therapy and as a health maintenance regimen; it was the forerunner of breathing exercises (qigong) and internal energy training (nei xing gong) and also was the foundation of the life nourishing (yang sheng) science of the Daoists.

Chen-style Taijiquan took the technologies of Daoyin and Tu Na, which were then combined in a coordinated way with the hands, eyes, whole body, and footwork, to become a "cultivation of both internal and external" internal energy training (nei gong quan) style of boxing. This not only is of beneficial use for strengthening the body, but was also a creative development in elevating the technology of barehanded boxing art and fighting skills.

4. Chen-style Taijiquan's Blending of Hardness and Suppleness

5. The Coordination of Consciousness, Breathing, and Movement

6. Realistic Combative Nature of the Competitive Activities of Two Person Push-Hands and Two-Person Dual Spear Training

Chen-style Requirements

The Head

In *An Illustrated Explanation on Taijiquan*, author Chen Xin writes, "The head is the leader of the six Yang channels (the head is where all Yang channels come together), and is master of the entire body, there is no part of the body [literally, the hundred bones and the five sense organs (ears, eyes, lips, nose and tongue) of the body] that does not manifest this dynamic fact." The *Boxing Treatise* states, "The baihui (acupuncture point "du 20" at the crown of the head) leads the entire body", and, "From beginning to end, the energy from the crown of the head can never be lost". It is also said, "When it is flexible and empty, energy is in the crown of the head", and, "Hang from the crown of the head". These passages describe how the position of the head can be used to prevent the "qi" from rushing upward and causing the muscles of the crown of the head to stiffen and clog.

From a mechanical point of view, the head is on a straight vertical line running from the top to the bottom of the body. From a physiological point of view, the brain is the central hub of the nervous system. If the head tilts to either side, this will affect the balance and the coordination of the entire body, and the beauty of the movements and, upright posture, will be lost. It will also affect the concentration of the spirit (jingshen).

When practicing, the head must lead and be in control to focus the spirit. Conscious instruction is behind every movement, every posture and every extension of the hands or feet, so that the entire body will be flexible and alive. If one does not practice in this manner, the spirit will be lost and scattered, and the movements will lose their completeness and coordination.

The specific demands include: The head must be kept erect, and the muscles of the crown of the head must be kept in a relaxed state, so it feels as if the head is suspended. One must not force the posture, be stiff, or tilt in any direction. When the body moves or turns, the head must stay in line with the torso and four limbs. The eyes are level and distantly focused. When moving, the eyes follow the tip of the middle finger of whichever hand is leading. The lower jaw is slightly tucked in, the teeth and lips are just touching. The tip of the tongue is at the roof of the mouth to increase the secretion of saliva. The ears are alert and listen to all sounds. Most important of all, everything should be naturally light and relaxed. There should not be the slightest thought of impatience or feeling of tension.

The Chest and Back

Chen family Taijiquan demands the chest to be concave (often mistranslated as hollow, it literally means "to hold in the mouth"), empty and relaxed. When the chest is concave and empty, and the collarbones and ribs are relaxed and sunken, the upper limbs will be empty and flexible, and the center of gravity will drop. This will also help with the critically important concept of all movements and changes arising from the ("turning in folds" or undulating) movement of the torso and waist.

Chen family Taijiquan demands the back to be extended, spread out, relaxed, sunken, and filled with "zhong qi" (internal energy associated with the spleen and stomach, and hence related to digestion and nutrition). According to acupuncture theory, the back is the passageway of the "du" channel, which is one of the six Yang channels. Pay special attention to the muscles of the back being extended, relaxed and sunken downward so they conform to the shape of the spine. Wherever there is a curve, the muscles extend to preserve the proper alignment of the vertebrae. This creates an unobstructed flow of "qi" and blood, until "the qi flows back and forth while adhering to the back," and then at the proper time, "the strength issues from the spine".

Some other styles require the back to be a "stretched back". However, use of the word "stretched" will cause people to make the mistake of stretching upward. When a person's spine stretches, no matter whether it stretches upward or forward, it causes the muscles of the broad of the back and the muscles between the ribs to stretch tautly and extend forward. This forces the chest to contract, and the shoulders to become hunched over in front, thereby producing the incorrect posture of a bowed back and hunched shoulders. It also affects and ruins the body's beauty, causes the diaphragm to feel pressure, and disrupts smooth and uninterrupted breathing.

The Waist and Spine

In the course of practicing Taijiquan, the spine and waist are the most important. Thus the expression, "The spine and waist are the number-one minister".

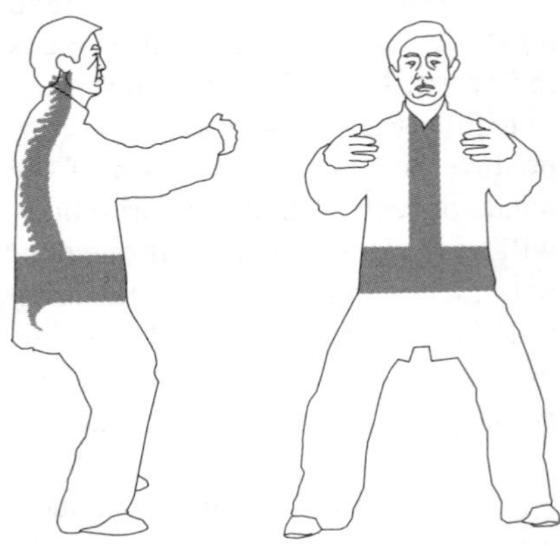

The single demand of Chen family Taijiquan on the waist is that the energy must sink. That is to say, the vertebrae of the waist should follow the curve of the spine; slightly tucked and sunken. The energy is from the sinking. The waist is the axis for twisting both the upper and lower parts of the body. When the chest is concave, and sinking has produced energy, then the "qi" of the heart will descend, settle, and become stable (firm). At the same time, one must slightly bring in the two sides of the chest. This is the "tied-up ribs" concept found in Chen-style Taijiquan theory. However, when sinking the energy of the waist, an excessive amount of force must not be used. If strength is used in the waist, then the muscles of the waist will contract and affect the flexible nature of turning movements of the upper and lower body.

When sinking the waist, one must straighten the spine of the lower back. This is the so-called "straight waist". The spine of an adult is composed of 24 vertebrae (according to Chinese medical theory). Because of our erect posture, the profile of the human body shows four physiological curves: the crown of the head, the chest, the waist, and the sacrum. Among the curves, only the spine in the area of the waist curves forward. Movements of the back are powerful; it can stretch and contract to a great degree because the joint cartilage and ligaments connect the vertebrae. However, the spine is easily pulled toward other muscles of the body, resulting in the appearance of bending, lifting or tilting. The "straight waist" is maintained for three major reasons: to lessen the tendency of the bend in the waist to incline forward; to avoid affecting the normal physiological state of the vertebrae when the body is relaxed; and to preserve the straightness of the body, thus making the spine and waist an even better wheel axle. The spine of the lower back should be as straight as a flag pole. In the course of practicing, the vertebrae of the chest and above the waist follow the movements. Although there are sometimes slight stretches and contractions, one cannot just shake and quiver as one wishes; one must pay attention to straightening the curves.

The Abdomen

Chen family taijiquan requires the abdomen to be "stretching inward" (often mistranslated as "close" or "contract"). The "dantian" is where the abdomen is located and is where the "qi" returns. When practicing taijiquan, all energy which goes in or out of the body does so at the "dantian". Some practitioners of taijiquan talk about a "relaxed abdomen" or "empty the

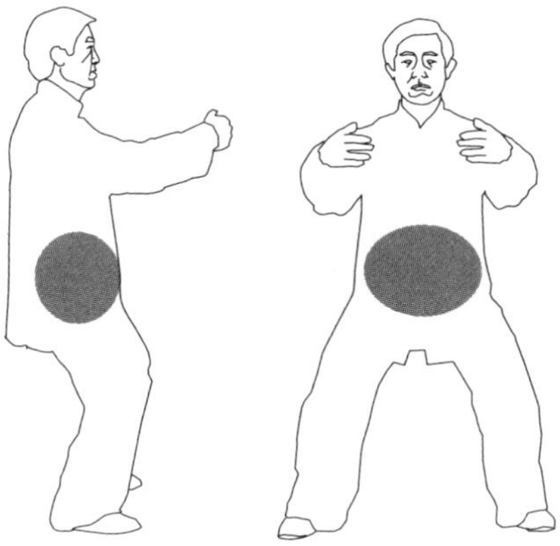

chest and fill the abdomen". In reality, the muscles of the abdomen follow the coming and going of the "zhong qi" at the "dantian"; sometimes expanding, sometimes contracting. "When the zhong qi is in the center then emptiness, flexibility, and concavity are all internalized."

The Buttocks

Chen family Taijiquan requires the buttocks to be "spread out". Coordinating the waist sinking, the abdomen stretching inward, the hips opening and stretching outward, the crotch rounding and opening, and the knees stretching inward, will cause the buttocks to spread slightly to the rear, and benefit the flowing of the "zhong qi" through the spine, and the movement of energy in the waist, crotch and legs. A spread out buttocks are certainly not a sagging buttocks nor are they protruding buttocks. Some styles of Taijiquan advocate the "restraining buttocks", that the buttocks should be pulled in. Restraining the buttocks certainly guards against the mistake of a sagging buttocks, however, if only the buttocks is pulled the front of the crotch will open wider, and the rear will become narrow. Then the energy of the crotch cannot be opened and rounded, thereby affecting the flexible and lively nature of the body's turns and movement.

Shoulders and Elbows

"Relax the shoulders and sink the elbows" is the common demand all styles of Taijiquan make on its practitioners. The shoulder joints should extend downward and outward, and be opened and relaxed, while the two elbow joints should sink and feel as if they are weighted down. The actions of relaxing the shoulders and sinking the elbows are

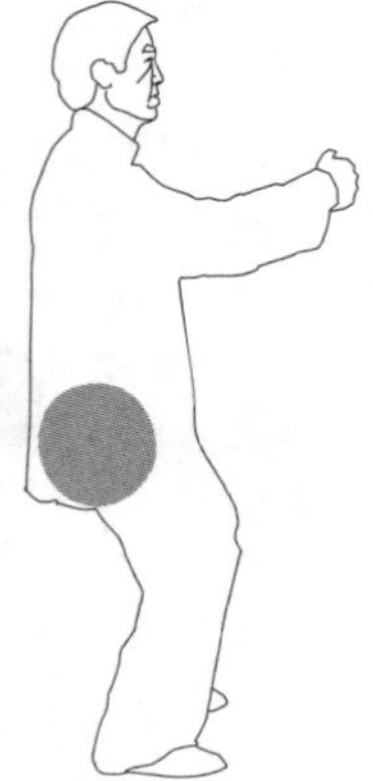

interrelated. Only when the elbows are sunk and the shoulders relaxed can the movements be natural, and the two arms be rounded, full, relaxed, and lively. The style's theory states, "The joint turns at the shoulder and folds at the wrist."

When the shoulder and elbow joints are clear and unobstructed, the internal energy can reach the fingers. If there are any obstructions in the shoulders or elbows, it will affect the movement of internal energy, and that in turn will affect the coordination of the body. When practicing, one must relax the shoulder joints and continuously extend them outward, so that the energy will slowly break free and sink. The elbows should appear as if weighted down, the actual purpose being to protect the ribs. A space of approximately one fist must always be maintained between the armpit and the body. This aids in the free turning of the arms.

The Wrist

Chen style Taijiquan has a vertical wrist, sitting wrist, broken wrist, and spiraling wrist. No matter how many changes occur, the wrist must be coordinated with the body's posture by moving and transforming in accordance with the "zhong qi". For the wrist to be flexible and lively, it must be more pliable. One must never allow the wrist to be floating or weak to make the movements better looking. If this occurs, the ward-off (peng) energy is lost, and when practicing push hands, it will be easier for your opponent to grab your wrists and control them.

The Hands

Chen family Taijiquan places great emphasis on the use of the hands. The theory of the style states, "Throughout this entire art, only the heart is used to move the hands, the hands lead the elbows, and the elbows lead the body". There are three different basic shapes for the hand to assume: open palm, fist, or hooked hand. See below for separate descriptions of each.

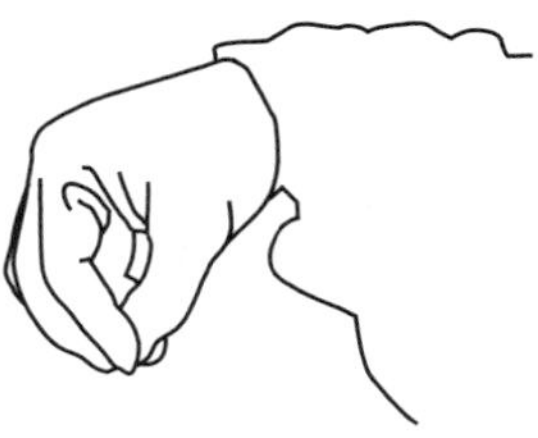

The Palm

Chen family Taijiquan requires the palm to be like a "row of roof tiles". That is to say, the thumb and the little finger are close to each other, while the index, middle, and ring fingers are all bunched slightly to the rear. All five fingers are slightly bunched together, but without using any strength. The

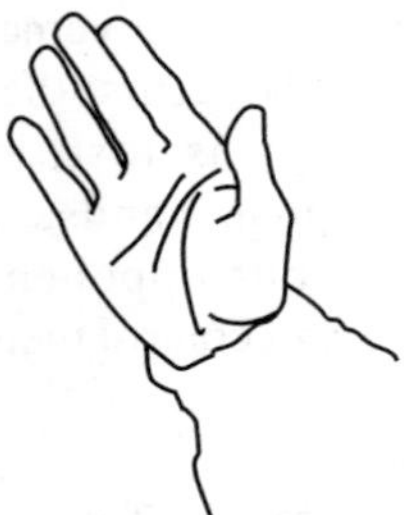

center of the palm is empty.

In addition, since Chen family Taijiquan "silk cocoon energy" runs in both clockwise and counter-clockwise directions, its manifestations in the two hands are also different. For example, when using counterclockwise silk cocoon energy (ni chansijin), the thumb leads the energy outward during a push (an). The internal energy passes through and fills each finger to its tip, going from thumb to index finger to middle finger. When using clockwise silk cocoon energy (shun chansijin), the little finger leads the energy to stretch inward, from the little finger to the ring finger to the middle finger; always recombining in the thumb. The energy follows the turning of the hands and arms to concentrate in the "belly of the fingers" (the first section from the fingertip). Only in Chen family Taijiquan does one concentrate one's thought, intention, and gaze on the middle finger, while following the turning of the arms and concentrating the energy in the belly of the fingers.

The Fist

If the fist is clenched too tightly, tension will increase in the hand, arm, and the muscles of that half of the body and will cause them to become stiff and rigid. Then the internal energy will not readily flow to the wrist. In other words, loose fists are maintained throughout to store energy, but in the instant it takes the practitioner to clench his fists, his energy rises up from his feet, travels through the legs, is directed by the waist, passes through the shoulders and elbows, then arrives at the fist. The energy travels through the body all at one go (literally translated as "one breath").

The Hook Hand

The fingers are bunched together, with the crook of the wrist relaxed and not a rigid curve. If one uses strength in making a rigid hook, it will cause the stiffening of the wrists and arms, a loss of flexibility and liveliness, and will block the flow of "qi ".

The Lower Limbs

The lower limbs are the

foundation that supports the body, and the source of the energy and strength which can be issued. The theory states, "Energy is rooted in the feet, issues through the legs, is controlled by the waist, and manifests itself in the hands and fingers."

The Groin

Chen style Taijiquan requires the groin to be rounded, empty, relaxed and lively. Avoid developing postures in which the groin protrudes, collapses or is without liveliness. The theory of Chen style states, "From within the groin comes a spring-like strength, so that if a bird should suddenly try to take off from it, it would have trouble doing so."

A rounded groin is created when the root of the hip and the knees work together to be opened by stretching outward and being rounded. Every time one starts to take a step, one leg becomes full and the other empty. The tip of the foot of the empty leg turns inward while the oblique muscle in the thigh rotates outward. In addition, the perineum (huiyin) [acupuncture point "ren 1"] rises slightly, and the groin is kept both rounded and empty. Only by doing this can emptiness and fullness be clearly differentiated. If the groin protrudes, one cannot make this distinction. A relaxed and lively groin can be attained by allowing the hip joint and the muscles of the buttocks to relax, and not press against the pelvis. The fullness and emptiness must freely interchange. The alternating of fullness and emptiness (from side to side) in the groin is like tracing parallel "infinity" symbols, twisting inside and turning outside. While moving from the front to the back it travels in a descending arc. In this way, one avoids the lack of movement found in a groin which is "dead". A collapsed groin occurs when the buttocks sink to the level of the knees. The knee joints will lock, the steps will not be light, and the joints will not be flexible. When practicing, the "baihui" acupuncture point and the "huiyin" acupuncture point work together so that the Yin and Yang become balanced through the flow of "qi", thereby straightening the standing body.

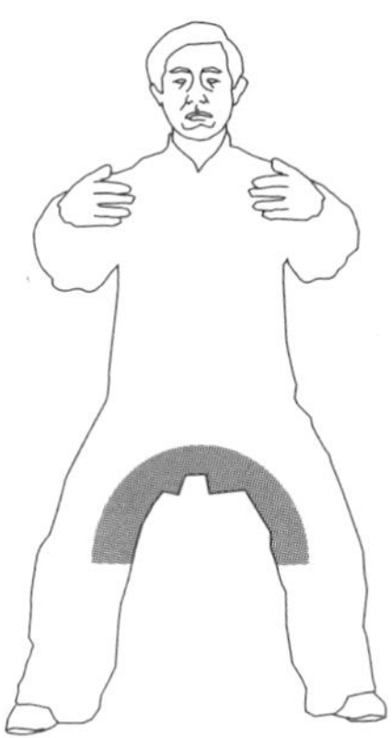

The groin must be

coordinated with the waist, hips and knees. When the waist is relaxed and sunken, the hips are stretched outward, and the knees are stretched inward, then the energy from the groin will naturally be rounded.

The Hips

Chen style Taijiquan demands that the roots of the hips be open and stretching outward; the hips should be relaxed, open and stretching outward. Turning the waist either left or right and alternating emptiness and fullness in the legs depends on whether the hip joints are relaxed and lively. If the hips are lifeless and stuck to the pelvis, the waist cannot act as a carriage axle.

Relaxing the hips is not easy to do because they support the weight of the upper body. When the hips are relaxed, the burden on the knee joints will increase. Beginners have trouble relaxing the hips because they usually have less strength in their leg muscles and their knee joints cannot support the weight of the body. Their knees then protrude forward, their belly sticks out, they extend their chests,and their body tilts backward. To preserve the straightness and (relaxed) stretching out of the torso while squatting, the knees must not go past the tips of the feet the hips and buttocks should appear as if sitting on a stool. The relaxing of the knee joints must be coordinated with the relaxing of the shoulders. If the hips are not relaxed, and the shoulders are stiff and hanging [against the body], the muscles of the ribs and abdomen will be pressed, thereby affecting the relaxation and sinking of the muscles of the ribs and abdomen, and the diaphragm. The ability of "qi" to rise and fall will also be hampered.

The Knees

The knees are very important in Taijiquan, because the uprightness of the standing body is maintained by bending the knees and relaxing the hips. When practicing the entire routine, the knee joints must maintain the same degree of bend from the beginning to the end. When the stance is high, the steps are small and there is only a light burden on the knee joint; when the stance is low, the steps are large and there is a heavier burden on the knee joint. When practicing the routine, both the amount of support the legs provide and the weight of the body are completely controlled by the knee joints.

Beginners should first practice in a high stance, one in which the legs can support themselves, then gradually (in due course) lower the posture. One must be conscious of protecting the knee joints. After practice, the speed of the circulation of blood in the joints and body increases, and the joints will feel warm. At this time, the pores are open and the "couli" (the space between the veins and skin in Chinese medical theory, perhaps identical with the "fascia" in Western anatomical terms) are relaxed. To avoid pain in the joints, skin and muscles caused by dampness, never bathe in cold water or allow the wind to blow on them after practice.

In two-person push hands, the legs (of the two persons) are side by side, the two knees stick together, and can be used to strike outward, hook inward or attack the knees of the opponent and force him to lose strength. They are also used to protect the groin and shin.

The Feet

The feet act as the body's foundation. The correct positioning of the feet is necessary to preserve the footwork's agility and steadiness. Chen family Taijiquan requires the feet to be firm and steady, with the toes, sole of the foot and heel all gripping the ground. The "bubbling well" acupuncture point located on the bottom of the foot is empty (like the center of a suction cup). The toes must not curl upward, and the center of the foot must not shift or lean in any direction. When walking or taking a step, one must first decide upon, then prepare for, the direction and position of the step. One strives to achieve "where the foot lands, it takes root." The foot cannot be carelessly placed anywhere. Only in this way can the steps feel clearly defined, sunken, stable and firm.

When taking a step to the front, left or right, one must bend the knees to relax the hips. The tip of the foot curls and stretches inward; the heel of the foot inclines to the inside, "shoveling" and sliding outward along the ground until it reaches the appropriate extension. Once the appropriate position is reached, the center of gravity is shifted, lowered and planted into the ground. When going backward, first the tip of the foot touches the ground, then the center of gravity is shifted, with the step gradually becoming full.

When turning to the left or

right, one foot supports the center of gravity, while the tip of the other foot bends upward and points outward or hooks inward. The outside of that heel then touches the ground and is placed in the proper direction and position. When the center of gravity is then shifted, the step becomes full. When the tip of the foot points outward or hooks inward, the legs should still provide the turning and twisting energy.

Combat footwork can be divided into hooking, linking, stamping, kicking and trampling. Hooking, linking (or trapping) and kicking are usually methods that employ the toes, while stamping and trampling use the center of the foot and heel.

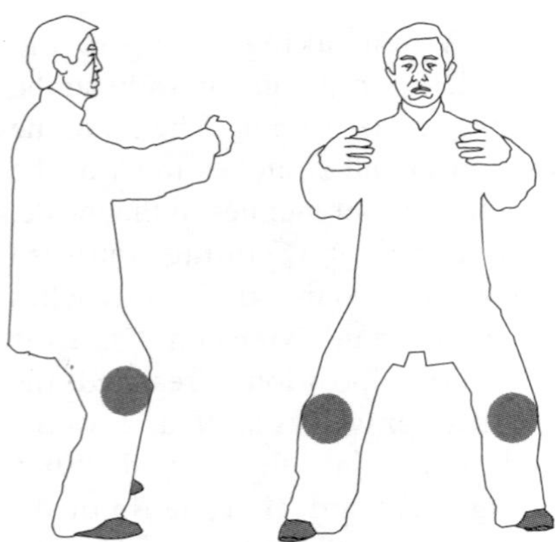

Conclusion

The demands on each part of the body are interrelated and interact with each other throughout the entire routine. Incorrect posture of any part of the body will affect the entire body. Any individual part can influence the whole. Likewise, the whole body can affect its individual parts.

One must first build a solid foundation on the basic skills, and only then will the positioning of each part of the body be appropriately coordinated. The speed, path and method of movement will eventually reach the point at which the body is upright, the footwork is stable, and all moves are rounded and lively, flowing in succession without interruption. The top and bottom halves of the body move together as one, and the body is coordinated in its movements. When one part moves, all parts move; they follow without interruption like flowing water. When there is stillness, it is like a mountain; movement can be as slow as floating clouds or as fast as electricity.

The Method and Progression of Chen-style Taijiquan Training

1. Familiarity with the set of forms, postures clearly executed:

The so-called set of forms (tao lu) indicates the complete set of forms. The so-called postures (zi shi) indicates the structure of movements in each form (jia shi). In the beginning, the main thing is to place emphasis on being familiar with practice of the set of forms and that the positions and directions are correct. At the same time, it is appropriate to pay attention to the standards concerning the postures. After practicing Taijiquan for a short while, when you are thoroughly familiar with the set, at this time you must place emphasis on the correct performance of the postures; in this way you will be able to produce internal energy (nei qi) and bring into play the health and barehanded combat effects. Presently, we will look at it from two aspects and discuss the training techniques and the items to pay attention to at this level.

1) In quietude there is motion; in motion there is quietude. In practicing Chen style Taijiquan you must keep your thoughts quiet, getting rid of all internal and external disturbances. Only in this way will you benefit, by restraining your internal energy (nei qi), and by guiding the rising up and movement of internal energy (yin dong gu dang). A boxing treatise says: "Quietude nourishes the 'ling gen', qi nourishes the spirit (shen)". The so-called root (gen) of "nourishing the root" is the fundamental nature, and is also the kidney. Chinese medical theory holds that "kidney is

the root of inborn nature" (shen wei xian tian zhi gen), and stores within it the original Yin and the original Yang, the animating force of life and movement in the human body. "Quietude nourishes the fundamental nature" (jing ze yang gen), this is to say that only when your consciousness is in a state of peace and quiet is it of any benefit to the flourishing and collection of your kidney qi (shen qi); therefore causing your five internal organs to function healthily, your internal energy (nei qi) to be full, your spirit nourished and your movements strong and vigorous.

2) Pay attention to body-mechanics (shen fa). In the beginning of your practice of Taijiquan, you shouldn't set your sights too high or train in great haste. This is similar to beginning to write Chinese characters, it's acceptable if you can just make your cross stroke horizontally level, your vertical brush stroke straight, your dot and hook, etc., forming characters within a square frame. In the beginning of your practice of Taijiquan, with respect to body mechanics, you are only required to keep your head naturally upright, stand straight, and don't lean over too far in any direction (bu pian bu yi). In your footwork (bu fa), you are only required to perform the bow and arrow stance (gong bu), empty step stance (xu bu), step out (kai bu), and draw back step (shou bu) well. If you know the position and direction of each it is acceptable.As for those errors that unavoidably crop up, like raising your shoulders or sticking out your elbows,filling your chest with unrestrained qi(heng qi),panting when you breathe, your hands and feet trembling,etc.—it is not advisable to delve into these phenomena too deeply. But, the direction of motion, the angles, and proper sequence must be absolutely correct. You should do everything you can do to make the movements (zi shi) soft (rou ruan) natural and balanced (da fang shun sui).

By keeping up with the practice of around ten sets a day, you can become familiar with the set of forms (tao lu). At this time, you should make progress in taking into account the requirements of the movements; from head to foot, undertaking correction of every form and movement. You should do as much as you can to slow down the speed of the movements in order to benefit the thought process in determining whether the movements are correct or not. Keeping to daily practice of ten sets, after a period of time, you can pass through this level and enter into the second level.

2. Adjustment of body mechanics, relaxing the whole body:

So-called body mechanics

(shen fa), indicates the principles of the requirements for each part of the entire body while practicing Taijiquan. If you want to adjust body mechanics you must first expend some effort (gong fu) on relaxation. In order to cause the joints to relax and open up (song kai), stretch the muscles (or tendons) and set the bones in proper alignment, you can select a few movements to practice such as "Jin Gang Dao Dui" (Pounding the Mortar), "Yan Shou Gong Quan" (Cover Fist and Punch), "Bai Jiao Die Cha"(Swing the Foot and Drop Down), etc., but you must do all that you can to relax and not use brute force (zhuo li).

The main defects of practice to appear at this level lie in not standing up straight, filling the chest with unrestrained qi (heng qi), lifting up the shoulders and sticking out the elbows, etc. There are two main causes that produce these defects: one is that there is not a sufficient understanding of the meaning of relax (fang song - to relax or loosen); the second is that the supporting strength of the legs is not sufficient, making it difficult to relax. A boxing treatise says: "The body must use upright posture as its fundamental principle. Use the whole body's natural alignment and movement as its subtlety." That is also to say that in practicing the forms of the set, in body mechanics you must use standing with upright posture as the cardinal principle. The upright (duan zheng) posture referred to also has two meanings: one indicates that the trunk and limbs and the head are all situated in an upright position; another is when the body is under a tilted or slanted circumstance, it maintains a relative balance, as for example, a movement like taking a step forward, with the upper body drawing in the attacker and the lower body advancing simultaneously. So-called relaxation (fang song), is to say that with the legs supporting the body, each part of the body relaxes in a natural and concerted way, with the qi sinking to the dantian. In the beginning, because there isn't understanding of or attention paid to these few problems, and in addition, one's strength is meager, therefore one unavoidably will experience the above mentioned defects.You can overcome the above mentioned defects through increasing the number of times you practice the set, increasing athletic capacity by making your postures lower to the ground, and performing some single or double leg squatting exercises, and standing meditation training (zhan zhuang gong) At the same time, paying attention to relaxing the hips (kua), bending the knees, rounding the crotch, and maintaining an upright posture. As the strength of the legs increases, and in body mechanics a loosening up or relaxing takes place; this will cause the chest or thorax (xiong bu), the back (bei bu), the ribs (lei bu) and the diaphragm (ge ji) to naturally sink downward, coordinating with the rise and fall of the motive force of qi within the body. The breathing will be natural, the vital capacity of the lungs will be enhanced, and the defects will be eliminated.

This level of practice requires a three to four month period of time. When the time comes, the body mechanics will have already been adjusted, the postures already basically correct; moreover, as the quality of the practice is raised, there will already be a perception of the movement of internal energy (nei qi).

3. Opening up energy channels - directing internal energy:

Energy channels and collateral channels (jing luo) spread throughout the body. Internally, they connect the internal organs, and, externally, they connect points on the skin's surface. Thus, linking up the upper and lower and the inside and outside of the body. These are the pathways that regulate the organism and along which internal energy (nei qi) moves. Qi is an almost imperceptible substance that forms and maintains life in the human organism. It is an infinitesimally small particle, very difficult to perceive from direct observation. It is only through the human sense organs, according to the changes that it goes through, that its existence is made known. The qi of the human body arises from the following several aspects: the first is a natural gift from our parents' "jing qi" (th eenergyf s perm and egg which combine to form the zygote or fertilized egg); the second is the energy that is produced by the transforming of what we eat and drink into "grain and water"(shui gu) refined energy (jing qi) and exists within the human body's"jing qi" (refined or sexual energy). Qi is produced through the combined physiological functioning of the spleen (pi), lungs (fei), and kidney (shen). A boxing treatise states: "Qi is the root source of life, "jing" (as in jing luo - channels and collateral channels) is the path of qi. If the pathways are blocked, then the qi does not travel along them." It is also stated, "Utilizing my body's unfettered original energy (yuan qi), to move (or move throughout) my body"; "Use qi to move the body, linking together all parts in one continuum of energy." This is an explanation of qi as the body's basic innate substance. Only under the condition that the channels and collateral channels (jing luo) are open and unblocked can you guide (yin dong) the movement of qi and expand and contract your energy at will, reaching a state of the constituent parts linked together in one continuous flow of energy (yi qi guantong), thus producing the results of preventing disease, maintaining good health, and fighting ability.

We have already discussed above, in the later part of the "adjusting of body mechanics relaxing the whole body" level, that there is already the feeling within the body of the movement of internal energy (nei qi), and the practice of Taijiquan also becomes (more) interesting. However, this feeling is like the rising and falling of the waves, at times it is there, at times it is not, sometimes hidden and sometimes manifest. After a short period of time, it can even reach the point where it is completely gone. This is due to the channels and collateral channels not flowing freely, the moving force of qi is unsuccessful in getting through, and, one's not guiding the movement of internal energy. Because of this, at this level of practice it is necessary to pay attention to mentally guiding internal energy. Under the direction of the conscious mind, using intellect to move the body, internal energy will penetrate throughout, segment by segment. If there is some part that presents difficulty, you can adjust your own body mechanics, with the obtaining of the free flow of useable energy (jing) as the criterion. It is advantageous to practice slowly and disadvantageous to practice quickly. For each and every technique and form, you should pay close attention to the energy, which should be active and ever flowing. Make every effort to keep the awareness of the undifferentiated state between internal energy and external form. By practicing and making progress in this way for a while, the internal energy will just naturally flow unobstructed. You will also slowly overcome the stiff energy (jiang jin) and brute force (zhuo li), gradually reaching a state of the whole body interlinked, continuous and unbroken movement, internal energy in accord with the demands of the barehanded boxing forms. A regulated expansion and contraction of internal energy will be produced, reaching the state of all of the constituent parts linked together in one energy continuum (yi qi guan tong).

4. Combining form and energy, like a circle with no end:

So-called form, indicates the body, and is also the external form of the barehanded boxing forms and movements. Qi indicates internal energy. From the point of view of medical theory, form (xing) and energy (qi) are united, are mutually interdependent, and one relies on the other for its function. A boxing treatise says: "using intellect to move the energy, you must be calm, settling the energy, and you will be able to infuse qi into your bones." It also says: "using qi to move the body, the body's movement must follow smoothly."That is, it requires that in each and every technique and posture, you must concentrate on using your intellect (yi) to lead the movement of qi, using the qi to move the body, in accord with what is natural, driving the external form.Through the repetitive practice of combining form with energy, the internal energy is caused to circuit the body and then start over again at the beginning, like a circle that has no end. Spare no effort to accomplish the following: the whole body as one, internal and external united, the external form driven by the movement of internal energy, once set in motion the entire body moves, once it is still the entire body becomes still, in movement and stillness, open and close, in rising and falling, revolving and rotating, there is nothing that is not in accord with what is natural.

During the course of practice, the body and the hands, inner and outer any parts that are not sufficiently coordinated will produce problems that can influence the flow of internal energy, thus causing the internal energy and intellect difficulty in combining with the external form or body. If the speed of the movements is too fast or slow, as well as the angles of the body position not sufficiently mastered, it will be difficult to achieve the desired effects. While practicing the movements of the set, it can cause the body to be slow while the hands are fast, the eyes not following the movement, etc, and other disorganized phenomena; you won't be able to combine body and hands as one, or coordinate the movement. There is a saying: "The hand arrives before the body, the strike will amount to little; the hand and the body arrive together, striking the opponent is like crushing dry grass." That is an explanation of the importance of combining form with energy, and the body and limbs following smoothly.

The practice at this level should place importance on combining thought (yi nian) with the postures of the body, and it is also the heart/mind (xin), thought or intention (yi), internal energy (qi), and form (xing) all reaching a single target simultaneously, causing internal energy to link together all parts into one uninterrupted flow of energy. At the same time, you should understand that the "open" or "closed"condition of any part of the body, is just a partial manifestation of the open or closed condition of the entire body. The overall defects of the whole body, can also be manifested in any part of the body. Because of this, it is the common practice, when adjusting the position of the parts, that you must pay attention to adjusting the whole body, thus reaching unity of intention and energy. The specific indications at this level are: you feel your skin expand, your fingers feel numb, your heels feel heavy, and you have the feeling that your "dantian" is getting heavy.

5. Reciprocally connected movement of the whole body, the unity of internal and external:

The meaning of"the interconnectedness of the whole body, unity of isnternal and external"indicates the whole body's forming an integrated system of movement. Chen Chang-xing, in his *Shi Da Yao Lun* (Essay on Ten Critical Points), said:

"Taijiquan, is ever changing and elusive, and ever powerful; although its postures are not all the same, in the end, their energy goes back to the same state of oneness. So-called one, from the top of the head to the feet; internally, there are organs, sinews and bones; externally, there is skin and muscle, the four limbs and all the bones of the body, all interconnected as one. Chop at it and it will not separate, strike at it and it will not break apart. When you want to move the upper body the lower body follows by itself, when the lower body wants to move the upper body commands itself to follow. The upper and lower move and the middle responds, the middle moves and upper and lower join together in movement with the middle. Internal and external are interconnected, the front and the back are dependent on each other, the so-called one is what connects them, how could it not be thus called?!"

This discussion specifically expounds on the interconnectedness of the whole body (zhou shen xiang sui), the matching of internal with external (nei wai yi zhi), and all the parts of the body linked together (yi qi guan tong) in one uninterrupted flow of internal energy.

In the interconnectedness of the whole body, unity of internal and external level, although internal energy already penetrates throughout and links together the body, the internal energy is very weak. While practicing Taijiquan, by slightly not paying attention or when conditions are not right for exercise (such as over-exhaustion or not being mentally up to it) all can influence the movement and linking up of the internal energy of the various parts of the body. In the previous level, if the body and hands, internal and external produce "contradictions" (mao dun), you can make use of adjustment of body mechanics (shen fa) to resolve them, causing the postures to follow smoothly and internal energy to penetrate throughout. However, in the present level, it is not permitted to use the solution of adjusting body mechanics to resolve defects or contradictions. This level requires that the whole body be reciprocally connected (xiang sui), using internal energy to drive the external form. If the qi is not there, the external form doesn't move; if the qi is there, the external form moves according to the internal energy. Use the mind to move the qi, use the qi to move the body. In each and every move and posture, the qi arises from the dantian. Internally, it moves throughout the internal organs and the bones of the body; externally, it moves along the skin and fine hairs. It moves throughout the whole body and then returns to the dantian, spiraling back and forth, circling at will. The core of the movements is "chan si jing" (twining silk energy), using qi as the overall "driver", forming a comprehensive system of movement. Chan si jing originates from the kidneys (shen) and arises from the dantian, spreading throughout the whole body. Each part of your body always has some, filling your four limbs to overflowing, soaking into the "hundred bones" of your body, reaching the ends of your four extremities and penetrating nine important points (jiu qiao). This increases your internal energy without limit, causing the internal energy to be infused into your bones, stretching your tendons and strengthening your bones. The internal energy and blood flow freely, aiding digestion of food and drink, curing disease and extending one's years. These are all beneficial results of working on "twining silk" internal energy. Twining silk internal energy is the essence of Chen style Taijiquan.

During this level, in addition to maintaining daily practice of the forms and sets, you can combine this with the practice of push hands, thus realizing the distinct energies of "adhere to, connect, stick to, and follow" (zhan lian nian sui), and, "ward-off, roll-back, press, and push" (peng lu ji an), testing whether or not your forms' movements are correct. You can also add the practice of several sets of "Paochui", in order to strengthen your stamina and explosive power. You can practice broadsword (dao), spear (qiang), double-edge sword (jian), and staff (gun) in order to test the coordination of the hand, eyes, body, and step. Therefore, causing your practice of Taijiquan to be a process bringing about unity of internal and external, and the whole body interconnected. You practice without having to think too deeply about it, and without having doubts or unanticipated results; grasping completely Taijiquan's requirements and rules of movement.

Passing through this level of

practice, you already have self-correcting ability and can manage to avoid pitfalls and follow the right path without the guidance of your teacher. Continue to delve deeply into the study of Taijiquan and you can gradually enter into the realm of profound mystery. Chen Xin said: "When you don't clearly understand the theory, engage a teacher who understands clearly; when the way is not clear, call on a good friend; when the theory is clearly understood and the way is clear, but you still aren't able, practice daily with all your effort and then continue without letup, and with the passage of time you will arrive by your own effort."

6. A stable foundation, substantial internal energy

The meaning of so-called stable foundation, substantial internal energy, indicates progressively stabilizing the lower body, and building upon the foundation established in the previous level, impelling internal energy to become substantial and full. A boxing treatise states: "when the root is firmly rooted the branches and leaves flourish." "Nourish the root and the branches and leaves will flourish on their own, prime the spring and the flow will increase on its own." Practicing forms is a method of nourishing the root and priming the source. The "root" indicated here has the meaning of foundation, and is also the lower body from the waist down. A boxing treatise states: "When the lower body is firm, the upper limbs are naturally light and flexible."The so described "lower body"(xia pan) indicates the lower half portion of your body or your legs. Relying on the supportive strength of your legs, with your two feet as a foundation, your crotch energy rounded and able to turn freely, you will sink into a stable stance.

Another theory has it that your root (gen ben) is your "original internal energy" (yuan qi). Original internal energy is stored in the kidneys. When the kidneys are full of internal energy, then "essential strength" (jing li) will be abundant. This is the so-called "solid root"(gen ben gu).

In the phrase "priming the spring", the so-called "spring" indicates the source (gen yuan) or origin (ben yuan). The "original qi" (yuan qi) with which your body is already endowed at birth is the origin of all the various internal energies, the source of which is the kidneys - in connection with the "dantian". Original qi is a natural endowment from pre-birth (xian tian) (pre-birth indicates the embryonic state of a living being, consisting of elements from both the father and mother) and it's also called the pre-birth source. It is the root of the five organs (heart, liver, spleen, lungs, and kidney) and the six viscera. The original Yin (yuan Yin) is used to nourish the Yin of the five organs, and the original Yang (yuan Yang) is used to nourish the Yang of the five organs.

Obtaining original Yang, the body uses it for warming; and obtaining original Yin, the body uses it for nourishing the Yin. Therefore, vitality flourishes, which in turn is good for helping the internal energy of the kidneys, filling the "dantian" to overflowing with qi. This kind of mutually beneficial process finishes a complete cycle and then starts anew; therefore, bringing about a solid root and priming the source.

After passing through the previous levels above, when you practice the barehanded forms, your whole body forms a holistic, completely integrated system of movement. However, in coordinating the breathing with the movement you still cannot manage to be appropriately natural and smooth.

In the first through the fourth levels above, because the movements and postures are stiff and not coordinated, internal energy and the external form are not combined, and, the requirement for matching up the movements with the breathing is not possible. When the fifth level is reached, although the whole body is interconnected, with the internal and external combined into one, if the movements speed up or change rapidly or alternate fast with slow, then it is difficult to match up the movement with the breathing. When you practice in this level, along with the raising of the quality of your barehanded practice, you must strictly match up the breathing with the movement. I want to especially point out that the abdominal style of breathing in this level is the opposite of the therapeutic medical style of abdominal breathing, that is, you should practice reverse abdominal breathing.

Under normal physiological conditions, breathing comes from the participation of the lungs, intercostal muscles, and diaphragm in completing the process of breathing. The main expression of this is upper thoracic breathing which, at the same time, involves the participation of the diaphragm. When a lung condition develops, because the functioning of upper thoracic style of breathing becomes limited, then, in a compensating way, the abdominal style of breathing becomes strengthened. The main manifestations of this type of abdominal breathing activity are: When you inhale, the diaphragm contracts, the abdominal cavity is shifted downward, pressure increases within the abdomen, and the abdomen protrudes toward the outside; when you exhale, the diaphragm slowly expands upward, with the abdominal cavity shifting upward, decreasing pressure within the abdomen, drawing the abdominal wall inward.

The "reverse abdominal breathing" of taijiquan is just the opposite of the situation described above. When you inhale, the belly draws inward, the diaphragm rises upward and the internal energy of the dantian (dantian zhi qi) rises upward from the belly. The stomach starts to bulge naturally, the thoracic cavity naturally expands, and the capacity of the lungs is increased; when you exhale, the belly protrudes, the diaphragm sinks downward, internal energy (nei qi) sinks down into the dantian, the stomach and thoracic cavity naturally returning to their normal state. There is a horizontal "rotation" (xuan zhuan - alternating expansion and contraction) of the kidneys at the back of the waist, due to the sinking of internal energy to the dantian and the inner horizontal "revolving" (zhuan) of the dantian. These are combined into one. When issuing energy (fa jin) in coordination with the breathing, you use one quick inhalation and one short exhalation to complete the action.

After you coordinate the breathing together as one, in addition to normal practicing of the solo sets, you still should practice a few supplemental training exercises (fu zhu gong) as well. Such as: practicing standing meditation postures (zhan zhuang) using any of the stances, such as horse stance (da ma bu), or bow stance (gong bu), or "T"step stance (ding bu), these are all acceptable. Hold the posture for 20 minutes before and 20 minutes after practicing taijiquan, in order to develop a firm and steady standing posture, good breathing and moving of "breath" or internal energy, developing your strength and endurance.

Practice shaking a long pole (dou ganzi), using a white waxwood pole with a diameter at the base or thick end of 6-8 cm and a length of three meters. Practice every day the three actions of open (lan), close (na), and thrust (zha) - 100 times each.

In addition, you still should take single energy-issuing (fa jin) actions from the set of forms and practice them individually, in order to increase your ability to store and release energy (under the conditions of already having a stable foundation of rooted postures and substantial internal energy).

7. An acute sense of touch knowing yourself and the opponent

8. The right timing and right position, following the opponent

9. Your body is like gunpowder, set off with one move

10. Limitless change, appearing and disappearing at will

Hand Forms and Stances of Chen-style Taijiquan

Fig. 1-1

Hand Forms

1. The Palm (zhang): The requirement of Chen-style Taijiquan for the palm is that it be a "roof tile palm" (wa long zhang). Your thumb and little finger should be held as if they are pulling closer together; your middle, index and third fingers should all slightly stretch out backward. Your four fingers should lightly draw in together, but you should not use force. Keep the center of your palm relaxed (literally "empty"). (fig. 1-1)

2. The Fist (quan): The Chen-style Taijiquan fist is formed by rolling up your four fingers together, with the tips of the fingers touching the center of your palm. Then roll up your thumb so that it is touching the middle segments of your middle and index fingers to make a fist. It is not beneficial to make an excessively tight fist, however, in order to avoid rigidity in your hand and arm. (fig. 2)

Fig. 1-2

3. The Hook Hand (gou shou): Bring together the tips of your five fingers, bending and relaxing your wrist. You cannot use force, creating a "dead" angle between your hand and forearm, because this will adversely affect your circulation. (fig. 3).

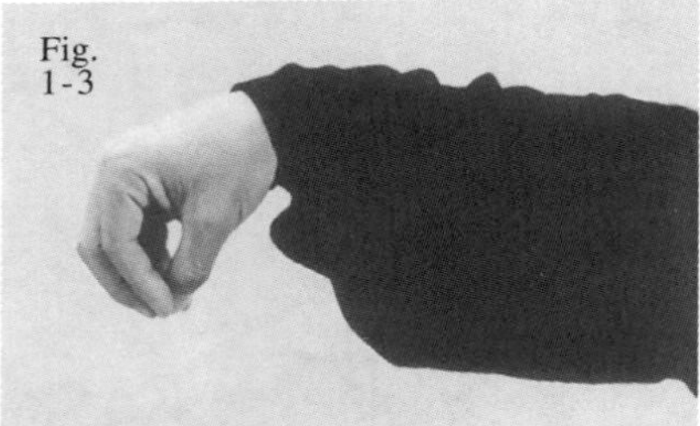
Fig. 1-3

Stances

Although there are some differences between the bow stance of Chen-style Taijiquan and other martial arts styles, they all have in common the requirement of bending the knees and relaxing the hip joints (kua).

1. Left Bow Stance (gong bu): The left leg is substantial and the right leg is "empty". The knee of the substantial leg is lined up vertically over the heel and facing in the same direction as the toes. The toes of the empty leg hook inward and the knee is slightly bent, yet, there is straightness within bending (ie. the leg appears to be extended straight out). 70 percent of your weight is supported on your substantial (bow) leg and 30 percent of your weight is supported on your empty (arrow) leg. Your hip joints are relaxed and your knees are bent. Your crotch pulls open and forms a round shape. That is, there is opening outward and coming together inward (ie. although the thighs of the upper leg rotate to open outward, the knees and calves rotate to close inward). "Within opening there is coming together, within coming together there is opening". This stance is used in the form Single-Whip. (fig. 4)

Fig. 1-4

2. Right Bow Stance: The right leg is substantial, the left leg is "empty". The other requirements are the same as the left bow stance, just the direction is different. This stance is used in the form Lazily Tying Coat. (fig. 5)

Fig. 1-5

3. Empty Step Stance (xu bu): In the empty set stance, one leg supports the weight of your body. The other foot is "empty", with just the toes lightly touching the ground. The empty leg supports only about a tenth of your body weight and serves to raise that limb upward. With your knee bent and the hip crease (kua) relaxed, the weighted side and the empty side are clearly differentiated. There are both left and right empty step stances; an example of the left style is seen in "White Goose Spreading Its Wings", and the right style in "Forward Technique" and "Backward Technique". (fig. 6)

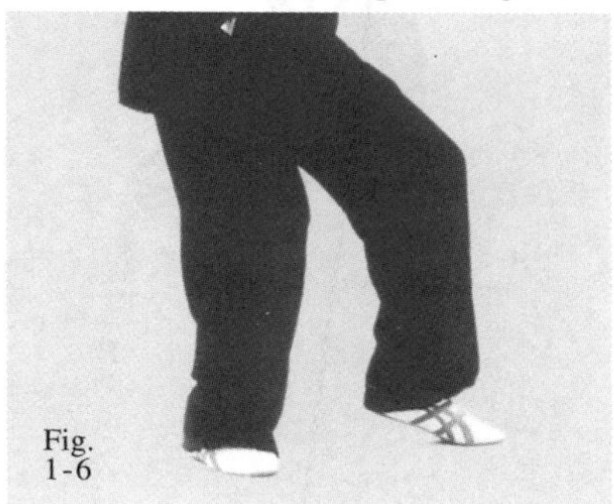
Fig. 1-6

4. Ground Stance (pu bu): The ground stance is a kind of low to the ground technique and is also called "Single Leg Take-down" (dan die cha). One leg squats down by bending at the knee and the other leg extends straight out along the ground. Your posture cannot be too immobile however. With your buttocks about four finger widths from the ground, you need to preserve the flexibility and turning power within your groin. This stance is one way of training the supportive strength of your legs. It is seen in the postures"Swing the Foot and Drop Down" and "Dragon Rolling Downward". (fig. 7)

Fig. 1-7

5. Single Leg Stance (du li bu): The single leg stance is a type of raising-upward stance. It is the opposite and complimentary counterpart of the ground stance, with one a high stance and one a low stance. One leg supports the entire weight of your body, the other leg rises upward with bent knee to hip level. The tip of the foot on the raised leg turns to point inside, below your crotch. The supporting leg stretches out but does not lock into a straight line and the stance is naturally firm and stable, like in the form "Golden Rooster Standing on

One Leg". (fig. 8)

Fig. 1-8

6. Left-Coiling Sitting Stance (zuo zuo pan): In this stance your right leg is in front and your left leg is behind. Your legs cross and "coil" as you sit downward—as in the form "Slapping the Left Foot". Your right leg supports your body weight and your left foot is "empty" of weight, with just the left toes touching the ground. Your knees bend as you squat down. (fig. 9)

Fig. 1-9

7. Right-Coiling Sitting Stance (you zuo pan): In this stance your left leg is in front and your right leg is behind. Your legs cross and coil as you sit downward—as in the form "Slapping the Right Foot". Your left leg supports your body weight with your right foot empty of weight, with just the right toes touching the ground. Bend your knees as you squat down. (fig. 10)

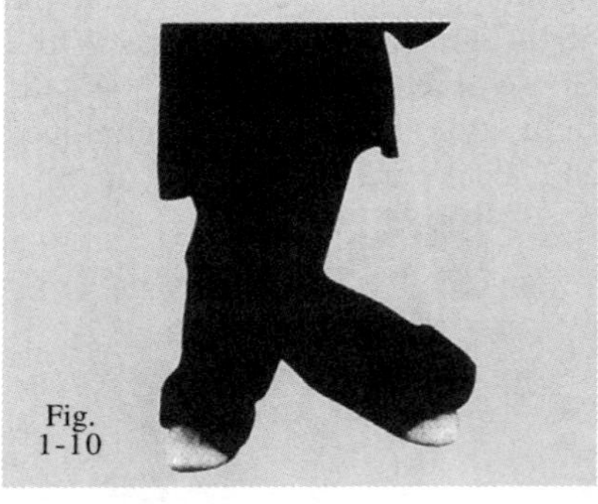

Fig. 1-10

Basic Movements and Chan Si Jin Exercises

Upper limb exercises: left single-arm rolling through clouds

ACTION 1: Step out into a left bow stance, warding off (peng) with your left hand as far as your left knee, at shoulder-high level. Grab your waist with your right hand, the thumb at the back and four fingers to the front of your waist. With your weight on the left, look at your left hand. (fig. 11)

Fig. 1-11

ACTION 2: Turning your body toward the right, shift your weight to your right leg. At the same time, your left hand sinks downward in an arc and settles inward in front of your lower abdomen. Your left hand twines inward (shun chan). (fig. 12)

Fig. 1-12

ACTION 3: Continuing to turn your body toward the right, shift your weight to your left leg. At the same time, "insert" your left hand, fingertips forward, to the upper right. Turn your hand over at a point in front of the right side of your chest. Your left hand now twines outward (ni chan). Look ahead toward the left side of your body. (fig. 13)

Fig. 1-13

ACTION 4: Relax your left hip crease (kua) and turn your body back toward the left. Your left hand twines outward (ni chan) and opens out to over your left knee at shoulder-high level, with your eyes looking at your left hand. At this point you have completed the whole Left Single-Arm Rolling Through Clouds movement. (fig. 14)

One closing (he) (actions 1, 4) and one opening (kai) (actions 2, 3) is one round (pai). Usually, for each type of single-movement solo-exercise you would practice 16 rounds to make up one section (jie). Then you would do the same section over again to practice more. At the beginning level you can practice

Fig. 1-14

carefully, according to the detailed instructions for the exercises in this text, in order to familiarize yourself with the directions of movement. Later, after you become more familiar with the exercises, you can perfect the weight-shifting, threedimensional revolving patterns of movement in your lower body; and speed up changing the left and right rotation of your waist and the natural (shun chan) and reverse (ni chan) twining of your hands and arms.

1. For the sake of simplicity, "shun chan" will be rendered throughout the text as "twines naturally" or "twines inward". This is a whole-body spiraling movement manifested as a clockwise rotation of the right hand and a counter-clockwise rotation of the left hand (with the little finger of either hand leading in the direction of the rotation), as if you are scooping something toward your center. "Ni

chan" will be rendered as "reverse twines" or "twines outward" which is a counter-clockwise rotation of the right hand or a clockwise rotation of the left hand (with the thumb of either hand leading in the direction of rotation) as if scooping something away from your center.

Only in this way can you go from beginning level to being thoroughly familiar, from thoroughly familiar to smooth and natural; gradually arriving at a state where your whole body is interconnected, (its moveme-nt) continuous, without any breaks.

2. Right single-arm rolling through clouds

ACTION 1: Step out into a right bow stance, ward off (peng) with your right hand as far as your right knee at shoulder-high level. Grab your waist with your left hand, the thumb at the back and the four fingers to the front. With your weight

Fig. 1-15

on the right, look at your right hand (fig. 15)

ACTION 2: Turn slightly to the left and shift your weight to your left leg. At the same time, your right hand sinks downward in an arc and comes in toward your lower abdomen. Your right hand twines inward (shun chan). Your eyes look toward the right front of your body. (fig. 16)

Fig. 1-16

ACTION 3: Continue turning your body toward the left while shifting your weight to the right. At the same time, insert your right hand, with fingertips forward to the upper left. Turning your palm outward at the left side of the chest, your right hand twines outward (ni chan). Your eyes look toward your right side. (fig. 17)

ACTION 4: Relax your right hip crease and turn your body toward the right. Your right hand twines outward (ni chan) and opens

Fig. 1-17

outward as far as your right knee at shoulder-high level. Your eyes look toward the front of your body. (fig. 18) Other requirements are the same as Left Single-Arm Rolling.

Fig. 1-18

3. Double-arm rolling through clouds.

ACTION 1: Starting from a single-whip posture (dan bian), with your two legs opening to a left bow stance and your two arms opened out. Your posture should be upright and balanced. Your eyes look to your front. (fig. 19)

Fig. 1-19

ACTION 2: Turning your body slightly toward the left, change your right hand to an open palm and twine it inward (shun chan), sinking it downward along an arc to in front of your lower abdomen. Your left hand changes to outward twining (ni chan) and wards off (peng) upward. Your eyes look toward your right front.

Fig. 1-20

(fig. 20)

ACTION 3: Turning your body, first to the left and then to the right, shift your weight from your left leg to your right leg. At the same time, your right hand moves to the left and then upward, changing to reverse twining (ni chan) and warding off (peng) toward the right. Your left hand twines inward (shun chan) in an arc, coming in to the inside of your left leg. Your eyes look toward the left front (fig. 21)

Fig. 1-21

In this way (you have returned to your original position) you can go through this cycle for many repetitions of the turning action, practicing rotating your crotch and turning your waist, the left and right silk-twining (chan si) actions of your two arms, and moving your whole body together as one unit. You can also combine this exercise with taking steps. You can take a side step followed by a closing step (bing bu); a step sideways, behind your other leg (tou bu); and a step sideways, in front of your other leg (gai bu) and turning your body (which uncrosses your two legs and leaves you facing 180 degrees in the opposite directiona second "tou bu" or "gai bu" followed by another 180 degree turn returns you to facing in the original direction).

4. Left and right roll back twining hands.

ACTION 1: Step out into a right bow stance (your right leg bent like a bow, your left leg straight like an arrow). Your left hand is situated in front of the left side of your chest at shoulder-high level. Your right hand is held against the right side of your waist. Your eyes look straight ahead. (fig. 22)

Fig. 1-22

ACTION 2: Turning your body slightly toward the left, shift your weight to your left leg. At the same time, your left hand reverse twines (ni chan) and rolls back (lu) downward to the left side of your waist. Your right hand first reverse twines (ni chan) and rolls back (lu), changing to natural twining (shun chan) as it turns over upward, warding off (peng) forward in front of the right side of your chest. Your eyes look forward. (fig. 23)

Fig. 1-23

ACTION 3: Turning your body slightly to the right, your weight shifts to the right. At the same time, your right hand reverse twines (ni chan) and rolls back (lu) to the right side of your waist. Your left hand first reverse twines (ni chan) and rolls back (lu), changing to natural twining (shun chan) as it turns over upward to finish up at the left front of your body. Your eyes look forward. (fig. 24)

Fig. 1-24

In this way you can cycle through many repeats. Use your body to lead your hands, your waist to drive your shoulders, your shoulders to drive your elbows, and then the energy goes through to your hands. Practice the rearward roll back (lu) energy with your whole body's action integrated into one. Note: Pay attention to not propping up your shoulders when you turn in transition to upward movement after you roll back.

5. Left and right twining with fists

ACTION 1: Starting from the same basic foundation of left and right roll back (in a left bow stance), your two hands form fists. The palm of your right fist faces inward and it is situated at shoulder-high level in front of your body. The palm of your left fist faces upward and is situated at the left side of your waist. The weight is on your left leg, and your eyes look to your right front. (fig. 25)

Fig. 1-25

ACTION 2: Turn your body toward the right, shifting your weight to the right. Reverse twine (ni chan) your right fist in an arc, first toward the left and then downward to beside the right side of your waist. Your left hand reverse twines (ni chan) in an arc toward your rear and then wards

Fig. 1-26

off (peng) upward. Your eyes look toward your left front. (fig. 26)

ACTION 3: Continuing to turn your body toward the right, your right fist reverse twines (ni chan) in an arc toward the rear and then wards off (peng) out to the right side. Your left fist changes to natural twining (shun chan) and moves in to the centerline of your body at chest-high level, the palm of the left fist facing inward toward you. Your eyes look toward the left front. (fig. 27)

Fig. 1-27

ACTION 4: Turn your body toward the left and shift your weight to the left. Reverse twine (ni chan) your left fist inward in an arc, with the palm facing downward. Your right fist changes to natural twining (shun chan) and turns upward. Your eyes look forward. (fig. 28)

Fig. 1-28

ACTION 5: Continue to turn toward the left, reverse twining (ni chan) your left fist to a position by the left side of your waist. Your right fist twines naturally (shun chan) and moves inward to the centerline of your body at chest-high level, the palm of your right fist facing downward. Your eyes look forward. (fig. 29)

Fig. 1-29

Practice in this way for a number of repetitions. A major point is to practice the (horizontal figure 8) revolution of your groin and the left and right turning of your waist; also the natural (shun) and reverse (ni) "silk-twining" (chan si) movements of your two fists, with the energy of your fists alternately moving inward and then warding off (peng) outward.

6. Double-arm twining

ACTION 1: First stand at attention in the Beginning Posture of Taijiquan, then raise your left leg and take a step forward. Ward off (peng) upward in an arc toward the front and then roll back (lu) toward the rear, twining both hands simultaneously —your left hand twining inward (shun chan) and your right hand twining outward (ni chan). (fig. 30)

Fig. 1-30

ACTION 2: Your two hands roll back (lu) and your body turns to the right. Then your weight shifts to your left leg. (fig. 31)

Fig. 1-31

ACTION 3: Turning your body toward the left, your two hands move in a downward arc, and then ward off (peng) forward, your left hand reverse twining (ni chan) and your right hand twining naturally (shun chan). (fig. 32)

Fig. 1-32

ACTION 4: Your two hands continue in an upward direction with the hands changing slightly to the right hand reverse twining (ni chan) and the left hand natural twining (shun chan). Your body turns slightly toward the right. (fig. 33)

Fig. 1-33

ACTION 5: Without stopping, turn your body toward the right and shift your weight to the right. Your two hands roll back (lu) toward the right rear. (fig. 34)

Continue repeating this cyclical in practicing more repetitions. You can also reverse the position of the legs, with your right leg in front and your left leg behind, alternating between the left forward and the right forward styles in turn. The vertical circles described by your

Fig. 1-34

two hands on both sides of your body mainly depend on the rotation of your waist and crotch, which drives the circular action of your two arms. Using your body to lead your hands, control your internal energy (qi) with the intention of your mind (yi).

Lower limb exercises: double-arm twining with forward steps

ACTION 1: Stand at attention with your feet together, your two arms hanging down at both sides. With your whole body relaxed, your conscious mind (yi) focuses on your dantian. Look straight ahead. (fig. 35)

ACTION 2: Shifting your weight to your right leg, raise up your left leg and take a step forward toward the left front with your left leg. At the same time, your two hands circle forward and upward in

Fig. 1-35

an arc, then roll back (lu) toward the rear, with your left hand twining inward (shun chan) and your right hand twining outward (ni chan). Your eyes look forward. (fig. 36)

Fig. 1-36

ACTION 3: Shifting your weight to your left leg, bring your right foot together with your left foot. At the same time, your two hands change to the left hand twining outward (ni chan) and the right hand twining inward (shun chan), to ward off (peng) forward along a descending arc. Your eyes look forward. (fig. 37)

Fig. 1-37

Then, step forward and roll back (lu) with your two arms (as in action two above). This mainly serves to train the coordination of hand and arm actions with stepping, and the coordination of your whole body.

2. Sideways advancing step with double-arm twining

ACTION 1: Stand upright with your two feet together and your two arms sinking downward at your sides. With your whole body relaxed, focus your conscious mind (yi) on you dantian. Look straight ahead. (fig.38)

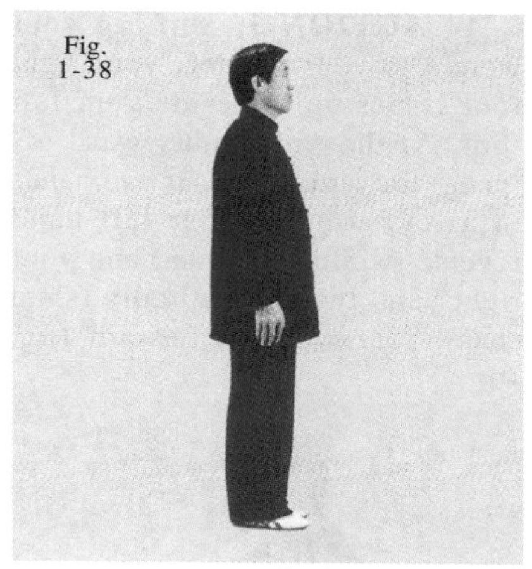
Fig. 1-38

ACTION 2: Shifting your weight to your right leg, raise your left leg and take a step forward to your left front. At the same time, your two hands circle forward and upward, then roll back (lu) to your rear. Your left hand twines inward (shun chan) and your right hand twines outward (ni chan). Your eyes look to the left front. (fig. 39)

Fig. 1-39

ACTION 3: Shifting your weight to your left leg, your right foot comes up to beside your left foot. At the same time, ward off (peng) forward with your two hands in a forward arc, your left hand reverse twining (ni chan) and your right hand twining naturally (shun chan). Your eyes look forward. (fig. 40)

Fig. 1-40

3. Left and right twining with retreating step.

ACTION 1: Stand upright with both feet together and look forward. With your left hand held at the left side of your waist, push (tui) forward with your right palm, the right palm facing forward. Let your elbows sink and your shoulders relax. (fig. 41)

ACTION 2: Shifting your weight to your left leg, raise your

Fig. 1-41

right leg so that just the toes of your right foot touch the ground. Bring your right leg back in an inward arc toward your left foot and toward your rear. At the same time, your right hand reverse twines (ni chan) in a downward arc, as your right leg steps back, and rolls back (lu) to your right rear. Your left hand turns over and pushes (tui) forward from behind. (fig. 42)

Fig. 1-42

ACTION 3: Shifting your weight to your right leg, raise your left leg and trace an arc inward toward your right foot with the toes of your left foot as you step backward with your left foot. At the same time as you are stepping back with your left leg, your left hand reverse twines (ni chan) in a downward arc and rolls back (lu) to your left rear. Your right hand turns upward from behind and pushes (tui) forward. Your eyes look forward. (fig. 43)

Fig. 1-43

This movement is called "Stepping Back and Whirling the Arms" and is for practicing the technique of coordinating your upper and lower body while retreating backwards. You can practice with 3, 5, or 7 retreating steps.

4. Left-opening step with single-arm twining.

ACTION 1: Stand upright with both feet together. With your right hand holding your waist, extend your left arm straight out from your side, the left palm facing left. Sink your elbows and relax your shoulders. Look straight ahead to the front. (fig. 44)

Fig. 1-44

ACTION 2: Turn slightly to the right and shift your weight to your right leg. Raise your left leg and step out toward your left side. At the same time, your left hand twines inward (shun chan) in a downward arc toward your body. Your eyes look to the left front. (fig. 45)

ACTION 3: Turn slightly to the left and shift your weight to your

Fig. 1-45

left leg. Raise your right leg and draw it in to your left leg to stand with both feet together. At the same time, your left hand continues in an arc toward your body, then turns upward, changing to reverse twining (ni chan) and extending out toward the left. Your eyes look toward the left front. (fig. 46)

Fig. 1-46

This is mainly an exercise for training left single-arm twining in a circle with a left-opening step. The foot goes out (kai) and the hand comes in (he). The hand coming in and the foot going out is a way to practice "leading the attacker in above while advancing below" (shang yin xia jin). You can practice by repeating in sets of 3, 5, or 7 steps.

5. Right-opening step with single-arm twining

ACTION 1: Stand straight upright with your left hand holding your waist and your right hand extended out to your right, the right palm facing to the right front. Sink your elbows and relax your shoulders. Look toward the right front. (fig. 47)

Fig. 1-47

ACTION 2: Turn your body slightly to the left and shift your weight to your left leg. Raise your right leg and take a sideways step out to the right side with your right hand moving downward in an arc toward your body at the same time. Your eyes look to your right front. (fig. 48)

Fig. 1-48

Fig. 1-49

ACTION 3: Turn slightly to the right and shift your weight to your right leg. Raise your left foot and bring it up to beside the inside of your right foot to stand with both feet together. At the same time, your right hand continues in an arc inward then upward, turning over toward the outside and reverse twining (ni chan) as it extends out to the right. Your eyes look toward the right front. (fig. 49)

The direction of this form is to the right, otherwise, all other requirements are the same as the left-opening step style above.

Standing Meditation Postures

Single Whip (dan bian)

With your head held naturally erect, let the top of your head rise up naturally as if it were suspended (xu ling ding jin). Stand upright in a balanced posture (li shen zhong zheng) with a level gaze and your teeth lightly touching. Your two elbows sink downward and your shoulders are relaxed. Your two hands draw or guide your internal energy (jin). Relaxing your hips and bending your knees, you must keep your groin rounded. Your left leg is weighted (shi) and your right leg is relatively without weight (xu). The tip of your left foot toes out and the tip of your right foot toes inward. Concentrating your consciousness, relax your entire body and let your internal energy (qi) sink to your lower abdomen (dantian) then descend down to the acupuncture point under the front part of your foot (yongquan) (fig. 50)

Fig. 1-50

With your head held naturally erect, let the top of your head draw upward as if it were being lightly drawn upward by a string attached to your crown (ding jin ling qi). Standing upright in a balanced posture, extend your right hand out to your right side and hold your waist with your left hand. Relax your shoulders and sink your elbows. Your left arm is rounded in shape with no sharp angle at the elbow. Relaxing your hips (kua) and bending your knees, you must keep your groin rounded open and not pinched together. Your right leg is weighted and your left leg is relatively without weight. The tip of your right foot toes out and the tip of the left foot toes in. 70% of your weight is on your right leg and 30% of your weight is on your left leg. (fig. 51)

Fig. 1-51

Lazily Tying One's Coat (lan za yi)

Take a diagonal step posture with your weight on your left leg. The tip of your left foot toes out and the tip of your right foot toes in. Relaxing your hips and bending your knees, the energy of your groin (dang jin) twines inward (nei kou) on itself. Stand upright and balanced. With your body rotated slightly to the left, your two arms are extended outward, perpendicular to a line intersecting your two feet. Your two feet and two hands are each oriented to one the four corners of a square. Your eyes look straight forward. (fig.52)

Fig. 1-52

Diagonal Posture(xie xing)

Concentrating your consciousness on a single point, your thoughts settle down and become tranquil. Standing naturally upright, your entire body relaxes. Your two arms form a circle, with your two palms facing inward toward your body and the fingers of each hand pointing tip to tip with the fingers of the opposite hand. Sink your elbows and relax your shoulders; your two feet about a half meter apart. Bending your knees and relaxing your hips (kua), squat down and keep your groin rounded by rotating your knees slightly inward. Lightly grip the ground with the ball, ridge and heel of each foot - keeping the center of your foot (yongquan) "empty" of weight. (fig. 53, 53 supplemental)

Fig. 1-53 Fig.1-53 supplemental

Primordial Posture (hun yuan zhuang)

These few standing meditation postures (zhong ding shen fa) above are also called standing post (zhuang gong) training. After every time you practice some basic exercises (such as chan si jing) you should stand for 5-10 minutes. At first stand in only one, then two, then more postures; starting with a short amount of time and gradually increasing to a longer amount of time; starting from a higher stance and gradually progressing to a lower stance—gradually increasing your athletic capability. When you practice standing meditation postures, there aren't any complicated movements so it is easy to concentrate your consciousness, making it possible for you to master standing upright in a balanced posture, relaxing your entire body, releasing the tension in you upper torso (xin qi xia jiang) and allowing your internal energy (qi) to sink to your lower abdomen (dantian).

The First Routine of Chen-style "Laojia" Taijiquan

The "old" (or big) frame style of the Chen family's Taijiquan was created by Chen Chang-Xing (of the 14th generation of the Chen family at Chenjiagou village) out of five routines of Taijiquan, one routine of cannon fist (paochui), and the 108-form routine of long boxing (changquan), which had been created by Chen Wang-Ting. Later, Chen Chang-Xing reduced the number of movements, arranged and compiled the first routine and the second routine (paochui) of the old frame of Chen style Taijiquan as we know it today.

The first routine mainly emphasizes softness, but also contains an element of hardness within. The second routine mainly stresses hardness or firmness, with an element of softness contained within. These two complimentary elements within the routines supplement each other, and each has its root in the other, up to the point where hardness and softness become blended together into a harmonious whole.

This chapter will introduce the first routine of the old frame style. Its special characteristics are: large movements, light yet steady footwork, naturally erect posture, internal energy governing the movements of the body, with the spiraling energy of "chan si jin" as the core, the waist as the central axis of movement, and each separate movement linked together in a continuous whole. When movement commences the whole body is set in motion, when movement ceases the entire body is still. All the movements in the routine are performed continuously like clouds moving across the sky and water running down a mountainside. When exerting force within the routine, one does so with a relaxed and elastic type of strength, and with an unbroken continuity of energy.

When practicing Taijiquan, the requirements for proper practice are as follows: keep the head erect naturally (as if it were suspended by a string attached to the top of the head) stand naturally upright, relax the shoulders and drop the elbows. Bring the shoulders slightly forward and lower the waist. Let the internal energy (qi) descend, and breathe naturally. With the hips relaxed and the knees bent, round the crotch (i.e. the legs should form a rounded shape). With solid and empty clearly separated, the upper and lower parts of the body move in harmony with each other, blending hard and soft, fast and slow movements smoothly. External movements of the body should describe an arc (i.e. should follow circular paths) with the internal energy within the body following a spiral path. With the waist as an axis, movement of the torso leads the movement of the limbs, with a spiraling or twining type of movement. Gradually, a type of internal energy is produced which is seemingly soft yet not soft, seemingly hard but not hard, which can easily change between extremely heavy or incredibly light action. Your movements appear outwardly soft but are inwardly firm, like iron wrapped in cotton. If in the entire set of movements there aren't any plane surfaces or any straight lines and there aren't any breaks in the continuity of movement or any motions that don't follow a smooth circular line, then that is the correct way.

The Names of the 74 Forms

1. Beginning Posture of Taijiquan (TaijiQiShi)
2. Pounding the Mortar (Jin Gang Dao Dui)
3. Lazily Tying One's Coat (Lan Za Yi)
4. Sealing Six Avenues of Attack and Closing Four Sides(Liu Feng SiBi)
5. Single Whip (Dan Bian)
6. Pounding the Mortar (Jin Gang Dao Dui)
7. White Goose Spreading Its Wings (Bai E Liang Chi)
8. Diagonal Posture (Xie Xing)
9. Holding Up the Knee (Lou Xi)
10. Stepping to Both Sides (Ao Bu)
11. Diagonal Posture (Xie Xing)
12. Holding Up the Knee (Lou Xi)
13. Stepping to Both Sides (Ao Bu)
14. Cover Fist and Punch (Yan Shou Gong Quan)
15. Pounding the Mortar (Jin Gang Dao Dui)
16. Hit and Drape Fist Over Body (Pie Shen Quan)
17. Blue Dragon Flying Out of the Water (Qing Long Chu Shui)
18. Pushing With Both Hands (Shuang Tui Shou)
19. Fist Under the Elbow (Zhou Di Kan Quan)
20. Stepping Back and Whirling the Arms (Dao Juan Gong)
21. White Goose Spreading Its Wings (Bai E Liang Chi)
22. Diagonal Posture (Xie Xing)
23. Turning Back with Arms Twining (Shan Tong Bei)
24. Cover Fist and Punch (Yan Shou

Gong Quan)

25. Sealing Six Avenues of Attack and Closing Four Sides (Liu Feng Si Bi)
26. Single Whip (Dan Bian)
27. Rolling Hands Through the Clouds (Yun Shou)
28. Patting the Horse's Back (Gao Tan Ma)
29. Slapping the Right Foot (You Ca Jiao)
30. Slapping the Left Foot (Zuo Ca Jiao)
31. Kicking with the Left Heel (Zuo Deng Yi Gen)
32. Walking Forward by Stepping to Both Sides (Qian Tang Ao Bu)
33. Punching Toward the Ground (Ji Di Chui)
34. Turning and Kicking Twice in the Air (Ti Er Qi)
35. Protecting the Heart with the Fist (Hu Xin Quan)
36. Whirlwind Kick (Xuan Feng Jiao)
37. Kicking with the Right Heel (You Deng Yi Gen)
38. Cover Fist and Punch (Yan Shou Gong Quan)
39. Small Grab and Hit (Xiao Qin Da)
40. Protecting the Head and Pushing the Mountain (Bao Tou Tui Shan)
41. Sealing Six Avenues of Attack and Closing Four Sides (Liu Feng Si Bi)
42. Single Whip (Dan Bian)
43. Forward Technique (Qian Zhao)
44. Backward Technique (Hou Zhao)
45. Parting the Wild Horse's Mane (Ye Ma Fen Zong)
46. Sealing Six Avenues of Attack and Closing Four Sides (Liu Feng Si Bi)
47. Single Whip (Dan Bian)
48. Jade Maiden Working Her Loom (Yu Nu Chuan Suo)
49. Lazily Tying One's Coat (Lan Za Yi)
50. Sealing Six Avenues of Attack and Closing Four Sides (Liu Feng Si Bi)
51. Single Whip (Dan Bian)

52. Rolling Hands Through the Clouds (Yun Shou)
53. Swing the Foot and Drop Down (Bai Jiao Die Cha)
54. Golden Rooster Standing on One Leg (Jin Ji Du Li)
55. Stepping Back and Whirling the Arms (Dao Juan Gong)
56. White Goose Spreading It's Wings (Bai E Liang Chi)
57. Diagonal Posture (Xie Xing)
58. Turning Back with Arms Twining (Shan Tong Bei)
59. Cover Fist and Punch (Yan Shou Gong Quan)
60. Sealing Six Avenues of Attack and Closing Four Sides (Liu Feng Si Bi)
61. Single Whip (Dan Bian)
62. Rolling Hands Through the Clouds (Yun Shou)
63. Patting the Horse's Back (Gao Tan Ma)
64. Reverse Sweep with Right Leg Crossing (Shi Zi Jiao)
65. Punch Toward the Crotch (Zhi Dang Chui)
66. Ape Picking Fruit (Yuan Hou Tan Guo)
67. Single Whip (Dan Bian)
68. Dragon Rolling Downward (Que Di Long)
69. Stepping Forward into Seven Stars Stance (Shang Bu Qi Xing)
70. Stepping Backward into Riding Stance (Xia Bu Kua Gong)
71. Turning Around and Sweeping with Both Legs (Zhuan Shen Shuang Bai Lian)
72. Cannon Right Overhead (Dang Tou Pao)
73. Pounding the Mortar (Jin Gang Dao Dui)
74. Closing Posture of Taijiquan (Shou Shi)

74 Small Forms Divided into 13 Large Forms *(after Chen Xin)*

I

1. Beginning Posture of Taijiquan (Taiji Qi Shi)
2. Pounding the Mortar (Jin Gang Dao Dui)

II

3. Lazily Tying One's Coat (Lan Za Yi)
4. Sealing Six Avenues of Attack and Closing Four Sides (Liu Feng Si Bi)
5. Single Whip (Dan Bian)
6. Pounding the Mortar (Jin Gang Dao Dui)

III

7. White Goose Spreading It's Wings (Bai E Liang Chi)
8. Diagonal Posture (Xie Xing)

IV

9. Holding Up the Knee (Lou Xi)
10. Stepping to Both Sides (Ao Bu)
11. Diagonal Posture (Xie Xing)

V

12. Holding Up the Knee (Lou Xi)
13. Stepping to Both Sides (Ao Bu)
14. Cover Fist and Punch (Yan Shou Gong Quan)
15. Pounding the Mortar (Jin Gang Dao Dui)

VI

16. Hit and Drape Fist Over Body

(Pie Shen Quan)

17. Blue Dragon Flying out of the Water (Qing Long Chu Shui)
18. Pushing with Both Hands (Shuang Tui Shou)
19. Fist Under the Elbow (Zhou Di Kan Quan)
20. Stepping Back and Whirling the Arms (Dao Juan Gong)
21. White Goose Spreading It's Wings (Bai E Liang Chi)
22. Diagonal Posture (Xie Xing)

VII

23. Turning Back with Arms Twining (Shan Tong Bei)
24. Cover Fist and Punch (Yan Shou Gong Quan)
25. Sealing Six Avenues of Attack and Closing Four Sides (Liu Feng Si Bi)
26. Single Whip (Dan Bian)

VIII

27. Rolling Hands through the Clouds (Yun Shou)
28. Patting the Horse's Back (Gao Tan Ma)
29. Slapping the Right Foot (You Ca Jiao)
30. Slapping the Left Foot (Zuo Ca Jiao)
31. Kicking with the Left Heel (Zuo Deng Yi Gen)
32. Walking Forward by Stepping to Both Sides (Qian Tang Ao Bu)
33. Punching Toward the Ground (Ji Di Chui)
34. Turning and Kicking Twice in the Air (Ti Er Qi)
35. Protecting the Heart with the Fist (Hu Xin Quan)
36. Whirlwind Kick (Xuan Feng Jiao)
37. Kicking with the Right Heel (You Deng Yi Gen)
38. Cover Fist and Punch (Yan Shou Gong Quan)
39. Small Grab and Hit (Xiao Qin Da)
40. Protecting the Head and Pushing the Mountain (Bao Tou Tui Shan)
41. Sealing Six Avenues of Attack

and Closing Four Sides (Liu Feng SiBi)

42. Single Whip (Dan Bian)

IX

43. Forward Technique (Qian Zhao)
44. Backward Technique (Hou Zhao)
45. Parting the Wild Horse's Mane (Ye Ma Fen Zong)
46. Sealing Six Avenues of Attack and Closing Four Sides (Liu Feng Si Bi)
47. Single Whip (Dan Bian)
48. Jade Maiden Working Her Loom (Yu Nu Chuan Suo)
49. Lazily Tying One's Coat (Lan Za Yi)
50. Sealing Six Avenues of Attack and Closing Four Sides (Liu Feng SiBi)
51. Single Whip (Dan Bian)

X

52. Rolling Hands Through the Clouds (Yun Shou)
53. Swing the Foot and Drop Down (Bai Jiao Die Cha)
54. Golden Rooster Standing on One Leg (Jin Ji Du Li)
55. Stepping Back and Whirling the Arms (Dao Juan Gong)
56. White Goose Spreading It's Wings (Bai E Liang Chi)
57. Diagonal Posture (Xie Xing)
58. Turning Back with Arms Twining (Shan Tong Bei)
59. Cover Fist and Punch (Yan Shou Gong Quan)
60. Sealing Six Avenues of Attack and Closing Four Sides (Liu Feng SiBi)
61. Single Whip (Dan Bian)

XI

62. Rolling Hands Through the Clouds (Yun Shou)
63. Patting the Horse's Back (Gao Tan Ma)
64. Reverse Sweep with Right Leg Crossing (Shi Zi Jiao)
65. Punch Toward the Crotch (Zhi Dang Chui)

66. Ape Picking Fruit (Yuan Hou Tan Guo)
67. Single Whip (Dan Bian)

XII

68. Dragon Rolling Downward (Que Di Long)
69. Stepping Forward into Seven Stars Stance (Shang Bu Qi Xing)
70. Stepping Backward into Riding Stance (Xia Bu Kua Gong)

XIII

71. Turning Around and Sweeping with Both Legs (Zhuan Shen Shuang Bai Lian)
72. Cannon Right Overhead (Dang Tou Pao)
73. Pounding the Mortar (Jin Gang Dao Dui)
74. Closing Posture of Taijiquan (Shou Shi)

The First Routine of Chen-style "Laojia" Taijiquan

1. Beginning Posture of Taijiquan

(Taiji Qi Shi)

ACTION 1: Stand at attention with your feet together, letting your arms hang naturally downward at your sides with your palms facing your body. Your head should be naturally erect and your lips and teeth lightly closed with the tip of your tongue touching the upper palate just behind your front teeth. Your eyes look forward, neither upward or downward. (fig. 2-1)

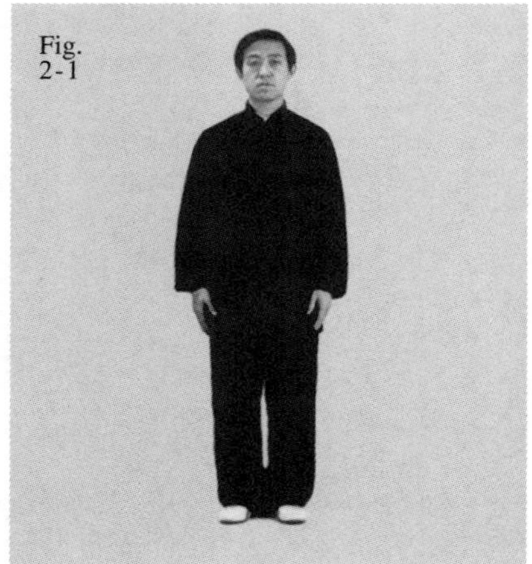
Fig. 2-1

Requirements: After assuming the standing posture, your mind should be concentrated, clear and calm, expelling any mundane thoughts. Your body's intrinsic energy (qi) should be directed downward and your breathing natural. Chen Xin's book on Taijiquan said, "When students begin to study Taijiquan, they should first rid their minds of extraneous thoughts, calm their mind and still their emotions, calmly awaiting any movement. After this state has been achieved, they can begin to study Taijiquan."

ACTION2: Bend your knees slightly, relaxing your hips and letting the weight of your body flow downward. Raise your left foot slightly and take a half-step sideways to the left so that your feet are now about as wide as your shoulders with your toes pointing very slightly outward. The parts of your foot that contact the ground (toes, ridge and heel) should grip the ground, and the acupuncture point which is located in the hollow of the foot (yongquan), should be weightless. Bring your shoulders slightly forward (i.e. as opposed to pulling them back and thrusting your chest outward) and drop your waist (pulling the spine into proper alignment). Relax your shoulders and let your elbows drop. Your body should be plumb with your head naturally erect as if it were suspended by a string attached to the top of the head. Your eyes look

forward. (fig. 2-2)

Fig. 2-2

Requirements: When stepping out to the left, first shift your weight onto your right leg. The toes of your left foot contact with the ground first, upon reaching the shoulder-wide position, and the whole foot should then be lowered into contact with the ground slowly. Your whole body should be relaxed, allowing your body's intrinsic energy (qi) to sink down to just below your navel (dantian). The qi should continue to descend all the way to the yongquan acupuncture point at the bottom of your foot, with your hips relaxed and your knees bent. Exhale as your internal energy (qi) descends. At this time your mind should be unperturbed by any thoughts and there is an outward appearance of equanimity.

ACTION 3: Slowly raise the hands, palm downward, to shoulder level. Let your elbows sink a little and relax your shoulders. While raising your hands, your body slowly sinks down, with your hips relaxed and knees bending. Your feet press downward and your eyes look ahead. (fig. 2-3)

Fig. 2-3

Requirements: While your hands are rising and your body descending, your chest, back, ribs and abdominal muscles should all be completely relaxed to promote the descent of internal energy (nei qi). Avoid raising your shoulders which can cause an over-abundance of internal energy (qi) in your chest. Inhale as your hands rise.

Internal Energy: Your body's internal, intrinsic energy (nei qi) sinks to your dantian; follows (shun) the inside of your legs and descends to the yongquan acupuncture point under the front part of your foot; the internal energy then moves upward along the outside of your legs; rises upward along the du mai (du channel or energy pathway up the center of your back) to your two shoulders and to your two elbows. The energy, passing through your relaxed shoulders and your dropped elbows, penetrates through to your two hands; your two hands slowly raising upward.

ACTION 4: Your body continues to sink down to a lower stance. Bend your knees and relax your hips, while at the same time pressing downward with the palms of your hands until they are on a level with your abdomen. The palms face downward and your eyes look forward. (fig. 2-4)

Fig. 2-4

Requirements: While pressing downwards with your palms, keep your body plumb upright. Avoid bending your waist and protruding your buttocks. Your hip creases should be relaxed, unconstricted, and open to circulation. When lowering your posture, it is as if you are sitting down on a stool. Exhale as your palms press downward.

Internal Energy: The internal energy (nei qi) rises upward along (shun) the du mai (governing meridian up the back); one portion of the energy moves (shun) to your two shoulders where it splits into your two arms. One portion passes over (rao) the feng chi (acupuncture point at the back of your head) rushes to the bai hui (acupuncture point on the centerline of your body near the top of your head) reaches the ren zhong (acupuncture point on the centerline, between your nose and upper lip) and descends along (shun) the ren mai (conception channel) to return to the dantian. In this way, internal energy (nei qi) rises up and drops down, passing through the ren channel, the du channel, and reaching to your four limbs, flowing unimpeded through the greater circulation (da zhou tian) and the lesser circulation (xiao zhou tian). From the limitless void (wuji) bringing the all-encompassing principle (taiji) into being, creating the two powers (Yin and Yang), opening up (shu tong) the channels and collateral energy pathways (jing luo), moving internal energy throughout the entire body, in one continuum of energy.

2. Pounding the Mortar

(Jin Gang Dao Dui)

ACTION 1: Turn slightly to the left, shifting your center of gravity to the right. With your right hand twining inward (shun chan) and your left hand twining outward (ni chan), push your palms upward in an arc to the left front with your left palm moving to eye level above your left knee with the palm facing outward and your right palm moving to a position in front of your chest, on the centerline of your body, with the palm facing upward. Your eyes look toward the left front. (fig. 2-5)

Fig. 2-5

Requirements: When raising your arms and turning your body, the energy of the waist and crotch should be combined by relaxing your hips and drawing in and lowering your waist slightly so that energy goes through to your palms. Inhale as you are performing this action.

Internal Energy: The dantian energy (qi) drops down to the yongquan acupuncture point as your body turns toward the left. The energy twines naturally (shun) from the right foot, along your right leg, up to your waist. The turning of the waist to the left sends the energy (jin) through your shoulders and elbows to your two hands, becoming upward ward-off (peng) energy .

Self-Defense Application: The upward pushing, ward off action is used to meet an attacker's right fist or palm strike. Your right hand grasps the attacker's fist and your left hand pushes against his elbow, warding off without losing contact.

ACTION 2: Turn your body 90 degrees to the right, shifting your weight from your right to your left leg, simultaneously turning your right foot so that your toes point outward. Pull both arms back to the right rear in a roll-back (lu) action with your left hand twining inward (shun chan) and your right hand twining outward (ni chan). Your eyes

look toward the left front. (fig. 2-6)

Fig. 2-6

Requirements: This action combines roll-back (lu), utilizing the energy of the waist, with ward-off energy (peng jin) added to the arms which follow an outward arc to the right rear. Shift your weight naturally, avoid raising your shoulders or lifting your elbows. Exhale during this action.

Internal Energy: The internal energy (nei qi) twines upward from your right foot to the dantian. One portion twines down to your left leg; another portion twines upward to your two arms and your two hands through the rotation of your lower spine (yao ji) to the right, becoming roll-back energy (lu jin).

Self-Defense Application: (Continuing from the application above) Turn swiftly as soon as the attacker's outgoing energy is spent, to unbalance him by leading him forward.

ACTION 3: Shift your weight to your right leg, raising your left leg and closing up your crotch area. Bend your knees and relax your hips, lowering your body and turning slightly to the right as your hands ward-off (peng) in a right upward direction. Your eyes look toward the left front. (fig. 2-7)

Fig. 2-7

Requirements: When your left leg is raised, your body sinks downward on your right leg, your upper (body) and lower (body) combining harmoniously. Avoid bending your waist and protruding your buttocks. Inhale during this action.

Internal Energy: Keeping ward-off energy (peng jin) in your two hands, continue to roll-back (lu) to the rear. The energy (jin) twines from your left leg to your right leg, raising your left knee and relaxing your hip (kua) or the crease where the leg meets the torso. Your energy (jin) combines (he) in your dantian.

Self-Defense Application: By raising your leg and turning your knee slightly inward you can protect the area of your crotch, and also you can kick the attacker's kneecap or shin with your heel or side of your foot.

ACTION 4: Let the inside of your left heel touch the ground and slide it toward the left front. Your weight is on your right leg while you continue to apply ward-off energy (peng jin) upward to the right. Your eyes look forward to the left front. (fig.2-8)

Fig. 2-8

Requirements: When stepping forward keep your body plumb upright, your two hands continue warding off upward to the right and your upper and lower body stay in balance. Exhale during this action.

Internal Energy: Your qi moves upward from the dantian, the energy (jin) driving into your two hands, adding ward-off energy (peng jin) to the hands. Your qi moves downward to your left foot.

Self-Defense Application: When your left leg goes out, it can be used to kick with the bottom of your foot (deng), to slide into the attacker's foot (chan), or kick sideways with the outer edge of your foot (chuai). It can be used to hook (gou) and control (guan) his foot and ankle joint.

ACTION 5: Shift your weight from your right leg to your left leg, turning your left foot outward and then placing your weight on it. As your weight shifts, your body turns 45 degrees to the left. Your two hands describe an arc downward and ward-off (peng) to the front, with your left hand twining outward (ni chan) and your right hand twining inward (shun chan). Your left hand wards off at chest level with your palm facing downward, and your right hand drops down to a position above and to the inside of your right knee with the palm facing outward and fingers pointing to the rear. Your eyes look forward. (fig. 2-9)

Fig. 2-9

Requirements: The three aspects of this action; turning your body, shifting your weight, and forward with your hands should be performed in a perfectly coordinated way. Lower your waist energy, and, your crotch area should follow a downward arc as it translates to the front. Keep ward-off energy (peng jin) in your left arm, preserving a circular shape. Don't allow your right arm to press too close to your body, it should remain a certain distance from the body throughout. Your left knee and your left heel should line up on a vertical axis and your right knee bends and your hip relaxes in order to keep your crotch area rounded. Your body should remain plumb upright. During this action first inhale and then exhale.

Internal Energy: Your energy (jin) twines inward (li chan) from your right leg. The crotch energy (dang jin) moves downward along an arc to your left leg, changing into outward twining (wai chan) as it moves to your left foot. Your waist energy (yao jin) rotates toward your left. Relaxing your shoulders and dropping your elbows, your energy (jin) moves toward the front in a splitting (lie) action through the reverse twining (ni chan) of your left arm and the natural twining of your right arm, becoming splitting energy (lie jin).

Self-Defense Application: The attacker cannot stand steadily when he is pulled forward and upward so he tries to pull back. Use splitting energy (lie jin) to attack at this moment.

ACTION 6: Your left palm twines forward then upward then back (making a circle in front of your chest) to a position in front of your chest with your palm facing downward. At the same time, your right palm and your right foot both move simultaneously to the front along an inward arc, with your right foot passing near the inside of your left foot and coming to rest with toes touching, forward of your left foot. Your right palm has lifted up forward to a position in front of the right side of your chest with the palm facing up. Your left fingertips are facing down on the inside of your right forearm. The weight is on your left leg, your eyes look forward. (fig. 2-10)

Fig. 2-10

Requirements: When stepping forward, bend your knees and relax your hips. The actions should be natural, light and nimble and also very stable. The intention is to combine the actions of your two arms with the rest of your body into one harmonious whole, the upper and lower parts acting in concert with each other. Inhale during this action.

Internal Energy: With the energy (jin) in your left leg, your waist turns slightly toward the left, sending your energy (jin) through to your left hand which flicks (liao) forward, and driving the movement of your right hand and your right foot. The energy (jin) goes through to the tip of your right foot and the fingers of the right hand. When you are able to practice to the point where your internal energy (nei jin) is plentiful and full, the internal energy can easily reach to your four extremities, circulating throughout your body as a whole.

Self-Defense Application: Lifting your right foot and stepping forward (shang bu) puts you in a position to kick the attacker in the groin, knee or calf. As your left palm moves forward it is in a position to strike the attacker's face and eyes to obstruct his vision. Lifting up your right palm forward can be used as a finger thrust to the attacker's throat.

ACTION 7: Your left palm twines inward (shun chan), turns over, and descends to a position in front of your abdomen with your palm facing upward. Your right hand forms into a fist and drops down into the middle of your upward facing left palm. The palm of your right fist also facing upward. Your eyes look forward. (fig. 2-11)

Requirements: There should be a space of about 8-10 centimeters between your forearms and your body. You should feel as though the round shape formed by your two arms is actively outward around its circumference. The energy of your

Fig. 2-11

Fig. 2-12

waist descends as your fist descends. Exhale during this action.
Internal Energy: The energy (jin) arises from your waist which drops downward. With your shoulders relaxed and elbows dropped, the energy goes through to your right fist. Your two arms ward-off (peng) outward along their circumference. Relaxing and sinking your entire body downward, your qi returns to your dantian.

Action 8: Raise your right fist upward to right shoulder level with outward-twining energy (ni chan). Bending the knee of your right leg and relaxing your hip, raise your right foot to a position below your crotch with the toes pointing naturally downward. Your eyes look forward. (fig.2-12)

Requirements: Your whole body sinks slightly when your leg is raised. The intention is to harmonize the action of your upper with the action of your lower body. When raising your fist upward your shoulders should be relaxed and your elbows dropped in order to promote the descent of internal energy (nei qi) and to keep your stance stable. Inhale during this action.

Internal Energy: Dropping your waist and relaxing your shoulders, the energy (jin) goes through to your right fist being raised upward. Dropping your waist and relaxing your hips (kua), your energy (jin) goes through to your right knee lifting upward.

Self-Defense Application: By rapidly raising your right fist upward, it is possible to strike the attacker's lower jaw or throat. By raising your knee upward, you are in a position to strike the attacker in the groin, abdomen or chest with your knee.

ACTION 9: Stamp downward with your right foot, the bottom of your foot level when it hits the ground. Your two feet should be at shoulder-wide distance from each other. Your right fist descends with inward-twining energy (shun chan) into the middle of your left palm. Your two arms forming a circular shape like the surface of a ball. Your eyes look forward. (fig. 2-13)

Fig. 2-13

Requirements: Your right fist and right foot descend simultaneously. Stamping your foot requires the exertion of energy (fa jin), your hips should be relaxed and your knees bent. The qi sinks downward to just below your navel (dantian). Exhale during this action.

Internal Energy: This action completes the form Jin Gang Dao Dui, with your internal energy (nei jin) returning to its state in the original posture, Beginning Posture of Taijiquan. Starting from the beginning form of Taijiquan, the internal energy (nei jin) issues from the dantian and moves internally throughout your five internal organs (wu zhuang) and skeletal structure (bai hai) and externally to your skin and fine hairs. After making one circuit of your body the qi still returns to the dantian; however, each technique and every form (yi zhao yi shi) must combine with the energy of your waist (jie he yao jin). Your waist is the seat of the kidneys (shen). Your mind (xin - literally the heart) is in command. Your kidneys are the source from whence the qi issues; your lower spine (yao ji) is like the axle of a car and your four limbs are like the wheels. Your waist serves as the hub; with just a movement of your waist, all the parts of your body move together in an interconnected way.

Self-Defense Application: One use of pounding your fist and stamping your foot is to stamp on the attacker's foot or toes. Another use of this action is to promote circulation and to achieve the effect of recovering from fatigue.

3. Lazily Tying One's Coat *(Lan Za Yi)*

ACTION 1: Turn slightly to the left and shift your center of gravity to the right. Your right fist changes to an open palm and twines outward (ni chan) as it wards off (peng) upward. Your left hand twines outward (ni chan) and pushes downward. Your eyes look to the left front. (fig. 2-14)

Fig. 2-14

Requirements: When your right fist changes into a palm and wards off (peng) upward, first drop and rotate your waist, using your body to drive your right hand to ward-off (peng) in an upward arc. Your left hand pushes (an) downward in conjunction with the action of your right hand. This action manifests a type of energy known as opening energy (kai jin). Inhale during this action.

Internal Energy: Your energy (jin) starts out from the dantian and, through the turning of your waist and relaxing of your shoulders, twines into your two arms. Your right hand wards off (peng) upward and your left hand pushes (an) downward, with all of your qi going through to the middle finger of both hands.

Self-Defense Application: Your two hands, the right upward and the left downward, separate the attacker's two hands and open him up for a shoulder strike. Your two hands can also be used to protect yourself, your right hand protecting the head area and your left hand protecting your body.

ACTION 2: Your two hands change from both twining outward (ni chan) to both twining inward (shun chan). Each hand describes an outward arc until both hands cross in front of your chest. Your right arm encloses your left arm, with the left palm facing outward toward the right and the right palm facing upward. Shift your weight to your left leg, raise your right leg and take a step sideways to the right, the inside of your right heel touching the ground and your right toes raised and pointing inward. Your eyes look toward the right front. (fig. 2-15)

Fig. 2-15

Requirements: The movement of your two hands and the movement of your leg should take place at the same time and in concert with each other so that each arrives at its final position simultaneously. In stepping toward the right be light, dexterous and natural. Exhale during this action.

Internal Energy: Combining with the action of your waist causes the energy (jin) to go through to your two arms. With your right arm playing the major role, the energy (jin) twines upward to your right hand, your little finger leading the energy. The energy (jin) twines downward into your right leg, reverse twining (ni chan) and turning inward (li he) as you step out (kai bu).

Self-Defense Application: This posture uses the method of drawing in the attacker above while advancing below (shang yin xia jin). While your upper limbs draw in the attacker's energy and redirect it, your legs can be used to trap (tao) by stepping behind and close against the attacker's forward leg, and control (guan) with your calf or foot the attacker's leg or foot. Your left hand, on top of your right arm and facing outward, can be used to protect your face.

ACTION 3: Turn to the left and shift your center of gravity to the right. Your right palm twines inward (shun chan) and wards off (peng) upward. Your eyes look toward the right front. (fig. 2-16)

Fig. 2-16

Requirements: When shifting your center of gravity to the right, your crotch traces an arc backward and to the right. The translation or movement of your crotch follows a figure eight pattern when shifting left and right and a downward arc when shifting forward and backward. Keep the intention to ward-off (peng) with your right elbow and don't allow your armpit to lose its circularity and thus restrict the circulation by clamping your arm against the side of your body, you should instead have the feeling that your armpit is empty and round. Inhale during this action.

Internal Energy: Your energy (jin) twines from your left leg to your right leg, dropping at the right side of your waist. Turning your body toward the left, the energy (jin) twines to your right shoulder. Your right hand draws the energy (ling jin).

Self-Defense Application: Your right shoulder can be used to strike the attacker in the chest with the technique of folding your back and striking with your shoulder (bei zhe kao).

ACTION 4: Turn over and twine your right palm outward (ni chan) while applying ward-off energy (peng jin) to your right forearm which wards off toward the right. Your left palm rotates, twining inward (shun chan) as it drops to a position just in front of your abdomen with the palm facing up. Your weight is on your right and your eyes should look toward the right front. (fig. 2-17)

Fig. 2-17

Requirements: While turning over your right arm to the right, relax your right hip and right shoulder, lower and turn your body slightly to the right, making sure not to raise your shoulders or lift your elbow. Exhale during this action.

Internal Energy: Your waist energy (yao jin) drops downward, turns toward the right and travels upward to your shoulders. When the energy reaches your shoulder, your shoulder relaxes. The energy can then penetrate through to your elbow.

Self-Defense Application: After using the technique of striking with your shoulder, concentrate your energy on your elbow which can then be used to strike the attacker.

ACTION 5: Turn your body to the right and twine your right palm outward (ni chan), opening your right arm out to a position with your right hand above your right knee. Relax your shoulder and let your elbow drop. Your right palm changing to slightly twining inward (shun chan) with your fingertips pointing upward at eye level. Your left palm twines outward (ni chan) to your left side where it holds your waist in a grip between the thumb and forefinger, fingers to your front and thumb to the back (palm facing downward). Your weight is on your right. Your eyes should follow the movement of your right palm and then look toward the front. (fig. 2-18)

Fig. 2-18

Requirements: When opening your right arm to the right, use the movement of your waist to make your shoulder move, and use the movement of your shoulder to make your elbow move. Your shoulders should be relaxed and your elbows dropped. The energy (jin) is driven upward from your waist to your shoulder, from your shoulder to your elbow, and from your elbow to your fingertips. Lower your waist and relax your hips (i.e. keeping your sacrum erect and opening your hip area to free circulation), opening and rounding your crotch. Your right leg is weighted or substantial and your left leg is relatively weightless or insubstantial. Your right calf should be vertical with your right knee on a vertical line above your right heel, neither inclining forward, backward or outward. Your left leg should be extended but not completely straight, with your knee slightly bent and your toes turning inward. Your posture should be plumb, as if balancing something on the crown of your head. The movement is large and outwardly expanding . Continue to exhale during this action.

Internal Energy: In this form, Lan Za Yi, the energy twines upward from your left leg to your waist and travels downward to your right leg. Moving your energy upward, use your waist to drive your shoulder, your shoulder to drive your elbow, and your elbow to drive your hand. Your left hand holds your waist with reverse twining (ni chan) energy.

Relax (fang song) your hip (kua), your shoulder, and your whole body. Your xin qi drops downward (xin qi is literally heart/mind energy; in Chen-style jargon it indicates dropping the energy from the sternum area of the upper torso into the waist). Your internal energy (qi) returns to your dantian.

Fig. 2-19

4. Sealing Six Avenues of Attack and Closing Four Sides *(Liu Feng Si Bi)*

ACTION 1: Turn your body toward the right and shift your center of gravity slightly to the right. Bring your left palm forward from your left waist in an upward arc until it comes near your right arm, in a position where it can act in conjunction with your right hand. There is the slight intention that the right palm should lead forward and downward. Your eyes look at the tip of your right middle finger. (fig. 2-19)

Requirements: While your two palms are in conjunction, their action combines with the turning of your body to the right and the shifting of your weight to the right, with your two palms standing upright, ready to receive an incoming force. Inhale during this action.

Internal Energy: Your energy (jin) starts out from your dantian, twining upward into your two arms, going through to your two hands, and dropping down to your waist and crotch.

Self-Defense Application: Both hands in conjunction meet the attacker's incoming hand(s) and arm(s) with the intention of warding off (peng) downward.

ACTION 2: Turn your body toward the left and shift your center of gravity to the left. Roll-back (lu) from the right toward the lower left with your left hand twining outward (ni chan) and your right hand twining inward (shun chan). Your eyes look

toward the right front. (fig. 2-20)

Fig. 2-20

Requirements: When rolling-back, lower your center of gravity and lower your waist. Keep the combining energy (he jin) in your two hands and add outward ward-off energy (peng jin). Exhale during this action.

Internal Energy: The energy (jin) drops downward to your waist and crotch and turns to the left, shifting from your right leg to your left leg and going through to your two hands.

Self-Defense Application: Use pulling energy (cai jin) and roll-back energy (lu jin) as you pull the attacker and roll-back to the lower left to make him fall flat on his face.

ACTION 3: (As this action is a transitional movement to action 4, even when you are practicing each action separately, there would be no stopping here.) Continue to turn toward the left with your two palms still twining, your left hand twining outward (ni chan) and your right hand twining inward (shun chan), and continue to roll-back (lu) to the left rear, but now in an upward direction. Shift your center of gravity to the right. Your eyes look toward the right front. (fig. 2-21)

Fig. 2-21

Requirements: When you roll-back (lu), don't move your hands back too far to your rear. Keep ward-off energy (peng jin) on your right arm. While your body continues to turn toward the left, your weight shifts to the right. Your spine serves as the axis. Inhale during this action.

Internal Energy: From your waist, the energy (jin) revolves left and twines upward to your two arms and your two hands. Traveling downward, it twines from your left leg to your right leg.

Self-Defense Application: Your arms continue to draw the attacker's energy harmlessly to your rear while your leg energy slowly advances in order to disrupt the attacker's center of gravity and cause him to fall over.

ACTION 4: Without stopping from the previous action, continue to shift your center of gravity to the right. Your two palms continue together in an upward arc with your left hand changing to inward twining (shun chan) and your right palm to outward twining (ni chan) until your two palms reach a position in front of your left shoulder. While both palms are moving together, your body turns toward the right in conjunction with the movement of your hands. Your eyes look toward the right front. (fig. 2-22)

Fig. 2-22

Requirements: When the action changes from roll-back energy (lu jin) to pushing energy (an jin), your two hands roll-back together and raise together due to the translation to the left of your waist and crotch and then the rotation of your waist and crotch toward the right. Your elbows drop downward and your shoulders relax, your wrists rotate and your arms turn along with your waist during this transitional movement; keeping contact without resistance (to the attacker's energy). The rotational motion is round and natural, drawing smoothly into folds. The change from roll-back energy (lu jin) to pushing energy (an jin) is totally regulated by the undulating action of your crotch, waist and torso. Continue inhaling during this action.

Internal Energy: Your energy (jin) continues turning toward the right. Drop your waist and relax your shoulders, turning your wrists and rotating your shoulders, twining the energy into your two hands.

ACTION 5: Lower your body and turn slightly toward the right, your two hands push downward (an) in an arc to the lower right with evenly matched strength. Draw your left foot into a position about 20 centimeters from the instep of your right foot with just the tip of your left foot touching the ground. Your eyes look downward toward the right front. (fig. 2-23)

Fig. 2-23

Requirements: While pressing downward with your two palms, relax your hips and lower your waist, relax your shoulders and drop your elbows. Your two hands should, in concert with the lowering of your body, push forward with combined strength, uniting the action of your body with that of your hands. Exhale during this action.

Internal Energy: The whole body's complete energy (jin), through the relaxing of your waist and hips (kua) and, sinking of your elbows and shoulders, goes through to your two hands, becoming pushing downward energy (an jin).

Self-Defense Application: The combined strength of your two palms can be used to push the attacker away or, by using ting jin (tactile sensation energy) and zhan nian jin (adhering energy) you can seal up all of the attacker's avenues of attack (up or down, front or back, left or right) and put him in a position vulnerable to your counter-attack.

5. Single Whip

(Dan Bian)

ACTION 1: Turn your body slightly toward the right, twining your two palms inward (shun chan) with your left palm rotating to face upward, forward of your right palm which also faces palm upward. Your weight is on the right. Your left leg and left knee rotate inward on your left toes which serve as an axis. Your eyes look at your two hands. (fig. 2-24)

Requirements: The rotation of your two palms should be completely round. Inhale during this action.

Internal Energy: Qi issues from your dantian, turning your waist to the right, the energy twines into your two arms and your two legs. The emphasis is on the natural

Fig. 2-24

twining (shun chan), inward turning of your right hand.

Self-Defense Application: The force generated by the rotation of your spine goes through to your hands. The main point for attention is to avoid having your right hand seized by the attacker.

ACTION 2: Turn your body toward the left. With your weight on the right, your left leg rests on the ball of the left foot. Your left knee turns along with your body outward toward the left. Your right hand twines outward (ni chan) and your five fingers meet at the fingertips (forming a hook hand). Your right hand follows an arc with your right wrist raising up to shoulder level. The palm of your left hand faces upward and moves together with the turning of your body, dropping down to a position in front of your abdomen with your palm still facing upward. Your left elbow keeps its ward-off energy (peng jin) throughout this action. Your eyes look at the right hand. (fig. 2-25)

Fig. 2-25

Requirements: When your right hand forms a hook and raises upward, it should follow the rotation of your body. Lower your waist, relax your shoulders and drop your elbows. Your waist should serve as the hub of all movement, with the motion of every part of your body affected by the motion of your waist. This is an opening (kai) movement. Exhale during this action.

Internal Energy: Use the rotation of your lumbar spine, sending the energy twining over your shoulder and elbow to your wrist. Your five fingers draw together with the wrist leading the energy.

Self-Defense Application: Your five fingers form a hook and the waist and the wrist rotate as a way of escaping from an attacker grabbing your right hand. After freeing your right hand you can strike the attacker in a vital spot with the back of your wrist.

ACTION 3: Turn to the right, shifting your entire weight to your right leg. Lift your left leg by bending your knee and turning it inward toward your crotch area. Your right wrist draws energy (ling jin) your left palm doesn't move. Relax your shoulders and drop your elbows. Let the actions of the upper and the lower body complement each other so that your whole body is balanced and stable. Your eyes look toward the left front. (fig. 2-26)

Fig. 2-26

Requirements: Your right leg supports the weight of your body and the upper and lower parts of your body should work together to keep your whole body balanced and stable. Guard against bending your waist and protruding your buttocks. This is a closing (he) action. Inhale during this action.

Internal Energy: With your right hand directing your energy (jin), the energy shifts to your right leg. Raising your left leg, your left hand drops downward in combination with the energy in the abdomen area (dantian qi), with the intention being to concentrate the internal energy of your whole body in the dantian.

Self-Defense Application: Lifting your left knee and turning it inward serves to protect your crotch area and also serves to avoid being caught by the attacker's leg technique. The raised left foot can also be used to kick the attacker sideways with the bottom of your foot (ce deng) or the side of your foot (chuai).

ACTION 4: With your weight on your right leg, the inside of your left heel touches the ground and slides to the left with the tip of your foot raised upward and turned inward. Your right wrist draws energy and your left hand descends to a position in front of your abdomen gathering or reuniting the energy (he jin) there. Your eyes look toward the

left front. (fig. 2-27)

Fig. 2-27

Requirements: Stand with upright posture, as if your body were suspended by a string attached to the top of your head. Keep ward-off energy (peng jin) in effect throughout this action. This is an opening (kai) action. Exhale during this action.

Internal Energy: Concentrate your dantian internal energy. Your right wrist draws upward and the internal energy twines naturally (shun) down your upper leg, downward to the inside of your heel; your big toe at the tip of the foot drawing the energy. Your left arm sinks lower, and then leads the energy (jin) toward the right.

Self-Defense Application: Use the technique of drawing in the attacker above while advancing below (shang yin xia jin) on the left side, with your left foot sliding along the ground to the left as if to uproot the attacker's foot. Your left foot and leg can be used to kick the attacker with the bottom of your foot (deng) or to control his foot and leg by encircling (tao) and controlling (guan).

ACTION 5: Turn your body slightly toward the right and shift your weight to the left, to form a left facing bow step (gong bu). Your left palm moves to the right, in the direction of your fingers, as it twines outward (ni chan), turning over and warding off (peng) upward to a position at the right side of your chest with the palm facing outward. Your eyes look forward but observe your left hand out of the corner of your right eye. (fig. 2-28)

Fig. 2-28

Requirements: When shifting your weight to the left, your crotch should follow a downward and outward arc as it rotates into the new position. Your left knee cannot extend beyond your left toes. When turning your left palm outward, pay attention to not raising your shoulders or lifting up your elbow. Inhale during this action.

Internal Energy: Using your waist to drive the movement, the energy (jin) reverse twines (ni chan) upward from the outside of your right foot to the acupuncture point situated between the tip of your coccyx and your anus (chang qiang). Then, twining naturally (shun chan) from the inside to the outside and on to the tip of your left foot. The tip of your left foot swinging outward (pivoting on the heel) and the tip of your right foot turning inward. Then, once again internal energy rises from your waist to your shoulders, from your shoulders to your elbows, and from your elbows to your hands. Your left thumb draws or directs the energy (ling jin).

Self-Defense Application: This action can be used to strike the attacker with your left shoulder or your left elbow.

ACTION 6: Turning slightly toward the left, twine your left palm outward (ni chan), opening your left arm to a position above your left knee at about shoulder-high level where the direction of rotation reverses so that your left palm now twines inward (shun chan), relaxes and sinks slightly downward. Your eyes follow the motion of your left palm until it reaches the left side, then turn to look toward the front. (fig.2-29)

Fig. 2-29

Requirements: The tip of your left foot points outward while your right foot points inward. Stand with upright posture, rounded crotch, hips relaxed and knees bent. Relax your shoulders, drop your elbows, and hold your head erect as if it were suspended from above. This posture has the intention of matching and combining your upper limbs (arms) and your lower limbs (legs) into a harmonious whole as in the three external correspondences - shoulder with hip, elbow with knee, hand with foot (wai san he). This action is an externally opening (kai) and internally closing (he) action. Exhale during this action.

Note: Boxing postures have the so-called three external harmonies and the three internal harmonies. The outer harmonies are: shoulder aligned with hip, elbow aligned with knee, and hand aligned with foot. The inner harmonies are: mind combined with intent, internal energy (qi) combined with strength, and tendons (the musculature) combined with the bones (the frame or skeleton).

Internal Energy: The energy (jin) rises from your dantian, moving along your left waist and into your left shoulder, elbow, and into your middle finger of your left hand. Relaxing and dropping downward, the internal energy returns to your abdomen area (dantian). Use intention (yi) to guide your internal energy (qi), utilize internal energy (qi) to move your body, moving it throughout your body and then beginning again, passing along this circuit over and over without ever coming to an end.

6. Pounding the Mortar

(Jin Gang Dao Dui)

ACTION 1: Turn your body to the left and shift your weight to the left. Your right hand, changing to a palm from a hook-hand, twines inward (shun chan) as it describes an arc, downward and up to a position near your left palm. Your eyes look toward the left front. (fig. 2-30)

Fig. 2-30

Requirements: The movement of your right hand is governed by the motion of your body, both hands coming into conjunction in perfect coordination with each other and with the movement of your body. First inhale and then exhale during this action.

Internal Energy: The energy (jin) goes from your dantian to your lumbar spine, twining into your two arms, on through to your hands, with both hands acting together in combination.

Self-Defense Application: Your two hands are used to intercept the attacker's right hand and elbow and then either roll-back (lu) or pull the arm forward and lock his elbow joint (cai, na).

ACTION 2: Turn your body to the right and shift your center of gravity from your left leg toward your right leg. Your left palm changes to an inward twining (shun chan) and your right palm to an outward twining (ni chan), applying outward ward-off energy (peng jin) to both hands. Roll-back (lu) to the right rear along a downward to upward arc, so that your palms now face outward away from your body. Your eyes look toward the left front. (fig. 2-31)

Fig. 2-31

Requirements: This action requires the action of your two hands pulling back to coordinate perfectly with the shifting of weight and the turning of your waist. Inhale during this action.

Internal Energy: Continuing from the previous action, your two hands combine in unison, together with shifting your center of gravity. The energy (jin) twines from your left leg to your right leg. As your waist turns toward the right, the energy (jin) goes through to your two hands which roll-back (lu) upward toward the rear.

Self-Defense Application: This posture uses upward roll-back (lu), leading the attacker upward so that he is inclined forward, loses his balance and falls over. (The posture Sealing Six Avenues of Attack and Closing Four Sides, in contrast, uses downward roll-back.)

ACTION 3: Turn your body toward the left and shift your center of gravity along a downward arc to your left leg. Turn your left foot to point outward, your kneecap on a line vertically above your heel, with your knee bent and hips relaxed. With your left palm twining outward (ni chan) and your right palm twining inward (shun chan), both hands move downward and then upward along an arc, warding off (peng) forward. Your left hand wards off (peng) to a position above your left knee, level with your chest, palm facing downward. Your right hand drops down to ward-off (peng) in front of your right knee with your palm facing outward. Your eyes look

toward the left front. (fig. 2-32)

Fig. 2-32

Requirements: Your body begins to move first. Relax your hips and shift your center of gravity along an arc. Keep ward-off energy (peng jin) in your two arms at all times during this action. Exhale during this action.

Internal Energy: Your energy (jin) reverse twines (ni chan) upward from your right leg and shifts to your left leg where it changes to natural twining (shun chan). The twining energy of your waist (yao jin) drives the reverse twining (ni chan) of your left arm which wards off (peng) forward. The energy (jin) goes through the outside of your left forearm to the outer edge of your left palm. Your right hand twines naturally (shun chan) together with the action of the outer edge of your left palm. The energy of the crown (ding jin) draws upward.

ACTION 4: Your left hand describes a circle in front of your chest with your palm first lifting up and then finishing up with your palm facing downward. Bring your right palm rapidly forward along a downward arc to in front of your chest with your palm facing upward. The fingers of your left hand facing the inside of your right forearm. Your right leg, moving along with the motion of your right hand, steps forward as it passes by the inside of your left foot and finishes the movement with just the toes touching the ground. At the same time, your body turns to the left 90 degrees. Your eyes look straight ahead. (fig. 2-33)

Fig. 2-33

Requirements: While turning your body, shifting your weight and stepping forward with your right foot, keep your torso erect and centrally balanced. Bend your knees and relax your hips. With your left leg supporting the weight of your body, the qi should not be allowed to float upward. Inhale during this action.

Internal Energy: Your waist energy (yao jin) drives a little toward the left, going through to your left fingers which flick forward (liao). Your right hand, drawing the energy, brings your right foot into a forward step posture (shang bu).

Self-Defense Application: Same as for the fifth action of the second form, Jin Gang Dao Dui.

ACTION 5: Relax your body and sink down lower. Turn your left palm over by twining it inward (shun chan) and dropping it to a position in front of your abdomen with the palm facing up. Form a fist with your right hand, drawing it toward your body and dropping it into your left palm with knuckles downward. Your eyes look forward. (fig. 2-34)

Requirements: When your fist drops into your palm, your fist and palm are about the distance of a fist from your abdomen (approximately 10 cm). Your two arms form a circular shape, and ward-off (peng) around their circumference, like a ball filled with air. The intention is to protect the acupuncture point just below the navel (dantian). Exhale during this action.

Fig. 2-34

ACTION 6: Lower your body still further while raising your right fist to the level of your shoulder, your right fist twining outward (ni chan). Bend your right knee and raise your right foot, letting your right foot relax and hang down below your crotch. Your left hand twines inward (shun chan) slightly and sinks downward, the palm facing upward. Your eyes look forward. (fig. 2-35)

Requirements: While raising your right fist and right leg, bend your knee and relax your hip, sink your shoulders and drop your elbows, coordinating the action of your upper body with the action of your lower body. Absolutely do not allow your body's frame to rise upward or the internal energy (qi) to float upward. This action serves to accumulate and store energy. Inhale during this action.

Fig. 2-35

Internal Energy and **Self-Defense Application:** Same as action eight of the second form, Jin Gang Dao Dui, above.

ACTION 7: Your right foot stamps downward to the ground, with your two feet shoulder-width apart. Your right fist drops into your left upturned palm, with your body assuming a half-squatting posture. Your eyes look forward. (fig. 2-36)

Requirements: While stamping the ground, your weight is still on your left leg, the entire bottom surface (heel, ridge, ball) of your right foot contacts the ground at once. Use whip-snapping energy (tan dou jin) in your legs to initiate the stamping action. Your qi sinks to your dantian. Exhale during this action.

Internal Energy and **Self-Defense Application:** Same as action nine of the second form, Jin Gang Dao Dui, above.

Fig. 2-36

7. White Goose Spreading Its Wings *(Bai E Liang Chi)*

ACTION 1: Your body first turns slightly toward the left and then turns slightly back toward the right. Your right hand changes from a fist to a palm and twines outward (ni chan), wards off (peng) upward to a position in front of your forehead. Your left hand, twining outward (ni chan), turns over and the palm pushes downward. Your weight shifts to your right leg. Your eyes look forward. (fig. 2-37)

Fig. 2-37

Requirements: When both hands rotate and part from each other, they each describe an arc. When your right hand is warding off (peng) upward, pay attention to not raising your shoulders or elbows so that your shoulders stay relaxed and your elbows dropped. Inhale during this action.

Internal Energy: The energy (jin) follows the turning of your waist to the left and then to the right, twining into your two arms. This opens (kai) the energy to the right with ward-off (peng) energy and to the left with push-down (an) energy.

Self-Defense Application: Your two hands follow circular paths in opposite directions in front of your body with the intention of the upper protecting your head and the lower protecting your body.

ACTION 2: Shift your weight to your right leg. Lift your left leg and take a step backward, with the toes of your left foot touching down first. Your body turns to the right as your left foot steps backward. Your two hands manifest opening energy (kai jin). Your eyes look forward. (fig. 2-38)

Fig. 2-38

Requirements: While taking a backward step, it is important to separate clearly which leg is weighted and which leg is without weight throughout the action; be light and nimble during the stepping backward movement. You may also perform this action simultaneously with the previous action.

Internal Energy: The energy (jin) shifts to your right leg and your left leg reverse twines (ni chan) in a backward step. Dropping your waist energy, the energy goes through to your two hands, with opening energy (kaijin).

Self-Defense Application: The purpose of the withdrawing step is to lead the attacker's energy forward. The main point to observe in leading the attacker's energy forward harmlessly (yin jin luo kong) is to understand the principles of Yin and Yang and to clearly distinguish between the substantial and the insubstantial. Chen Zhao-Pi said, "If you do not distinguish between substantial and insubstantial, then you cannot utilize the principle of mutually coordinated action of the upper and lower parts of your body; if you cannot utilize the principle of mutually coordinated action, then you cannot lead the attacker's energy forward harmlessly; if you cannot lead the attacker's energy forward harmlessly, then you cannot borrow the attacker's incoming energy and turn it back against him."

ACTION 3: Shift your weight to your left leg. Your right foot steps backward one step, with your right foot passing by the inside of your left foot. Both hands twine inward (shun chan) with each describing an arc to cross in front of your chest, the fingers of your left hand pointing upward and the palm facing outward. The fingers of your right hand face forward with the palm facing upward. Your eyes look forward. (fig. 2-39)

Fig. 2-39

Requirements: When stepping backward, your eyes keep looking out to the front and your ears listen for anything happening behind. Your footwork should be light and nimble with your torso held erect. First exhale during this action and then inhale.

Internal Energy: Continuing from the above action, the energy (jin) twines from your right leg to your left leg and then raises your right leg to take a step backward using reverse silk-twining energy (ni chan si jin). Relax your hips and drop your waist. The energy (jin) goes through to your two arms, which twine naturally toward each other and come together to cross in front of your chest.

Self-Defense Application: The action of the light retreating step can be used to trap or encircle (tao) and control (guan) the attacker's leg and foot. As the energy (jin) twines from your waist through to your back, your shoulder can be used to strike backward and lean into the attacker. Your two hands crossing in front of your chest serve to protect and close your middle gate (zhong men) to attack.

ACTION 4: Your weight shifts backward to your right leg with your body turning toward the right. Separate your two hands by twining both outward (ni chan), your left hand pushing (an) downward with the palm facing down, and your right hand wards off(peng) upward with the palm facing outward. Each arm should form a semi-circular shape. Your left foot draws back to a position to the left front of your right foot with just the toes touching the ground. Your eyes look forward. (fig. 2-40)

Requirements: The shifting of weight to the right and the separation of your hands should follow the turning of your body and also combine with the energy of your waist. Continuing from the previous posture, first inhale and then exhale.

Internal Energy: From your lumbar spinal area the energy (jin) turns toward the left. Your center of gravity shifts to your right leg. The energy (jin) twines upward to your two shoulder blades, passing through your shoulders, elbows, and on through into your two hands. Relaxing your entire body and sinking downward, your energy combines and returns again to your dantian.

Fig. 2-40

Self-Defense Application: This action draws the posture of White Goose Spreads It's Wings to completion. The attacker is drawn deeply into a position where danger awaits him.

8. Diagonal Posture

(Xie Xing)

ACTION 1: Your feet stay in the same position as in the previous posture. Your body turns to the left with your left hand twining outward (ni chan) and swinging toward the rear. Your right hand twines inward (shun chan), with your elbow dropped and your shoulder relaxed, in an arc toward the left front. Your eyes look toward the left front. (fig. 2-41)

Fig. 2-41

Requirements: Let your body's action lead the action of your hands. Your two arms are compelled to circle, as if they were willow branches driven by the wind. Inhale during this action.

Internal Energy: The energy (jin) issues from your dantian, twining from your waist to your right shoulder. It goes through your shoulder and your elbow into your hand (mainly the right hand). Your right hand twines naturally (shun chan) in front of your face and describes an arc. Your left hand reverse twines (ni chan) as it describes an arc toward the rear.

Self-Defense Application: If an attacker were to try to strike your chest or face with his fist, you could quickly turn your body sideways toward the left and block his strike with your right arm.

ACTION 2: Turn your body toward the right, turning your right toes slightly outward toward the right. Your left knee turns inward with just your left toes touching the ground. As your body turns, your left hand describes an upward arc from the left rear to a position in front of your nose, on the centerline of your body. Your left hand is a standing palm with the fingers pointing upward and the palm facing toward the right. Your right hand twines outward (ni chan) while describing an arc and pushing (an) downward to a position outside your right thigh with the palm facing downward. Your eyes look toward the left front. (fig. 2-42)

Requirements: When your two hands are circling, let your waist serve as the axis and keep your head and neck erect. Exhale during this action.

Internal Energy: Using your waist as a pivot point, the energy

Fig. 2-42

Fig. 2-43

(jin) rotates from the left to the right and twines into your right hand which describes an arc to push downward (an). Your left hand twines naturally (shun chan) to settle in front of your chest.

Self-Defense Application: If the attacker continues to attack with another strike, and your right arm has just blocked, turn quickly toward the right with your right hand pushing downward and your left hand now blocking in front of your face, protecting your middle gate (zhong men).

ACTION 3: Shift your weight to your right leg and lower your body. Bend your left knee and raise your left leg. Your two hands ward-off (peng) upward to the right. Your eyes look toward the left front. (fig. 2-43)

Requirements: With your two hands warding off (peng) upward and your body being lowered, the entire weight of your body is supported on your right leg. Your knee should be bent and your hip joint/crease (kua) area relaxed. The upper and lower parts of your body working in harmony (i.e. when raising your leg, lower your body to preserve balance). Inhale during this action.

ACTION 4: Continue lowering your body. Slide your left heel along the ground toward the left front with the tip of your left foot raised upward. Your two hands continue warding off (peng) upward. Your eyes look toward the left front. (fig.2-44)

Requirements: When stepping out to the left (kai bu), the

Fig. 2-44

inside surface of your left heel slides along the ground as if to scrape the surface of the ground. Your two hands ward-off (peng) upward and the energy of your waist descends, thus achieving the intention of upper and lower being in balance with each other. Exhale during this action.

Internal Energy: Your right hand reverse-twines (ni chan) upward with ward-off energy (peng). Your left hand twines naturally (shun chan) upward with ward-off (peng) energy. Lift your leg with inward twining (li chan) energy while taking a step outward (kai bu). Sink your elbows and relax your shoulders, the energy (jin) recombines in your waist.

Self-Defense Application: The upward ward-off (peng) of your two hands can be used either to roll-back (lu) with (i.e. leading the attacker's energy forward harmlessly) or block (dang) a strike. Your raised leg can be used to kick with your heel (deng), the side of your foot (chuai), or can be used to hook (gou) or suspend (gua) the attacker's leg. Your left shoulder is prepared to strike the attacker with a backward stroke (bei kao).

ACTION 5: Turning your body toward the left, shift your weight to your left leg. Your left hand twines outward (ni chan), and, moving with the turning of the body toward the left, describes a downward arc to a position below the outside of your left knee. Your right hand, twining inward (shun chan), circles to the rear and then changes to an outward twining (ni chan) as it reaches a position below your right ear. Your eyes look toward the left front. (fig. 2-45)

Fig. 2-45

Requirements: Turning your body and shifting your weight should be performed in a perfectly coordinated way. This posture can be performed with three differing degrees of difficulty; large, medium, and small. In the small degree of difficulty: with a smaller stance and a higher body position, your left hand moves from a position level with your waist. In the medium degree of difficulty: same as above, but, your left hand moves from a position below your left knee. In the large degree of difficulty: your left elbow moves from a position below your left knee; therefore, there is a seven inch elbow strike and a seven inch shoulder strike . Or, in other words, your elbow or your shoulder operate at a distance of seven inches (seven Chinese inches or about 25 centimeters) from the ground. First inhale and then exhale during this action.

Internal Energy: Utilizing the left-turning rotation of your waist, the energy (jin) twines downward and combines in your left leg. The energy (jin) from the left side of your waist twines upward to your left shoulder, left elbow, and left hand. Your right hand reverse twines (ni chan), revolving your right wrist around to a position in front of the right side of your chest.

Self-Defense Application: This posture places its main emphasis on the left side of your body, with the right side playing a supporting role. Your left side has pressing energy (ji jin) that goes in turn to your shoulder, to your elbow, and to your hand. Your right hand is like a shield at the rear, ready to be brought into action in an instant.

ACTION 6: Continue turning your torso toward the left with the weight on your left side. Bring the five fingers of your left hand together to form a hook hand (gou shou) and, describe an upward arc with your left hand as it rises to shoulder level. Your right hand is a standing palm, with fingers pointing upward and wrist bent back, and guards in front of your chest. Your eyes look forward. (fig. 2-46)

Fig. 2-46

Requirements: While raising your left hand, keep your left wrist relaxed so that the energy can flow through to your wrist. Your right hand waits in reserve. With your waist dropped and your hips relaxed, the energy accumulates on the right side of your waist. Inhale during this action.

Internal Energy: Drop your waist, relaxing your shoulders and sinking your elbows; sending the energy (jin) through to your left wrist.

Self-Defense Application: Bringing the five fingers of your left hand together in a hook hand (gou shou) prevents them from being grabbed and bent backward by the attacker. The action of raising your left wrist upward can be used for striking the attacker under the jaw.

ACTION 7: Turning your body toward the right, your right arm pulls open (la kai) to the right, with your right hand twining outward (ni chan) while describing an arc toward the right. Relax your shoulders and drop your elbows. Drop your waist and round your shoulders slightly forward. Relax your hips and bend your knees. Your eyes look forward. (fig.2-47)

Fig. 2-47

Requirements: In this posture, your two hands and your two feet are positioned to all four corners. You should keep an upright posture with an expansive quality to the movements of your limbs, opening and rounding the area under your crotch. Your head should be held erect as if suspended from above or as if balancing an object on your crown. The central equilibrium of your body is undisturbed by forces acting from above or below, the four sides and the eight directions. This is called body technique of central equilibrium (zhong ding shen fa). Exhale during this action.

Internal Energy: With the emphasis on your right hand, your waist energy turns toward the right and twines to your right shoulder. The energy reaches your relaxed shoulder, and then twines to your right elbow. The energy reaches your sunken elbow, and then twines to your hand. The energy reaches your bent wrist (zuo wan) or standing palm, and goes through to the tip of your middle finger. At the completion of the form, your knees should be bent and your hip creases (kua) relaxed. Your chest should be slightly compressed and your waist dropped. Your posture erect in a state of central equilibrium, with energy drawing upward from above [as if your head is suspended, or as if balancing a book on top of your head]. Your entire body should relax, returning your qi to your dantian.

Self-Defense Application: This posture utilizes the central equilibrium body technique (zhong ding shen fa), with the intention to withstand a force coming from any direction. When opening the posture toward the right, there is the potential to use a right shoulder technique or a right elbow technique.

9. Holding Up the Knee (*Lou Xi*)

ACTION 1: Let your body sink downward, relaxing your hips and bending your knees, into a squatting posture. First, draw your two hands slightly upward with an outward twining (ni chan) action, then bring your two hands downward together with an inward twining (shun chan) action to a position above your left knee. Your weight is on your left leg. Your eyes look forward on a downward angle. (fig.2-48)

Fig. 2-48

Requirements: When your two hands come downward together, your posture should remain erect and your hands should lower as your body lowers. Your two hands should come together as though cupping the hands to hold water, keeping them linked together with combining energy (he jin). First inhale and then exhale during this action.

Internal Energy: Your waist energy drops downward, the energy combining with your left leg; the energy moves upward to your two shoulders, with your shoulders relaxed and your elbows sunken, and combines in your two hands.

Self-Defense Application: The action of bringing your two hands downward together can be used to strike the temples (tai yang xue) of an attacker trying to grab your leg. You can also strike downward to the back of his head, causing his face and your knee to smash into each other.

ACTION 2: Your two hands, drawing energy upward, ward-off (peng) upward. With your left hand in front and your right hand behind the left, both hands form standing palms in front of your chest on the centerline of your body. While raising your hands, shift your weight backward to your right leg. Your left foot draws back to a position to the left front of your right foot, with just the toes touching the ground. Bend your knees and relax your hips. Your eyes look forward. (fig. 2-49)

Fig. 2-49

Requirements: Your weight shifts back to your right leg along a downward arc. You should perform the action of drawing your left leg back smoothly and naturally. Inhale during this action.

Internal Energy: The energy shifts from your left leg back to your right leg. Drop your waist and relax your hip creases (kua). Your two hands draw energy to combine in front of your chest on the centerline of your body.

Self-Defense Application: Your two hands rise up to seal off and protect your middle gate, waiting at the ready for any action. The tip of your left foot just touches the ground without weight, allowing for endless possibilities to move in any direction.

10. Stepping to Both Sides *(Ao Bu)*

ACTION 1: Turn your body slightly toward the right. Your two hands both twine outward (ni chan) and roll-back (lu) downward toward the right. Bend your left knee and raise your left leg, with your weight on your right leg. Your eyes look forward. (fig. 2-50)

Fig. 2-50

Requirements: When you roll-back (lu) downward, you must keep the ward-off energy (peng jin) in your two hands. When raising your left leg, your upper and lower body must act in concert to achieve equilibrium, and your right leg must stand firmly. Exhale during this action.

Internal Energy: The energy follows the turning of your waist to the right, twining upward to your shoulders and going through to your two hands. Relax your hip creases (kua) and send the energy twining down to your left knee.

Self-Defense Application: Your two hands roll-back (lu) downward, bringing the attacker falling forward as you raise your left knee to hit against his chest and abdomen region.

ACTION 2: Turning your body slightly toward the left, take a step forward with your left leg (shang bu). Your left heel touches the ground with the toes raised up off the ground and your weight on your right leg. Your two hands ward-off (peng) upward and forward, your left hand twining outward (ni chan) and your right hand twining inward (shun chan). Your eyes look forward. (fig. 2-51)

Fig. 2-51

Requirements: Taking a step toward the front must be done smoothly and naturally. Your two hands ward-off (peng) upward and roll-back (lu) downward while describing an arc and must combine naturally with the overall movement of your body. Inhale as your two hands are turning the circle in an upward direction, exhale as they are turning the circle in a downward direction.

Internal Energy: The energy follows the turning of your waist, turning first to the right and then to the left. The energy twines to your left leg, your foot making contact at the heel with the ground. Your big toe turns upward slightly, drawing energy. The energy travels upward through your two arms, going through to your two hands. Your left reverse twines (ni chan) and your right twines naturally (shun chan) while warding off (peng) forward.

Self-Defense Application: Taking a step forward, your two hands ward-off (peng) forward and hit the attacker in the face.

ACTION 3: Turn your body toward the left and shift your weight to your left leg. Your left hand, after twining outward (ni chan), pushes (an) downward. Your right hand twines outward (ni chan) and pushes (tui) toward the front. Bend your right knee and raise your right leg. Your eyes look forward. (fig. 2-52)

Fig. 2-52

Requirements: Your footwork is firm and steady; at the same time, your step forward should be light, nimble and natural. First exhale and then inhale during this action.

Internal Energy: As your waist turns toward the left, the energy shifts from your right leg back to your left leg. Raise your right leg and take a step forward (shang bu). Your left hand reverse twines and rolls-back (lu) downward. Your right hand reverse twines (ni chan) and wards off (peng) forward.

Self-Defense Application: The continuous action of stepping forward and striking with your palm, with your two hands and arms describing circular paths on either side of your body, is used to protect the left and right sides of your chest (your rib-cage) and your facial area from attack. The circular action of rollback (lu) downward and ward-off (peng) forward follows from the stepping forward action.

ACTION 4: Your right leg steps forward to the right front, your heel touching down with the toes raised. With your weight on your left leg, turn your body slightly toward the left. Your left hand swings to the rear with the palm facing backward and your right hand wards off (peng) forward. Your eyes look forward. (fig. 2-53)

Fig. 2-53

Requirements: The stepping forward (shang bu) should be performed like the walk of a cat, light, nimble and entirely natural. The circular, twining movement of your hands and arms on both sides of your body should follow the lead of your waist, with your waist as the axis. Exhale during this action.

ACTION 5: Turn your body toward the right, and shift your weight to your right leg. Turn the tip of your right foot outward and lower it to the ground. Your right hand twines outward (ni chan) while describing an arc to push (an) downward beside the outside of your right thigh. Your left hand twines inward (shun chan) as it describes an arc, turning over upward to push (tui) forward. Your eyes look forward. (fig. 2-54)

Fig. 2-54

Requirements: When your left hand turns over on an upward arc, pay attention not to raise up your shoulder. The energy of your waist should drop downward. Continue to exhale during this action (continuing from the posture above).

ACTION 6: With your weight on your right leg, turn your body slightly toward the right. Bend your left knee and raise your left leg. Your left hand forms a standing palm (li zhang) in front of your nose on the centerline of your body and your right hand pushes (an) downward. Your eyes look toward the left front.

(fig.2-55)

Fig. 2-55

Requirements: When raising your leg, your body sinks downward. With your knees bent and your hips relaxed, the upper and lower parts of your body are in balance. Inhale during this action.

ACTION 7: Your left leg steps forward (kai bu) and the inside of your heel touches down with the toes raised and turned inward. Your body lowers and your two hands remain in the same relative position but are augmented with ward-off energy (peng jin). Your eyes look toward the left front. (fig. 2-56)

Requirements: With upright posture, guard against bending your waist (wan yao) and protruding your buttocks (tu tun). Exhale during this action. (Because actions 4, 5, 6, and 7 are similar, in action and use, to the

Fig. 2-56

stepping forward action in actions 2 and 3, the details are not repeated here.)

11. Diagonal Posture

(Xie Xing)

ACTION 1: Shifting your weight to your left leg, turn your body slightly toward the left. Your left hand twines outward (ni chan) as it describes a downward arc to a position in front of your left knee. Your right hand twines inward (shun chan) and turns over outward, describing an upward arc from the rear to a position below your right ear where it changes into an outward twining (ni chan) action. Your eyes look toward the left front. (fig. 2-57)

Fig. 2-57

Requirements: Turning your body and shifting your weight while your hands are revolving, requires you to combine the above actions with the energy of your waist and sink your buttocks downward. Continue to exhale during this posture.

ACTION 2: Continue turning your body toward the left with your weight on the left. The five fingers of your left hand come together to form a hook hand (gou shou) and raise in an upward arc to the level of your shoulder. Your right hand, in a standing palm (li zhang), lowers to a position in front of your chest. Your eyes look forward. (fig. 2-58)

Requirements: With your waist as the axis, all parts of your body and its movement are linked together into one continuous whole. The energy goes, in succession, from your waist to your shoulder, from your shoulder to your elbow, and from your elbow to your hand. Your left wrist draws energy, and your right hand accumulates energy and is held at the ready. Inhale during this action.

Fig. 2-58

ACTION 3: Turn your body toward the right. Your right hand twines outward (ni chan) and pulls open in an arc to the right. With your shoulders relaxed and elbows dropped, round your shoulders slightly forward and drop your waist. Your hips are relaxed and your knees are bent. Your eyes look forward. (fig. 2-59)

Requirements: In this posture, your two hands and your two feet occupy positions at the four

corners, requiring an upright posture and a relatively wide-open and expansive positioning of the limbs. Your crotch is open and rounded, your neck and spine are in an upright alignment as if you were being drawn upward by a string attached to the top of your head. This posture is stable from every direction (above and below, the four sides and eight directions) and is called body technique of central equilibrium (zhong ding shen fa). Exhale during this action.

Internal Energy: Your waist energy revolves to the right, twining to your right shoulder. The energy reaches your relaxed right shoulder and then twines to your right elbow. The energy reaches your sunken right elbow, and then twines to your right hand. The energy reaches your right sitting or dropped wrist (zuo wan) [or standing palm] and goes to the tip of your middle finger. Upon completion of the form, your knees should be bent and your hip creases (kua) relaxed. Enclose your chest slightly (han xiong) and drop your waist (ta yao). Standing with upright posture, the energy of your crown lifts or draws your crown upward. Your entire body relaxes and your internal energy (qi) sinks to your dantian.

Self-Defense Application: The same as for the seventh action of the eighth form Side Posture.

12. Holding Up the Knee (*Lou Xi*)

ACTION 1: Lower your body by relaxing your hips, bending your knees and squatting down lower. Your two hands first twine outward (ni chan) and draw slightly upward, then, your two hands twine inward (shun chan) and move downward together to a position above your left knee. Your weight is on your left leg. Your eyes look forward on a downward angle. (fig. 2-60)

Requirements: When your two hands move downward together, keep your body's posture upright, with your two hands descending as

Fig. 2-60

your body descends. Keep combining energy (he jin) in your two hands as if you were cupping water in them. First inhale and then exhale during this action.

Internal Energy: The waist energy drops, combines with the energy of your left leg, and travels upward to your two shoulders. With your shoulders relaxed and your elbows dropped, the energy combines in your two hands.

Self-Defense Application: Same as for the first action of the ninth form, Lou Xi.

ACTION 2: Your two hands draw energy upward and ward-off (peng) upward with your left hand forward and your right hand in back of the left hand. Both hands forming a standing palm in front of your chest on your body's centerline. Your weight shifts to your right leg as your hands are drawing upward. Your left foot draws back to a position to the left front of your right foot, with just the toes of your left foot touching the ground. Your knees should be bent and your hips relaxed. Your eyes look forward. (fig.2-61)

Fig. 2-61

Requirements: The requirements and the Self-Defense Application is the same as for the second action of the ninth form, Lou Xi.

13. Stepping to Both Sides (Ao Bu)

ACTION 1: Turning your body slightly toward the right, your two hands both twine outward (ni chan) and roll-back (lu) downward toward the right. Bend your left knee and raise your left leg, with your weight on your right leg. Your eyes look forward. (fig. 2-62)

Fig. 2-62

Requirements: When performing the action of roll-back (lu), keep ward-off energy (peng jin) continuously in your two hands. When raising your leg, the upper and lower parts of your body should be kept in equilibrium. Your right leg must be firmly planted in the ground. Exhale during this action.

Internal Energy: Your energy follows the turning of your waist toward the right and twines upward to your shoulders, going through to your two hands. Relaxing your hip creases (kua) and dropping your waist sends the energy twining downward to your left knee.

Self-Defense Application: Your two hands roll-back (lu) downward, bringing the attacker falling forward. At this time you can raise your left knee to hit his chest or abdomen.

ACTION 2: Turn your body slightly to the left and take a step forward with your left leg (shang bu), your left heel touching the ground first with the toes of the left foot raised upward. Your weight is on your right leg. Your two hands ward-off (peng) upward and forward, your left hand twining outward (ni chan) and your right hand twining inward (shun chan). Your eyes look forward. (fig.2-63)

Fig. 2-63

Requirements: Step forward smoothly and naturally. Your two hands ward-off (peng) upward and roll-back (lu) downward, describing a circular shape; these actions should combine naturally with the overall movement of your body. Inhale as your hands turn upward (shang fan), exhale as they roll-back (lu).

Internal Energy: The energy follows the rotation of your waist, first to the right and then to the left, twining into your left leg. With the heel of your left foot touching the ground, your big toe raises slightly, drawing energy. The energy travels upward through your two shoulders, through your two elbows and goes on through to your two hands. Your left hand reverse twines (ni chan) and your right hand twines naturally (shun chan) while warding off (peng) forward.

Self-Defense Application: Same as for the second action of the tenth form, Ao Bu.

ACTION 3: Turning your body toward the left, shift your weight to your left leg. Your left hand twines outward (ni chan) and then pushes (an) downward. Your right hand twines outward (ni chan) and pushes (tui) forward (fig. 2-64), followed by the raising of your right leg. Your eyes look forward. (fig. 2-65)

Fig. 2-64

Fig. 2-65

Requirements: The requirements and the Self-Defense Applications are the same as for the third action of the tenth form, Ao Bu.

ACTION 4: Your right foot steps forward (shang bu) to the right front, your heel touching down with the toes raised upward. With your weight on your left leg, turn your body slightly toward the left. Swing your left hand toward the back with your palm facing backward and push (tui) forward with your right hand.

Your eyes look forward. (fig. 2-66)

Fig. 2-66

Requirements: The requirements and the Self-Defense Application are the same as for the fifth action of the tenth form, Ao Bu.

ACTION 5: Turn the toes of your right foot outward and shift your weight to your right leg. Raise your left leg and take a step forward (shang bu) to the left front. As you step forward, turn your body 90 degrees from the left toward the right. Your right hand twines outward (ni chan) and sinks downward. Your left hand twines inward (shun chan) as it turns over upward, describing an upward arc. As your left hand passes your left ear it changes into an outward twining (ni chan) action. Your two hands meet in front of your chest, forming a cross, and your weight tends toward your right leg. Your eyes look forward. (fig. 2-67)

Fig. 2-67

Requirements: When shifting your weight and taking a step forward, you cannot raise up your body. When your two hands cross in front of your chest, the ward-off energy (peng jin) keeps the shape formed by your two arms rounded. Your body's posture should be kept upright and balanced. Continuing from the above action, first inhale and then exhale during this action.

Internal Energy: Your waist turns to the right and your internal energy (nei jin) twines downward into your right leg, the bottom of your foot pressing downward and gripping the ground. As your left leg raises and takes a step forward (shang bu), your left hand changes from natural (shun) twining to reverse (ni) twining, matching the action of your right hand. Your two arms are full of ward-off energy (peng jin) and the energy of your crotch (dang jin) is round and natural.

Self-Defense Application: In this action one takes a defensive posture, calmly awaiting any movement by an attacker.

14. Cover Fist and Punch *(Yan Shou Gong Quan)*

ACTION 1: Turn your body slightly toward the right, shifting your weight toward the left. Both hands twine outward (ni chan) while separating downward, your left hand moves to the left and your right hand moves to the right. Your eyes look forward. (fig. 2-68)

Fig. 2-68

Requirements: When separating your hands, let your body's movement lead the movement of your hands. Lower your center of gravity and stand firmly; all movements should follow a circular path. Continuing from the above action, continue to exhale.

Internal Energy: The energy shifts to the left by utilizing the rotation of your waist and crotch to the right. Your two hands reverse twine (ni chan) and separate outward. Your energy wards off (peng) to the outer edges of your forearms and the outside edges of your palms.

Self-Defense Application: If the attacker tries to use his two palms to strike you, you can send your energy to both of your forearms and palm edges to separate his two arms and neutralize the attack.

ACTION 2: Shift your weight toward the right and turn your body slightly toward the left. Your right hand twines inward (shun chan) as it rises, turns over and becomes a fist at the right side of your waist with the center of the palm facing upward. Your left hand changes from outward twining (ni chan) to inward twining (shun chan) and ends up as a standing palm (li zhang) in front of your chest on the centerline of your body. Your eyes look forward. (fig. 2-69)

Fig. 2-69

Requirements: While forming a fist and combining energy (he jin), your body is upright and sinks lower, with your hips relaxed and your knees bent. Your energy gathers into your right leg, ready to issue forth. Inhale during this action.

Internal Energy: Relaxing your hip creases (kua) and dropping your waist, the energy from your dantian passes through the chang qiang, an acupuncture point at the base of your spine, and rushes up along the du mai (median governing vessel up your back) to the feng chi (acupuncture point situated in the neck) and through to the bai hui (acupuncture point situated along the centerline of your head, five inches back from the front hairline or about 16 cm.) and then on to the ren zhong (an acupuncture point on the centerline below your nose and above your upper lip). The energy divides and travels to your two shoulders. With your two shoulders relaxed and your elbows dropped, your right fist twines naturally (shun chan) in to the right side of your waist. Your left hand twines naturally (shun chan) to in front of your chest.

Self-Defense Application: Your left palm acts as a screen, hiding your right fist which is at the right side of your waist. In use, your right fist rushes out forward from under the left palm, which is why this action is called Cover Fist and Punch.

ACTION 3: Your right foot presses down against the ground and your right leg rotates slightly inward while rapidly turning your body toward the left with your left hip relaxed. Your right fist rushes forward, twining outward (ni chan) with a spiral corkscrew action. Pull your left elbow back to the rear, exerting force (fa jin). Your eyes look in front of your right fist. (fig. 2-70)

Requirements: When exerting force (fa jin), twist your crotch and turn your waist. Your fist suddenly rushing forward and your elbow pulling backward is done at the same moment, in the same burst of energy. Exhale as you exert force.

Internal Energy: The energy twines inward (li chan) from your

Fig. 2-70

right foot's pressing against the ground. Your waist rapidly revolves toward the left, the energy corkscrews through your shoulder and elbow, driving through to the tip of your fist (quan ding). Your left elbow twines naturally (shun chan) toward the rear with explosive force (fa jin), in combination with the action of your right fist. Therefore it is said of the movement of internal energy (nei jin) that it: originates in the kidneys; starting out from the foot, and travelling up the leg, it is directed by the waist; going through the shoulder and elbow, it drives the hand.

Self-Defense Application: The fist in front and the elbow in back are like a scale in balance; with the waist as the hub and qi (your body's intrinsic energy) as the wheel, totally using the rotational energy of your waist and crotch as the driving force. Therefore, it is said, there is a spring-like energy within the crotch; once it is set into motion even a bird would have difficulty flying away.

15. Pounding the Mortar

(Jin Gang Dao Dui)

ACTION 1: Sink your body lower, with your weight on the left. Your right fist changes to a palm and twines inward (shun chan), turning toward the inside (li he). Your left hand twines outward (ni chan) to a position at the inside of your right forearm. Your eyes look forward. (fig. 2-71)

Fig. 2-71

Requirements: When your right arm sinks and turns inward, don't bend your waist and don't bend your right arm at the elbow too much. Keep ward-off energy (peng jin) in your arms. Inhale during this action.

Internal Energy: Drop your waist, relax your shoulders and sink your elbows. Your right arm twines naturally (shun chan) causing the energy of your right arm to sink downward and turn inward (li he).

Self-Defense Application: In preparation for an attack from the rear, rapidly turn your body toward the left, sinking your right elbow and relaxing your right shoulder, drawing in the attacker's energy harmlessly. This method contains the technique of folding the back for a shoulder strike, and using the elbow for ward-off (peng) upward.

ACTION 2: Turn your body toward the right and shift your weight to the right. Your right hand twines outward (ni chan), turning over outward and warding off (peng) upward to a position beside your right temple (tai yang xue) acupuncture point. Your left hand twines outward (ni chan) and pushes (an) downward to a position above your left knee, with your left foot turning inward. Your eyes look toward the left side. (fig. 2-72)

Fig. 2-72

Requirements: Keep ward-off energy (peng jin) in both hands. When turning the toes of your left foot inward you should relax your left hip, and avoid locking the hip joint. Turning your toes inward allows you to change the direction of movement. Exhale during this action.

Internal Energy: Your waist turns toward the right and the energy ascends up the back along the governing meridian (du mai) to your two shoulders. Your right hand reverse twines (ni chan) and wards off (peng) upward, your left hand twines naturally (shun chan) and pushes (an) downward. Your dantian qi travels downward, causing your hip crease of the left leg to relax and your leg to turn inward (li he). The tip of your left foot turns inward, compressing or combining the energy of your crotch.

Self-Defense Application: The upward ward-off (peng) roll-back (lu) leads the attacker's body forward. You can use your left hip to strike the attacker and your left hand can thrust downward to strike upward against the attacker's crotch. You can use the da bei shuai technique to throw the attacker to the ground.

ACTION 3: Turning your body toward the right, shift your weight to your left leg. Your right foot circles past the inside of your left foot and takes a step forward (shang bu) with just the toes touching down. Your right hand twines inward (shun chan) on a downward arc and then lifts up in front of the right side of your chest with the palm facing upward. Your left hand twines inward (shun chan), turns upward and changes to an outward twining action (ni chan) as it comes to a position above your right forearm with the palm facing downward, at chest level. Your eyes look forward. (fig. 2-73)

Requirements: When shifting weight to the left or to the right, your step should be light, nimble and natural with your whole body relaxing and lowering. Inhale when your two hands are coming together, and exhale after they have come together and you are lowering your body.

Fig. 2-73

Internal Energy and **Self-Defense Application:** Same as the sixth action of the second form Jin Gang Dào Dui.

ACTION 4: Your left hand twines inward (shun chan), turns over outward and drops downward to a position in front of your lower abdomen with the palm facing upward. Your right hand forms into a fist and drops downward into the center of your upturned left palm with the center of the fist facing upward. Your eyes look forward. (fig. 2-74)

Requirements: The requirements, internal energy and self-defense applications are the same as for the seventh action of the second form, Jin Gang Dao Dui.

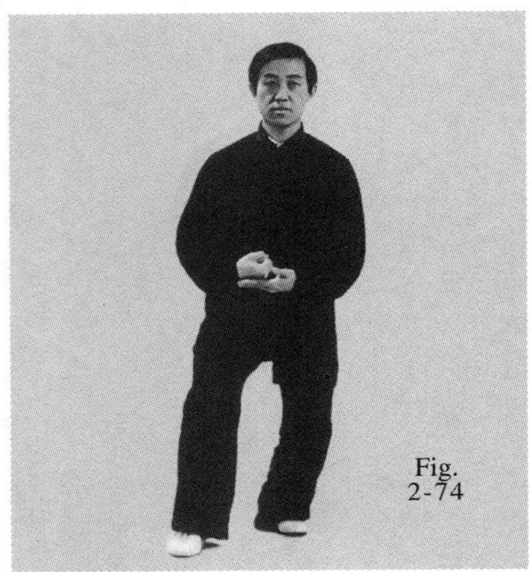

Fig. 2-74

ACTION 5: Your right fist, twining outward (ni chan), raises up to shoulder level. Bending your right knee and relaxing your right hip, raise your right leg with the foot hanging below your crotch and the tip of your right foot naturally hanging downward. Your eyes look forward. (fig.2-75)

Fig. 2-75

Requirements: When raising your right leg, lower your body. There is the intention of combining upper with lower and achieving balance. When raising your fist, you should let your elbow drop and relax your shoulder. Your qi should be directed downward and your stance made stable. Inhale during this action.

Internal Energy and **Self-Defense Application:** Same as the eighth action of the second form, Jin Gang Dao Dui.

ACTION 6: Stamp downward with the ball of your right foot hitting the ground level and your two feet shoulder-wide apart. Your right fist twines inward (shun chan) as it drops into the upturned palm of your left hand. The shape formed by your two arms is circular, like the surface of a ball. Your eyes look forward. (fig. 2-76)

Requirements: Your right fist and your right foot drop at the same time. Exert force (fa jin) when stamping the ground. Your hips are relaxed and your knees bent, the qi sinks to your dantian. Exhale during this action.

Internal Energy and **Self-Defense Application:** Same as the ninth action of the second form.

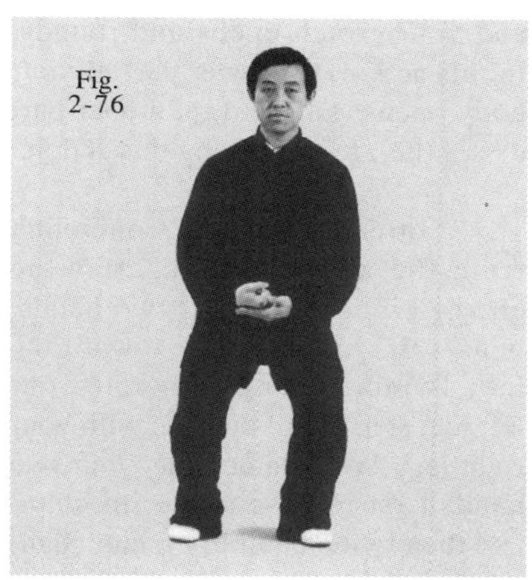

16. Hit and Drape Fist Over Body *(Pie Shen Quan)*

ACTION 1: First turn your body slightly toward the right and then slightly to the left. Your two hands, in front of your abdomen, first ward-off (peng) upward slightly and then sink downward. With your right fist changing into an open palm, each of your two hands simultaneously describe a downward arc, separating to the left and right sides of your body with your two palms facing toward each other. Your eyes look forward.(fig.2-77)

Requirements: Apply receiving energy (jie jin) in both hands when your hands are separating downward and sink your xin qi (i.e. direct the energy from your upper torso to sink into your lower abdomen, lowering your center). Your body should have the feeling that it is sinking downward. Inhale as your two hands rise upward and when you apply receiving energy (jie jin) and exhale when your two hands separate.

Internal Energy: The energy issues forth from your dantian, travelling downward through your legs and travelling upward along the governing meridian (du mai) to your two shoulders, going through to your two hands.

Self-Defense Application: The back of your wrists or back of your hands can be used to strike upward (liao da) into the groin area of attackers on both sides of you.

ACTION 2: Keeping your posture balanced and erect, lower your body. Shift your weight to your left leg and, raising your right leg, stretch out toward the right with your right foot. At the same time, your two hands first twine inward (shun chan) and then twine outward (ni chan) as they turn over and rise in an upward arc to a position in front of your chest where they cross, right inside the left. Your eyes look forward. (fig. 2-78)

Fig. 2-78

Requirements: The action of your two hands lifting upward in an arc to the point where they cross and the action of taking a step out toward the right are to be performed simultaneously, in perfect coordination with each other. Your waist energy (yao jin) sinks (xia sha) and your crotch opens and rounds. In this action, the lower part of your body opens (kai) and the upper part closes (he). Inhale during this action.

Internal Energy: Continuing from the above action, after the energy twines into your two hands, your waist turns slightly toward the left. Twining your energy into your left leg, step out to the side with your right leg. At the same time, your two hands first reverse twine (ni chan) and then twine naturally (shun chan) to come together in front of your chest. The energy then drops again into your waist.

Self-Defense Application: After striking outward to the two sides with both hands, your two hands guard in front of your chest.

ACTION 3: With your weight still on your left leg, turn your body toward the left. From in front of your chest, your two hands extend upward to the left with your left hand twining outward (ni chan) and your right hand twining inward (shun chan). Your eyes look toward the left side. (fig.2-79)

Requirements: In extending your two arms, you cannot straighten them completely. When your body turns, the movement of your two arms should combine in unison with the movement of your waist. Exhale

during this action.

Internal Energy: The energy twines into your two hands from the left rotation of your waist. Your left hand reverse twines (ni chan) and your right twines naturally (shun chan).

Self-Defense Application: In this action, when you want to go right, first go left. You want to turn toward the right but you first open or extend to the left. The intention is to feint to the east but strike to the west (sheng dong ji xi).

ACTION 4: Turning toward the right, shift your weight to your right leg. At the same time, your right hand twines outward (ni chan) as it describes a downward arc past your right knee to a position at the outside of your right knee. Your left hand changes to inward twining (shun chan) and pushes toward the front past your left ear to a position in front of your nose, on the centerline of your body, where it changes to outward twining (ni chan). Your eyes look toward the right front. (fig. 2-80)

Requirements: When turning downward and to the right with your right hand, the energy of your waist and crotch should sink downward. If you are going to practice the da shen fa (low frame), you must go even lower. Your shoulder and elbow must both turn to the right below the level of your right knee. This action of using your right shoulder to strike an attacker is also described as a seven inch shoulder strike. When you rotate downward toward the right, you must first draw inward above. Inhale as you lead in above and exhale as you rotate downward toward the right.

Internal Energy: Dropping your waist and relaxing your hip creases (kua), your waist turns toward the right, with your right side playing the major role. The energy goes from your waist to your shoulder, from your shoulder to your elbow, and on into your hand. The energy of your crotch (dang jin), twines inward (li chan) in your left leg to your right leg where it changes to outward twining (wai chan), your two knees and your two feet coordinated together. Your left hand changes from natural twining (shun chan) to reverse twining (ni chan) and comes in to in front of your chest.

Self-Defense Application: In this action, your waist propels your shoulder. Depending on the circumstances, you can use either a high or a low posture, and, a shoulder strike or an elbow strike.

ACTION 5: Shifting your weight to your left leg, turn your body toward the left. Your left hand twines outward (ni chan) to roll-back (lu) to a position just below your left knee. Your right hand twines inward (shun chan) to ward-off (peng) upward. Your eyes follow the movement of your right hand. (fig. 2-81)

Fig. 2-81

Requirements: Your two feet press firmly against and grip the ground. This action depends entirely on the left and right coiling of your crotch energy (dang jin) and the left and right rotation of your waist leading the spiraling, entwining action of your two arms. First inhale and then exhale during this action.

Internal Energy: The energy twines inward (li chan) from your right leg to your left leg, where it changes to outward twining (wai chan). The energy of your waist rotates toward the left, reverse twining (ni chan) into your left arm which sinks downward. Your right arm twines naturally (shun chan) as it moves inward. The energy of your crown (ding jin) draws upward.

Self-Defense Application: The rotation of your body toward the left follows the energy of your crotch and waist, which goes through to your shoulder and elbow. It has the potential to be used as either a fold the back and strike with the shoulder (bei zhe kao) technique or as a left ward-off (peng) upward with the elbow technique.

ACTION 6: With your weight on the left, continue turning your body toward the left. Your left hand twines outward (ni chan) to hold the left side of your waist, with the thumb holding the back of your waist and the four fingers the front. Your right hand twines inward (shun chan) with the little finger drawing energy and leading it forward, crossing in front of your body from right to left front, parallel to the ground. Your eyes follow the movement of your right hand to the left front. (fig. 2-82)

Fig. 2-82

Requirements: When rotating your body, your lower spine (yao ji) serves as the axis of movement. Your movements should therefore be continuous, circular, and be able to match exactly the movements of an attacker. In connection with the above action, continue to exhale during this action.

Internal Energy: Continuing from the above action, your internal energy doesn't break off and continues turning to the left.

Self-Defense Application: Practicing the coiling or turning energy of your crotch and waist and combining it with the spiraling, entwining action of your arms causes the movement of your entire body to start from the feet take shape in your legs and be controlled by your waist. Passing through your shoulders and elbows, it is manifested in the spiraling movement of your fingers. Gradually you will arrive at that point where there the mystery is revealed and others cannot fathom your movements, you alone can fathom theirs (i.e. others cannot see the internal spiraling of energy or predict its course).

ACTION 7: Shift your weight to your right leg and turn your body 130 degrees toward the right, turning the toes of your left foot inward. Your left hip should be relaxed and the knee slightly bent. Your right hand, changing to a fist, twines outward (ni chan) and turns over to the outside.

Your right fist wards off (peng) upward toward the right to a position next to your right temple (tai yang acupuncture point). Your left arm forms a rounded shape like the surface of a ball, and, your left elbow turns toward the inside. Your eyes sight along the tip of your left elbow to the tip of your left foot. (fig. 2-83)

Fig. 2-83

Requirements: When rotating your body, twist your waist and turn your crotch. Although your body inclines slightly forward here, the internal energy (zhong qi) stays upright (i.e. continues to function in a normal, balanced manner). Your right fist, the tip of your left elbow, and the tip of your left foot form a single line, all parts of your body combining to function as a whole. Don't bend your waist or protrude your buttocks. Inhale during this action.

Internal Energy: The energy is controlled by your waist and shifts from your left leg to your right leg. Following along with the shifting of your center of gravity and turning of your waist, the energy goes through to your right shoulder, and on to your right elbow, in combination with the energy going to your left shoulder and your left elbow. You should have the idea of matching up your left shoulder energy and your right hip energy, with your left elbow energy and your right knee energy also linked together.

Self-Defense Application: When the energy goes from your crotch and waist through to your right shoulder, there is the potential to use it for the backward shoulder strike (bei kao) or upward lifting elbow (shang tiao zhou) techniques. Your left shoulder and elbow, drawing downward slightly, can be used to draw in an attacker's energy harmlessly, and you could also apply a downward pull with elbow (xia cai zhou) technique.

17. Blue Dragon Flying out of the Water *(Qing Long Chu Shui)*

ACTION 1: Turn your body

toward the right and shift your weight to your left leg. Your right fist twines inward (*shun chan*) as it descends downward along an arc to a position at the right side of your waist. Your left hand first twines inward (*shun chan*) and then twines outward (*ni chan*), from the left side of your waist to a position in front of your chest. Your eyes look toward the right front. (fig. 2-84)

Fig. 2-84

Requirements: Place your weight on your left leg, relax your hips and bend your knees. Hold your right fist at the right side of your waist and keep your posture upright and centrally balanced. Exhale as your right fist is moving downward along an arc and inhale as it draws inward to your right side.

Internal Energy: The energy combines (*he*) in your left leg from your right leg, twining inward (*li chan*) in your left leg and twining outward (*wai chan*) in your right leg. Your waist energy turns to the right. Your right arm twines naturally (*shun chan*), with your shoulder relaxed and elbow dropped, settling to a position by the right side of your waist.

Self-Defense Application: In case an attacker suddenly pushes you from behind, you can rapidly turn toward the left and drop your right elbow and relax your right shoulder, causing him to miss his mark. Your right elbow can then be used to strike backward to the right at the attacker's chest. If the attacker, from the right side, grabs your right arm, you should rapidly drop your right elbow and relax your right shoulder. Revolve your right wrist and rotate your right arm to break the attacker's grip and then use your elbow or fist to strike him.

ACTION 2: Turn your body rapidly toward the left and shift your weight rapidly to your right leg. Your right fist, twining outward (*ni chan*), forcefully (*fa jin*) punches downward from the right side of your waist to a spot in front of your right knee. Your left hand twines inward (*shun chan*) and draws back to a position below your left ribs, forming a half-fist (*ban quan*) as it does so. Your left elbow forcefully withdraws toward the left, simultaneously with your right hand shooting out forward. Your eyes look downward toward the right. (fig. 2-85)

Fig. 2-85

Requirements: Use the spring-like energy (*tan huang li*) of your crotch and the turning energy of your waist to propel your fist outward with all of your force focused on one point, your entire body mobilized to act as a single unit. Open and round your crotch. Exhale during this action.

Self-Defense Application: Your fist strikes downward to the attacker's crotch or abdomen. In addition, on the foundation established by the previous form, your right fist could be used to twine inward (*shun chan*) while moving upward, then burst (*beng*) toward the rear with the energy of the back and shoulder (*bei kao jin*). The saying twining inward then bursting outward (*li chan wai beng*) describes this technique.

18. Pushing with Both Hands *(Shuang Tui Shou)*

ACTION 1: Your right fist changes to an open palm and wards off (*peng*) upward, with your right hand drawing in to the front (*qian yin*). Your left hand changes to an open palm and, following together with your body's turning to the right, moves to a position close to your right hand. Your eyes look toward the right front. (fig. 2-86)

Fig. 2-86

Requirements: When your two hands come together, the energy of your waist combines with your two hands. Inhale during this action.

Internal Energy: The energy goes from your waist through to your two hands. Your crotch energy sinks downward.

Self-Defense Application: The intention is to meet the attacker's energy with receiving energy (*jie jin*) and roll-back (*lu*) downward.

ACTION 2: Turn your body toward the left and shift your weight slightly toward the left from your right leg, with the toes of your left foot turning outward. Your two hands roll-back (*lu*) downward with your left hand twining outward (*ni chan*) and your right hand twining inward (*shun chan*). Your eyes look toward the left front. (fig. 2-87)

Fig. 2-87

Requirements: Your crotch moves downward along an arc toward the left. Keep outward ward-off (*peng*) in your two hands as they roll-back (*lu*) downward. Your head and neck are held erect as if pulled upward by a string attached to the top of your head. The posture of your body is upright and centrally balanced. Exhale during this action.

Internal Energy: The energy of your waist corkscrews and sinks downward, turning inward (*li he*) in your right leg and twining outward (*wai chan*) in your left leg. Your two hands roll-back (*lu*) downward with the energy reverse twining (*ni chan*) in your left hand and twining naturally (*shun chan*) in your right hand.

Self-Defense Application: Roll-back (*lu*) downward with the attacker's left arm, causing him to fall down face-forward.

ACTION 3: Shift your weight to your left leg as you continue to turn toward the left. Lift your right leg and bring it forward along an arc, past the inside of your left foot. Take a step forward (*shang bu*) to the right front, with the heel of your right foot touching down. The toes are raised upward and your foot is turned inward. Your two hands continue to roll-back (*lu*) toward the left, your left hand twining outward (*ni chan*) and your right twining inward (*shun chan*), moving along with the rotation of your body toward the left. Your eyes look toward the right front. (fig.2-88)

Fig. 2-88

Requirements: When shifting your weight and taking a step forward, keep roll-back energy (*lu jin*) in your two hands and keep your body's posture upright and centrally balanced throughout. Continuing from the above action, exhale during this action.

Internal Energy: The energy shifts to your left leg from your right leg, twining outward (*wai chan*) in your left leg. Your right leg takes a step forward (*shang bu*), the tip of your foot leading the energy and turning inward. Turning your waist to the left, the energy reaches your two hands, warding off (*peng*) outward and rolling-back (*lu*) to the rear.

Self-Defense Application: Turning your body and stepping forward with roll-back (*lu*) constitute one of the touching and adhering to, continuing and following (*zhan nian lian sui*) techniques. An attacker should get the impression that when advancing, the goal gets farther away; when retreating, there is no escape; when moving upward, that which is sought is higher still; when moving downward, that which is sought is deeper still.

ACTION 4: Shift the weight to your right leg and continue turning your body toward the left. Your two hands change, from the left hand twining outward (*ni chan*) and the right hand twining inward (*shun chan*), to your right hand twining outward (*ni chan*) and your left hand twining inward (*shun chan*) while moving along an upward arc toward the upper left rear. Both hands finish at a position in front of the left side of your chest. Your eyes look toward the right front. (fig. 2-89)

Requirements: When shifting your weight, your crotch moves from the left side toward your right leg. The action of your two hands should be perfectly round and natural as they change from roll-back (*lu*) to pushing energy (*tui an jin*) without any break in the energy continuum. Inhale during this action.

Fig.289 supplemental

Fig. 2-89

Internal Energy: The energy twines into your right leg from your left leg. Your waist energy turns to your left. Relax your shoulders and drop your elbows. Both your chest and your waist undulate (*yun hua*), moving in folds. Revolving your wrists and rotating your upper arms, the energy goes through to your two hands, combining at the left side of your chest and changing to pushing energy (*an jin*).

Self-Defense Application: Changing from roll-back (*lu*) into pushing technique (*tui an fa*), push forward parallel to the ground.

ACTION 5: Turning your body toward the right, relax your hips (*kua*) and sink lower as your two hands push forward with combined strength. Your left foot draws to the inside of your right foot with just the toes touching the ground, the weight on your right leg. Your eyes look forward. (fig. 2-90)

Fig. 2-90

Requirements: Relax your hips and drop your waist. Push forward with combined strength. Exhale during this action.

Internal Energy: Enclosing your chest (*han xiong*) and dropping your waist (*ta yao*), your waist energy turns slightly to the right. Relaxing your shoulders and dropping your elbows, the energy goes through to your two hands.

Self-Defense Application: Use the combined strength of your two hands to seal up (*feng*) the attacker's two arms. Push (*tui*) forward at chest-level.

19. Fist Under the Elbow

(Zhou Di Kan Quan)

ACTION 1: Turn your body toward the left, with your center of gravity on the right. Your left hand twines outward (*ni chan*) and sinks to the left side of your body. Your right hand twines outward (*ni chan*) and rises slightly upward. Your eyes look toward the left front. (fig. 2-91)

Fig. 2-91

Requirements: Your feet don't move and the movement of your hands is lead by the rotation of your body. With your spine as the axis, your body turns toward the left. Your left knee, following the movement of your body, swings outward. Inhale as you apply receiving energy (*jie jin*) in your two hands and exhale as your left hand sinks downward to your left side.

Internal Energy: Using your lower spine as a pivot, the energy goes through to your two hands.

Self-Defense Application: The left side of your body yields to and directs (*yin jin*) the attacker's incoming energy.

ACTION 2: Turn your body toward the right. As your body turns, your left knee turns inward. Your right hand changes into a fist. Twining inward (*shun chan*) it drops down and draws inward to a position in front of your abdomen. Twining your left hand inward (*shun chan*), bring your left hand forward along an upward arc from behind your body to a position in front of the left side of your body, level with the top of your head. Your eyes turn to look to the front. (fig. 2-92)

Fig. 2-92

Requirements: While your left hand is turning over upward (*shang fan*), keep your central equilibrium and upright posture. Don't allow your shoulders to raise up. Inhale during this action.

Internal Energy: Use your lower spine (*yao ji*) as a pivot to drive the revolving of your two arms. With your right arm above and your left arm below, there is the intention of bringing them together.

ACTION 3: Continuing from the above action, your weight is on your right leg, with just the toes of your left foot touching the ground. With your knees bent and your hips relaxed, round your shoulders toward the front slightly (*han xiong*) and drop your waist (*ta yao*). Drop your left elbow downward and raise your right fist upward so that the two come together in close proximity to each other. Your eyes look forward. (fig.2-93)

Requirements: Keep your posture upright and combine the actions of the upper and lower parts of your body harmoniously. Exhale during this action.

Internal Energy: From your dantian, the internal energy goes through to your left elbow and your right fist.

Fig. 2-93

Self-Defense Application: By combining the upward and downward actions in combination, you can hold or grasp (*na*) the attacker. The action of bringing the elbow downward can be used to strike the attacker's upper back and the back of his heart.

20. Stepping Back and Whirling the Arms (*Dao Juan Gong*)

ACTION 1: Turning your body toward the right, change your right fist into an open palm. Drop your right hand along an arc to the right side of your body while twining your right hand outward (*ni chan*). With your weight completely on your right leg and just the toes of your left foot touching the ground, push (*tui*) forward with your left hand. Your eyes look forward. (fig. 2-94)

Fig. 2-94

Requirements: When you drop your right hand down to your right side, use the turning of your right shoulder toward the right to lead the action of your right hand downward. First inhale and then exhale during this action.

ACTION 2: Bring your right hand forward to a position in front of the right side of your chest by turning it over upward and twining it inward (*shun chan*). Turn your body slightly toward the left. Lift your left knee upward and take a step backward (tui bu) with your left foot. Your toe touches down first. Your left hand lowers downward slightly as its energy drops (*ta jin*). The weight is on your right leg. Your eyes look forward. (fig. 2-95)

Fig. 2-95

Requirements: When taking a step backward with your left foot, you must wait until your right hand has just about reached a position in front of the right side of your chest and then take a step backward. This action has the intention of one hand going toward the front and one hand simultaneously going toward the rear in perfect opposition to each other. Inhale during this action.

Internal Energy: Using your waist as a pivot, the energy in your right hand changes from reverse twining (*ni chan*) to natural twining (*shun chan*). Following along with the rotation of your waist energy, your right hand rises to a position in front of the right side of your chest. The waist energy then turns to the left, raising your left leg. The energy in your left leg twines inward (*li chan*) and your left leg steps backward (*tui bu*). The tip of your foot touches down to the ground first.

Self-Defense Application: Step Back and Whirl the Arms is a method for defending yourself while retreating backward at the same time.

ACTION 3: Shift your weight to your left leg and turn your body toward the left. Your left hand twines outward (*ni chan*) as it rolls-back (*lu*) toward the rear. Your right hand twines outward (*ni chan*) as it pushes forward. Your eyes look forward and backward taking everything in. (fig. 2-96)

Fig. 2-96

Requirements: Your weight is shifted as your left hand rolls-back (*lu*) toward the rear and your right hand pushes (*tui*) forward at the same time, all in perfect coordination. Your body should be upright and centrally balanced throughout. Exhale during this action.

Internal Energy: With your waist as a pivot, the energy shifts from your right leg to your left leg. As your waist turns to the left, your internal energy twines to your left shoulder, elbow, and hand; then changes to reverse twining (*ni chan*) and roll-back (*lu*) toward the rear. Your right hand energy reverse twines (ni chan) and pushes (*tui*) forward.

ACTION 4: Shifting your weight to your left leg, your left hand changes from outward twining (*ni chan*) to inward twining (*shun chan*). Moving together with the rotation of your waist toward the left, your left hand moves along an upward arc from the rear to a position in front of your left shoulder. Raise your right leg and take a step backward (*tui bu*) along an arc. Your right hand twines inward (*shun chan*) a little and sinks down slightly. Your eyes look forward. (fig. 2-97)

Requirements: When stepping back toward the rear, your foot twines inward (*li chan*) and steps backward along an arc as your weight shifts. Your hip joint (*kuan guan jie*) should be relaxed and flexible. Inhale during this action.

Fig. 2-97

Fig. 2-98

Internal Energy: The energy issues from your dantian and is directed by your waist. Following along with the turning of your waist, it moves downward into your legs and moves upward into your arms. In this way, and in every action, your whole body is combined together by the movement of internal energy.

ACTION 5: Turning your body toward the right, shift your weight to your right leg. Your right hand twines outward(*ni chan*) as it rolls-back(*lu*) downward. Your left hand twines outward(*ni chan*) as it pushes toward the front. Your eyes look forward. (fig. 2-98)

Requirements: Keep your body's posture upright and centrally balanced. Let the movement of your body lead the movement of your hands. Exhale during this action.

Internal Energy: Using your waist to direct your energy, the energy twines from your left leg to your right leg as your left leg moves inward. As your waist directed energy moves upward, make use of body mechanics to drive the reverse twining (*ni chan*) downward roll-back (*lu*) action of your right hand and the reverse twining (*ni chan*) forward push (*tui*) of your left hand.

ACTION 6: Shifting your weight to your right leg, your right hand changes from twining outward (*ni chan*) to twining inward (*shun chan*) as it arcs backward and upward to a position in front of your right shoulder. Now, turning your body slightly toward the left, raise your left leg and take a step toward the rear with the toes of your left foot touching down first. At the same time, your left hand sinks downward slightly. Your eyes look forward. (fig. 2-99)

Fig. 2-99

Requirements: When taking a retreating step backward (*tui bu*) with your left foot, your weight is on your right leg and the action should be natural and light. When your right hand reaches its position in front of your chest, step down (*luo bu*) toward the rear. Combine and integrate the actions of your arms and upper body with the actions of your waist and legs. Inhale during this action.

Internal Energy: The energy shifts to your right leg. Your left leg energy twines inward (*li chan*) and your left leg takes a step backward (*dao bu*). Your right hand energy changes from reverse twining (ni chan) to natural twining (*shun chan*) as your right hand moves upward to a position in front of your right shoulder. Your waist energy drops downward (*xia ta*).

Self-Defense Application: Step Back and Whirl the Arms is one method of withdrawing. There is however, defensive action contained within the withdrawing action and attacking action contained within the defending action. The important point is to use your lower spine as the axis of your body's movement. Bending your knees and relaxing your hips, step back naturally with a nimble step and whirl your arms on both sides of the body to protect your vital points. Your two hands alternately pushing forward can be used to strike an advancing attacker atwill.

Note: Step Back and Whirl the Arms is one continuous movement. However, in order to facilitate teaching, it is broken down here into separate movements. When the student is proficient, the movements should be performed continuously, all at one go.

In practicing this form according to the proper requirements, starting from a step backward with the left foot, you take a total of five steps backward until you arrive back at the original action of the left foot stepping backward. If the prac*f*oce area is small, you could step back just once or just three times - an odd number of times so as to end up with the left foot stepping back.

21. White Goose Spreading Its Wings *(Bai E Liang Chi)*

ACTION 1: Shift your weight slightly toward the left, stepping down with your left foot. Turn your body slightly toward the left and push forward with your right hand, dropping your left hand to a position inside of your right arm, your two palms opposed as if holding something between them. Your eyes look toward the right front. (fig. 2-100)

Fig. 2-100

Requirements: Drop your waist and relax your hips. Your left palm faces right and your right palm faces left as if holding something between them. Continue inhaling during this action.

Internal Energy: The energy twines upward from your right leg. It passes through your right shoulder and elbow, and through to your right hand, which pushes forward and drops downward. Your two hands act in concert with each other. Your waist energy turns slightly to the left. From your right leg, the energy shifts slightly toward the left.

Self-Defense Application: This posture can be used to roll-back (*lu*) downward an attacker's strike.

ACTION 2: Turn your body slightly toward the left and shift your weight to your left leg. Lift up your right leg and take a step backward (*tui bu*) to the right rear. At the same time, your left hand twines outward (ni chan) and rolls-back (*lu*) downward, changing to inward twining (*shun chan*) as it moves upward and forward along an arc. At the same time, your right hand twines inward (*shun chan*) as it rolls-back (*lu*) downward and then upward to a position in front of your chest with the palm facing upward. Your left and right hands cross in front of your chest on the centerline of your body, the left hand on top of the upturned right arm with your palm facing outward (to the right). Your eyes look forward. (fig. 2-101)

Fig. 2-101

Requirements: In shifting your weight and stepping down to the rear, with your two hands each describing an arc until they cross, you should keep your center of gravity stable and stand with an upright posture. When you take a retreating step backward it should be natural and light, keeping upper and lower in balance. Exhale as your two hands roll-back (*lu*) downward and inhale as they rise up to cross in front of your body.

Internal Energy and **Self-Defense Application:** Same as for the third action of the seventh form, *Bai E Liang Chi.*

ACTION 3: Shift your weight to your right leg and turn your body toward the right. Your right hand twines outward (*ni chan*) to ward-off (*peng*) upward to the upper right front at eyebrow level. Your left hand twines outward (*ni chan*) as it pushes down (*an*) to a position above your left knee. Raise your left knee and draw your left foot back to a position to the left front of your right foot, the heel of your left foot raised and just the toes touching the ground. Your eyes look forward. (fig. 2-102)

Fig. 2-102

Requirements: Bending your knees and relaxing your hips, stand with upright posture, as if suspended by a string attached to the crown of your head. Your two arms form a circular shape, like the surface of a ball, to ward-off (*peng*) outward around their circumference. Exhale during this action.

Internal Energy: The energy follows the turning of your waist to the right, moving upward to your shoulder (relaxed shoulder) then driving to your elbow (dropped elbow) and going through to your fingers (the middle finger of your right hand drawing or leading the energy). Your left hand drops down, the energy penetrating through to your fingers. The energy then returns to your *dantian*.

Fig. 2-103

22. Diagonal Posture

(Xie Xing)

ACTION 1: Without moving your feet, turn your body toward the left. Your left hand, twining outward (*ni chan*), swings with the palm facing in the direction of movement to the rear of your body. Your right hand twines inward (*shun chan*), dropping your elbow and relaxing your shoulder, and moves with the palm facing in the direction of movement along an arc toward the left front. Your eyes look toward the left front. (fig. 2-103)

Requirements: Use the movement of your body to lead the movement of your hands and to propel the movement of your arms, just like willow branches moving in the wind. Inhale during this action.

Internal Energy: The energy issues forth from your dantian. From your waist it twines to your right shoulder, passing through your shoulder, elbow and on to your hand (with the main emphasis on your right hand). Your right hand energy twines naturally(*shun chan*),describing an arc in front of your face; your left hand energy reverse twines (*nichan*), tracing an arc to the rear.

Self-Defense Application: If an attacker tries to use his fist to strike your face or chest, you can turn rapidly toward the left and use your right arm to block or deflect the strike from reaching its target.

ACTION 2: Turning your body toward the right, slightly turn the toes of your right foot outward to the right. Your left knee turns inward, with just the toes of your left foot touching the ground. As your body rotates, your left hand moves from the left rear of your body upward along an arc and forward to a position in front of your nose, on the centerline of your body. Your left hand forms a standing palm(li zhang) with the palm facing the right. Your right hand twines outward (*ni chan*) along an arc, pushing downward (an) to a position outside of your right thigh with the palm facing downward. Your eyes look toward the left front. (fig.2-104)

Requirements: When your two arms revolve around your body, use your waist as the hub and keep your whole body aligned to the vertical, as if you were suspended from above by a string. Exhale during this action.

Fig. 2-104

Internal Energy: Using your waist as a pivot, the energy turns from the left to the right, twining to your right hand which pushes downward along an arc. Your left hand twines naturally (*shun chan*) to a point in front of your chest. Then, rapidly turning your body toward the right, your right hand pulls down (*xia bo*) and your left hand blocks (*dang*) your face, guarding your middle gate (*zhong men*).

ACTION 3: Shift your weight to your right leg while lowering your body. Bend your left knee and raise your left leg, with both hands warding off (*peng*) toward the upper right side of your body. Your eyes look toward the left front. (fig. 2-105)

Fig. 2-105

Requirements: Your two hands ward-off (*peng*) upward, your body sinks lower, and your right leg supports the entire weight of your body. Your knees are bent and your hips relaxed, with upper and lower in harmony (i.e. when you raise your left leg and ward-off upward you also lower your body to keep your posture stable). Inhale during this action.

ACTION 4: Sink your body a little lower. With just the heel of your left foot touching the ground, slide your left foot along the ground toward the left front with the toes lifted upward. Your two hands continue to ward-off (*peng*) upward. Your eyes look toward the left front. (fig.2-106)

Fig. 2-106

Requirements: When opening your stance (*kai bu*), the inside edge of your heel scrapes the ground as it goes out. Your two hands both ward-off (*peng*) upward while the energy of your waist (*yao jin*) drops downward. The intention of this is to keep the upper and lower parts of your body in balance with each other. Exhale during this action.

Internal Energy: Your right hand energy reverse twines (*ni chan*) to ward-off (*peng*) upward. Your left hand energy twines naturally (*shun chan*). Your left leg energy twines inward (*li chan*) and raises your leg upward to take a step sideways (*kai bu*). Sinking your elbows and relaxing your shoulders, the energy settles to your waist.

Self-Defense Application: The action of your two hands warding off (*peng*) upward can be used to roll-back (*lu*) with an attacker's strike or can be used as a block (*dang*) to deflect his strike. Your raised left leg can be used to strike the attacker with your heel (*deng*) or the outer edge of your foot (*chuai*) or to hook his leg (*gou*) or to hold up his leg with yours (*gua*). Your left shoulder has the potential to be used for a backward shoulder strike (*bei kao*).

ACTION 5: Turn your body toward the left and shift your weight to your left leg. Your left hand twines outward (*ni chan*). Moving along with your body's rotation toward the left, it moves downward in an arc to a position below your left knee. Your right hand twines inward (*shun chan*) as it turns a circle toward the rear and then changes to an outward twining (*ni chan*) as it comes into a position below your right ear. Your eyes look toward the left front. (fig. 2-107)

Fig. 2-107

Requirements: When turning your body and shifting the center of gravity you must move your body as a wholly integrated unit. This posture may be performed with either large,medium or small movements. For a detailed explanation, you may consult the explanation for action five of the eighth form, *Xie Xing*, above.

Internal Energy: Using the turning of your waist to the left, your energy moves downward, twining into and concentrating in your left leg. Moving upward to the left side of your waist, it twines to your left shoulder, left elbow, and into your left hand.Your right hand reverse twines (*ni chan*), the wrist revolving around to a position in front of the right side of your chest.

Self-Defense Application: This form places emphasis on the left side of your body, with your right side in a supporting role. The left side of your body is suffused with pressing energy (*ji jin*). The energy goes to your shoulder, from your shoulder it goes to your elbow, and from your elbow it goes into your hands. Your right hand stays back as a rear guard, ready to be brought into play at any time.

ACTION 6: Continue turning your body toward the left and shift your weight to your left leg. The five fingers of your left hand come together to form a hook hand and rise up along an arc to shoulder level. Your right hand forms a standing palm (*li zhang*) in front of your chest. Your eyes look forward. (fig. 2-108)

Fig. 2-108

Requirements: In raising your left hand, your left wrist should be relaxed and should draw the energy upward. Your right hand stores up energy for later use. Relaxing your hips and dropping your waist, energy accumulates at the right side of your waist. Inhale during this action.

Internal Energy: Drop your waist, relax your shoulders, and sink your elbows, sending the energy to your left wrist.

Self-Defense Application: Bringing the five fingers of your left hand together is a defense against having your fingers grabbed by an attacker. Raising up your left wrist can be used to strike the attacker upward under his lower jaw.

ACTION 7: Turning your body toward the right, your right hand twines outward (*ni chan*) and pulls open in an arc toward the right. Your shoulders are relaxed and rounded slightly forward, and your elbows sink downward. Your waist sinks downward with your hips relaxed and your knees bent. Your eyes look forward. (fig. 2-109)

Requirements: In this posture, your two hands and your two feet are situated to the four corners. You should keep your posture vertical and balanced at the center, with your limbs opening in an outwardly expansive way. Open and round your crotch, and keep your

Fig. 2-109

head and neck upright. The object is to maintain balance in the face of forces acting from any direction, or centrally stabilized body mechanics (*zhong ding shen fa*). Exhale during this action.

Internal Energy: With the main emphasis on your right hand, your waist energy turns to the right, twining to your right shoulder. Reaching your relaxed shoulder, it then twines to your right elbow. Reaching your sunken right elbow, it then twines to your right hand. Reaching your bent right wrist (*zuo wan*), it goes through to the tip of your right middle finger. When the form is completed, your knees should be bent and your hip creases (*kua*) relaxed. Enclose your chest (*han xiong*) and drop your waist (*ta yao*). Standing with upright posture, the energy of your crown draws upward (*ding jin ling qi*). Your whole body relaxes and the internal energy (*qi*) returns to your *dantian*.

Self-Defense Application: This posture with centrally stabilized body mechanics, is intended to be stable at the center no matter from which direction a force acts on it. Opening the posture toward the right can be used as a right shoulder or right elbow striking technique.

Fig. 2-110

23. Turning Back with Arms Twining *(Shan Tong Bei)*

ACTION 1: Turn your body slightly toward the left and shift your weight slightly to the left. Your left hand changes to a palm and rises upward as it draws the energy upward. Your right hand twines inward (*shun chan*) as it moves along an arc from right to left, with the intention of meeting up with and acting in conjunction with your left hand. Your eyes look at the tip of the middle finger of your left hand. (fig. 2-110)

Requirements: Drop your waist energy and relax your hips. As your body turns slightly toward the left, your weight shifts slightly forward. You should guard against bending your waist and leaning your body forward. Inhale when your two hands come together during this action.

Internal Energy: The energy twines inward (*li chan*), rising upward from your right foot. Moving along with your waist turning left, it twines upward through your shoulders, going through your elbows, and arriving at your two hands. You should have the intention of bringing your two hands into combined action.

Self-Defense Application: When your two hands coming together make contact with the attacker's right arm, you can apply roll-back energy (*lu jin*).

ACTION 2: Turn your body toward the right and shift your weight to your right leg. Bend your left knee and draw your left leg in, with just the toes of your left foot touching the ground. At the same time, your two hands follow the action of your body turning to the right and roll-back (*lu*) downward and outward toward the right. Your left hand twines inward (*shun chan*) and your right hand twines outward (*ni chan*), with both palms facing outward toward the right. Your eyes look toward the left side. (fig. 2-111)

Fig. 2-111

Requirements: The energy in your hands is closing or compressing energy (*he jin*). The roll-back (*lu*) action is performed as your weight shifts to the right. Your waist energy (*yao jin*) descends and, your entire body moves together as a unit. Exhale during this action.

Internal Energy: Your waist turns right and the energy goes through your two shoulders from your waist, reaching your two hands with combined force and changing to roll-back energy (*lu jin*). On your other side, your left shoulder compresses downward and your right shoulder strikes (*kao*) toward the upper rear. The energy penetrates through your body from your left shoulder and arrives at your right shoulder.

Self-Defense Application: An attack from the front is met by your two hands which meet the attacker's incoming force and direct it harmlessly toward your rear with roll-back (*lu*). Your left shoulder lowers, helping to direct the incoming energy harmlessly away. Your right shoulder can be used to strike the attacker, with the technique of *bei zhe kao* (folding the back and striking with the shoulder, i.e. a wind up and a strike).

ACTION 3: With your weight on your right leg, your left foot is weightless with just the toes touching the ground. Turning your body toward the left, your left hand twines outward (*ni chan*) to ward-off (*peng*) upward in an arc. Your right hand twines inward (*shun chan*) along a downward arc to a position in near your left knee. Your eyes look toward the right front. (fig. 2-112)

Fig. 2-112

Requirements: Your waist serves as the axis of your body's rotation toward the left and right. As your right shoulder settles downward, your left hand wards off (*peng*) upward. The intention is for the combination of your right hand and your left knee, your right shoulder and your left hip, to work together jointly. Inhale during this action.

Internal Energy: The energy turns left from the turning of your waist. Your left hand energy, with your elbow sunken and your shoulder relaxed, reverse twines (*ni chan*) to ward-off (*peng*) upward. Your right hand twines naturally (*shun chan*) to come inward below. Then your energy goes through your body from your right shoulder, arriving at your left shoulder.

Self-Defense Application: First roll-back (*lu*) toward the right then, as the attacker withdraws, strike against his retreating energy.

ACTION 4: Turn your body slightly toward the right. With your weight on your right leg, bend your left knee and raise your left leg. At the same time, twine your right hand inward (*shun chan*) while moving it upward and then drawing it inward to the right side of your waist. Your left hand twines outward (*ni chan*) in a downward direction, with the five fingers pressing together, hidden behind your back. Your eyes look forward.(fig.2-113)

Fig. 2-113

Requirements: When raising your left leg, keep the upper and lower parts of your body in balance by keeping your right knee bent and not raising up your body as you raise your left leg. Your right leg supports the weight of your body and should be entirely stable. Continue to inhale during this action.

ACTION 5: Turn your body slightly toward the right, with the weight still on your right leg. Your left leg takes a step forward (*shang bu*) setting down with the heel touching the ground and the toes raised upward. Your eyes look forward. (fig. 2-114)

Fig. 2-114

Requirements: With your weight still on your right leg, take a step forward naturally with your left foot. Continue inhaling during this action. Actions four and five may be performed continuously without stopping.

ACTION 6: Shift your weight to your left leg and turn your body slightly toward the left. At the same time, your right hand twines inward (*shun chan*) slightly as it thrusts forward and upward as a piercing palm (*chuan zhang*). Your eyes look forward and upward. (fig. 2-115)

Fig. 2-115

Requirements: When thrusting with your palm, screw your right foot downward into the ground. The energy of your waist goes through to your fingers. Exhale during this action.

Internal Energy: The energy starts from your foot, moves in your leg and is controlled directed at your waist. It passes through your shoulders and elbows, penetrating to your fingers; with your whole body connected.

Self-Defense Application: Your right piercing palm can be thrust straight into the attacker's larynx or into his eye. Your left hand at the rear of your body, with the five fingers joined, can be used for the purpose of shaking off an attacker's grabbing technique or for striking at an attacker's crotch.

ACTION 7: With your weight on the left, turn your body quickly toward the right while bending your right knee and raising up your right leg. Your right hand rapidly twines outward (*ni chan*) and turns over to face outward, warding off (*peng*) upward. It then rolls-back (*lu*) to a position in front of and above your face. Your left hand changes to a palm and twines inward (*shun chan*) to ward-off (*peng*) upward on the left side of your body. Your eyes look toward the left front. (fig. 2-116)

Fig. 2-116

Requirements: The movements of raising your two hands to ward-off (*peng*) upward in an arc, raising your right leg and rapidly turning your body must all be performed simultaneously and blend harmoniously into a single movement. This is a transitional movement. After you become familiar through practice there is no stopping during this action. Inhale during this action.

Internal Energy: From your waist, the energy does a somersault (*gun fan*) toward the right, twining into your revolving arms. Going through to your two hands with roll-back energy (*lu jin*). Your arms withdraw upwards in an arc and then move downward, stopping at the waist.

Self-Defense Application: Rapidly turning your body toward the back, you can use a shoulder strike or strike forcefully (*fa jin*) backward with elbow energy. You could also not raise your right leg, ward-off (peng) upward the attacker's arm and put your left hip into his crotch area, causing him to fall. This technique is the same as the hip throw *Kua Bei Shi* in *Shuaijiao* or Chinese wrestling.

ACTION 8: Stamp downward to the ground with your right foot, with your body continuing to turn toward the right. Raise your left foot and take a sideways step (*mai bu*) to the left front, your weight tending toward your right side. Your two hands descend together from above to a position in front of your abdomen where they cross. Your body is now facing 180 degrees away from the position in action six. As your body turns your eyes turn to look forward. (fig. 2-117)

Fig. 2-117

Requirements: After you become familiar with practicing this form, you don't have to stop, but can perform it continuously, all at one go. As you put weight down on your right foot and step sideways with your left foot your stance should be stable. Relax your hips, bend your knees, and drop your waist energy downward. The action of your two hands combines with the turning of your waist into one unified action. Continue inhaling during this action.

Internal Energy: The energy combines in your waist, sinks to your feet, and goes through to your hands.

Self-Defense Application: This form, *Shan Tong Bei* (Turn Back with Arms Twining), is also known as *San Tong Bei* (Thrice Circuiting Through the Back). The body technique is to turn or dodge toward the left in a flash and to turn or dodge toward the right in a flash with the internal energy (*nei jin*) making three orderly (*shun*) circuits of the front (*ren mai*) and the back (*du mai*) channels. On the left and on the right side of your backbone, making three circuits of your back, thus it is called Thrice Circuiting Through the Back (*San Tong Bei*). With *shan,* a quick dodge or lightning fast rapid movement, you can take a force attacking from behind and lead it harmlessly and, just as quickly, throw the attacker down.

24. Cover Fist and Punch

(Yan Shou Gong Quan)

ACTION 1: Turning your body slightly toward the right, shift your weight toward the left. Your two hands separate downward, both twining outward (*ni chan*). Your eyes look forward. (fig. 2-118)

Requirements: The action of separating your two hands downward occurs as your weight shifts. You should separate your

hands as your body turns slightly toward the right, with the movement of your body leading the movement of your hands. Exhale during this action.

Internal Energy: The energy twines from your right leg to your left leg. Your two arms, following along with the turning of your waist energy, reverse twine (*ni chan*) and separate downward.

ACTION 2: Shift your weight from your left leg to your right leg and relax your right hip. Your two hands change to twining inward (*shun chan*) along an upward arc and then settle lower. Your right hand forms a fist and your right elbow bends, bringing the fist to a position at the right side of your waist with the center of the palm facing upward. Your left palm comes in to a position in front of your chest on the centerline of your body, the center of the left palm facing forward and the fingertips pointing upward. Your eyes look forward. (fig. 2-119)

Requirements: With your weight settled on your right leg, drop your waist energy and relax your hips (*kua*). Each part of your entire body is connected one to another, all parts joined together as one. Your mind is concentrated, using stillness in awaiting any movement (*yi jing dai dong*). Your posture is poised to the point where just a light touch will set the release of energy in motion. Inhale during this action.

Internal Energy: Your waist energy drops downward. Enclose your chest and bind your ribs, relaxing your shoulders and sinking your elbows. Your energy combines in your fist but don't clench your fist tightly. The tip of your right foot turns inward, your right hip crease (*kua*) relaxes and sinks downward. This causes your right leg to form a spiraling, silk twining type of energy. Just like a spring, the more it is compressed the greater the release energy will be.

Self-Defense Application: Concentrate the energy of your entire body without releasing it. When internal energy (*nei jing*) has filled your body to the point of overflowing, you can strike forcefully with your shoulder, your elbow, your palm, or your fist. Once you have mastered this technique of combining and concentrating your body's energy (*he jin*), you can use it at will.

ACTION 3: Rapidly shift your weight from your right leg to your left leg and rapidly turn your body toward the left. Your right fist twines outward (*ni chan*) as it shoots forward in a burst of energy (*fa jin*) and your left elbow simultaneously shoots back rapidly in the same burst of energy (*fa jin*). Your left fist forms a half fist (*ban quan*) and is drawn in to the left side of your ribs. Your eyes look forward. (fig. 2-120)

Fig. 2-120

Requirements: When releasing energy (*fa jin*), your right foot presses down into the ground. The energy of your crotch is kept contained while twisting your waist and turning your crotch. With your lower back as the axis of movement, and your body's posture vertical and centrally balanced, force is released by a rotational movement. The energy of your fist issues forward and the energy of your elbow issues backward, with the two energies in balance. Exhale in coordination with the release of energy (*fa jin*).

Internal Energy: Your dantian energy sinks to your right foot, then issues forth from your right foot pressing the ground. The energy moves along your right leg, twining inward (*li chan*) to your left leg. Your waist energy turns rapidly to the left, twining upward to your right shoulder and elbow, then reverse twines (*ni chan*) to reach the top or striking surface of your fist (*quan ding*). Your left elbow issues forth with energy (*fa jin*) in support of your right fist shooting forward, causing your whole body to be integrated into one action.

Self-Defense Application: Shooting your fist spiraling forward can be used to strike an attacker's chest, and your left elbow can be used to strike backward; you could strike an attacker trying to grab you from behind in the ribs with your left elbow.

25. Sealing Six Avenues of Attack and Closing Four Sides *(Liu Feng Si Bi)*

ACTION 1: Turn your body slightly toward the right and shift your weight slightly toward the left. Your right fist changes to a palm and turns a small circle, with receiving energy (*jie jin*). Your left hand changes to an open palm and moves in an upward arc until it comes into conjunction with your right hand. Your eyes look toward the right front. (fig.2-121)

Fig. 2-121

Requirements: When your two hands come together with receiving energy (*jie jin*), use the action of your waist to propel your left hand and your right hand into conjunction. Guard against moving just one arm alone and don't lean your body forward. Inhale during this action.

Internal Energy: When your body turns to the right, your waist energy goes through to both your left and right hands in combination.

Self-Defense Application: Your two hands meet the attacker with receiving energy (*jie jin*), in preparation for roll-back (lu) downward.

ACTION 2: Shift your weight slightly to the right and turn your body toward the left, turning your left toes outward. Your two hands roll-back (lu) toward the lower left with combined strength, your left hand twining outward (*ni chan*) and your right hand twining inward (*shun chan*). Your eyes look toward the right front. (fig. 2-122)

Fig. 2-122

Note: This action is a transitional movement within a continuous form. In order to show it clearly, it is broken down like this into separate segments. When practicing it, you may do so without stopping.

ACTION 3: Shift your weight to your left leg. Raise your right foot and bring it forward past the back of your left foot and step forward (*shang bu*) to the right. The heel of your right foot touches down to the ground with the toes raised. At the same time, continue to turn your body toward the left and continue to roll-back (*lu*) toward the left. Your eyes look toward the right front. (fig. 2-123)

Fig. 2-123

Requirements: Shifting your weight and taking a forward step (*shang bu*) should be done smoothly and naturally. Keep ward-off energy (*peng jin*) in your two hands as they roll-back (*lu*).

ACTION 4: Without stopping after the above action, shift your weight toward the right. Your two hands describe an upward arc to a position in front of your left shoulder, your left hand changing to inward twining (*shun chan*) and your right hand to outward twining (*ni chan*). As your two hands come together in front of your shoulder, turn your body toward the right. Your eyes look toward the right front. (fig. 2-124)

Requirements: When changing from roll-back (*lu*) to push (*an*), your two hands roll-back (*lu*)

Fig. 2-124

downward and then combine upward. The movement all comes from the translation (lateral movement) of your waist and crotch to the left and their rotation to the right. Relax your shoulders and sink your elbows, rotating your wrists and upper arms in order to keep contact without breaking off the energy. Your arms and the hands rotate freely. Their rotational movement is like drawing smoothly into folds. Continue inhaling during this action.

Internal Energy: Your energy continues to turn to the right. Dropping your waist and relaxing your shoulders, the energy twines into your two hands.

Self-Defense Application: The change from roll-back energy (*lu jin*) to pushing energy (*an jin*) is regulated and transformed by the undulating movement of your crotch, waist, and torso.

ACTION 5: With your weight on the right, your body lowers and turns slightly toward the right. Your two hands push (*an*) downward in an arc toward the lower right front with combined strength. Your left foot draws inward to a position about 20 centimeters from the inside edge of your right foot, with just the toes touching the ground. Your eyes look on a downward angle toward the right front. (fig. 2-125)

Fig. 2-125

Requirements: When pushing, relax your hips and drop your waist energy, relax your shoulders and drop your elbows. Your two hands push downward with combined strength as your body sinks down, all parts of your body moving in perfect coordination with each other. Exhale during this action.

Internal Energy: The integrated energy of your whole body passes through a relaxed waist and your hip creases (*kua*), sunken shoulders and elbows, and goes through to your two hands, taking the form of pushing energy (an jin).

Self-Defense Application: The combined strength of your two hands is used to push out the attacker, or, use tactile sensation energy (ting jin) and adhering energy (zhan nian jin) to seal up the attacker's ability to attack you.

26. Single Whip

(Dan Bian)

ACTION 1: Turn your body slightly toward the right. Both hands twine inward (shun chan) with your left hand revolving to the front and your right hand revolving to a position behind your left hand. With your weight on the right side, your left leg turns on the toes of your left foot, turning your left knee inward as your body turns. Your eyes look at the two hands. (fig. 2-126)

Requirements: When your two hands revolve, the movement is perfectly circular and should not be angular or disjointed. Inhale during this action.

Fig. 2-126

Internal Energy and **Self-Defense Application:** Same as for action two of the fifth form, Dan Bian.

ACTION 2: With your weight on the right, turn your body toward the left. With the ball of your left foot touching the ground, your left knee turns outward along with the turning of your body toward the left. Your right hand twines outward (ni chan) and the five fingers gather together, with the wrist drawing energy upward. Your right hand raises upward along an arc to a position at shoulder level. Your left hand, with the palm facing upward, descends to a position in front of your abdomen as your body turns toward the left. The movement of your body leads the movement of your left hand. Keep ward-off energy (peng jin) in your left elbow. Your eyes look at the right hand. (fig. 2-127)

Fig. 2-127

Requirements: Your right hand changes to a hook hand (gou) and raises upward. As your body turns, drop your waist energy. Relax your shoulders and drop your elbows. Your waist serves as the hub of movement and all parts of your body are linked together. When one part of your body moves, all parts of your body move in turn, like the spokes and rim of a wheel following the rotation of the hub. This is an opening (kai) movement. Exhale during this action.

Internal Energy and **Self-Defense Application:** Same as for action two of the fifth form, Dan Bian.

ACTION 3: Turn your body toward the right and shift all of your weight onto your right leg. Bend your left knee and raise up your left leg, turning your left knee inward. Drawing energy to your right wrist, raise your right hand as if a string attached to the back of the wrist is lifting it upward. Your left hand doesn't change position. Relax your shoulders and sink your elbows, keeping the upper and lower parts of your body in balance. Your eyes look toward the left front. (fig. 2-128)

Fig. 2-128

Requirements: With your right leg supporting the weight of your body and the upper and lower body balanced, don't bend your waist and stick out your buttocks. Inhale during this closing (he) action.

Internal Energy and **Self-Defense Application:** Same as for the third action of the fifth form, Dan Bian.

ACTION 4: With the weight of your body on your right leg, slide your left foot along the ground toward the left, with the inside edge of your left heel touching the ground and the foot turned inward with the toes raised. Keep your right wrist drawing energy upward. Let your left hand sink lower, concentrating energy (he jin). Your eyes look toward the left side. (fig. 2-129)

Fig. 2-129

Requirements: Stand with an upright, centrally balanced posture and keep ward-off energy (peng jin) in all parts of your body. Exhale during this opening (kai) action.

Internal Energy: Gathering together the internal energy (qi) in your dantian, it draws your right wrist upward, and twines downward along your thigh to the inside edge of your heel, the big toe drawing the energy. Your left arm sinks down and then leads the energy toward the right.

Self-Defense Application: Same as for the fourth action of the fifth form, Dan Bian.

ACTION 5: Turn your body slightly to the right and shift your weight to the left, forming a left bow stance (gong bu). Your left hand wards off (peng) as it thrusts upward to a position in front of the right side of your chest, twining outward (ni chan) and turning over to face outward. Your eyes look forward, watching your left hand out of the corner of your eye (with peripheral vision). (fig. 2-130)

Fig. 2-130

Requirements: When shifting your weight, your crotch travels along an outward and downward arc, rotating as it shifts. Your left knee cannot cross over a vertical line drawn upward from the tip of your left foot. When your left hand turns over outward, pay attention that you don't raise your shoulder or stick out your elbow. Inhale during this action.

Internal Energy: Using your waist to drive your movement, the energy rises, reverse twining (ni chan) inward from the outside of your right foot to the chang qiang (acupuncture point at the base of your spine). Then, naturally twining (shun chan) from inside to outside, it twines to the tip of your left foot. The tip of your left foot turns outward and the tip of your right foot turns inward. Your energy then moves upward from your waist to your shoulder, elbow, and hand. The thumb of your left hand draws the energy (ling jin).

Self-Defense Application: In this action your left side has the potential to be used for folding the back and striking with the shoulder (bei zhe kao) and for striking with the elbow.

ACTION 6: Turning your body slightly to the left, open your left arm outward toward the left. Your left hand twines outward (ni chan) until it reaches a line drawn upward from your left knee and then changes to inward twining (shun chan) as it relaxes and sinks lower. Your eyes follow your left hand until it reaches its final position, then they turn to look forward. (fig. 2-131)

Fig. 2-131

Requirements: Your left foot is turned outward and your right foot is turned inward. Your hips are relaxed, your knees are bent, and your crotch is rounded. Your posture is upright and centrally balanced, with your neck held erect as if drawn upward by a string attached to the crown of your head. Your shoulders are relaxed and your elbows dropped. There is a correspondence between the position of your two arms and your two legs [i.e. three outer harmonies (wai san he), shoulder lined up with hip, elbow lined up with knee, and hand lined up with foot]. Exhale during this action.

Internal Energy and **Self-Defense Application:** Same as for the action six of the fifth form, Dan Bian, above.

27. Rolling Hands through the Clouds *(Yun Shou)*

ACTION 1: Turn your body slightly to the left and shift your weight a little to the left. Your right hand changes to a palm and twines inward (shun chan) as it sinks downward along an arc to a position in front of your abdomen. Your palm faces toward the left and your fingers point toward the front. Your feet don't move, and, your left hand draws energy. Your eyes look toward the right side. (fig. 2-132)

Fig. 2-132

ACTION 2: Turning your body to the right, shift your weight to your right leg. Your right hand changes from twining inward (shun chan) to twining outward (ni chan), turning over outward as it wards off (peng) upward along an arc to the upper right front. Your left hand twines inward (shun chan) as it moves downward along an arc, settling to a position in front of your abdomen. Your eyes look toward the left front. (fig. 2-133)

Fig. 2-133

ACTION 3: Turning your body slightly to the left, your left hand changes from twining inward (shun chan) to twining outward (ni chan) and describes an upward arc as it turns over outward and wards off (peng) upward. Your right hand changes to inward twining (shun chan) as it moves downward along an arc, settling to a position in front of your abdomen. At the same time, shift your weight to your left leg and take a step (bing bu) toward the left with your right foot to a position next to the inside of your left foot. Your eyes look toward the right front. (fig. 2-134)

Fig. 2-134

ACTION 4: Turning your body slightly to the right, your right hand changes from inward twining (shun chan) to outward twining (ni chan) as it turns over and wards off (peng) upward. Your left hand twines inward (shun chan) and moves downward along an arc to a position in front of your abdomen, drawing inward sightly toward your abdomen. At the same time, shift your weight to your right leg. Raise your left leg and step out (kai bu) toward the left, with your left heel touching down to the ground and the toes raised upward. Your eyes look toward the left front. (fig.2-135)

Requirements (and Explanation): Yun Shou uses your

Fig. 2-135

waist as a hub, with your two hands describing circles in front of your body, to the left side and to the right side in turn, revolving like a rolling wheel with upper becoming lower and lower becoming upper. According to requirements stated in the Quan Lun, or Taijiquan Classic, the circular movement of your two arms should not go any higher than eyebrow level or any lower than your navel. The action of your arms should follow from your steps and the rotation of your body.

The three methods for practicing Yun Shou are: using bing bu and kai bu (closing step and opening step), using tou bu (or cha bu) where your right leg steps to the left behind and past your left leg, and gai bu where your right leg steps to the left in front of and past your left leg. Ordinarily, you use the bing bu method. The opening step and closing step technique is to raise your right foot and then draw it in to a position next to the inside of your left foot; that is one bing bu. After this, your weight shifts again to your right leg and your left foot takes an opening step (kai bu) to the left. This cycle of bing bu followed by kai bu repeats for as many cycles of Yun Shou that you perform.

When you are practicing, you should arrange your steps suitably according to the size of your practice area. If your practice area is large enough, ordinarily you would choose to perform three closing steps and three opening steps. If the area is narrow and cramped, then you could perform two closing steps and two opening steps or one closing step and one opening step. However, you should pay attention to the fact that you should finish with an opening step made by your left foot. You can also use the tou bu or gai bu styles to move back and forth to the left and to the right (i.e. stepping past, either behind or in front of the opposite leg and turning your body 180 degrees). In other words, you can change your footwork according to the changing conditions that present themselves during your practice. The illustrations in this book only show a closing step followed by an opening step (yi bing yi kai) style, it is up to your discretion which method you should use. Exhale during the closing step phase of yun shou and inhale during the opening step phase.

Internal Energy: The internal energy (qi) sets out from your dantian. Using your waist as a hub, it revolves upward into your two arms and downward into your two legs. The changing steps are light and nimble. The swinging movement of your two arms follows from the turning of your body. The energy penetrates through to the tips of your four extremities (si shao).

Self-Defense Application: Yun Shou is a method of practicing shifting to the left and to the right that combines nimble footwork with a constant cycle of moving from the left to the right and from the right to the left with your hands. You can move to the left or to the right, advance or retreat, turn your body around with tou bu and gai bu, and perform these actions at any speed. This form emphasizes defense, but, within defense there is attack, and within attack there is defense. Yun Shou takes into account both attack and defense. This form is also a method for practicing light and nimble footwork.

28. Patting the Horse's Back *(Gao Tan Ma)*

ACTION 1: Turn your body slightly to the left and shift your weight to your left leg. Draw your right foot in to a position next to the instep of your left foot. With your hip relaxed and your knee bent, your right foot is in an empty step (xu bu), without weight and with just the toes touching the ground. Your left hand twines outward (ni chan) and your right hand twines inward (shun chan), with each describing a circular path. Your left hand circles upward and your right hand circles downward, crossing in front of your chest with your left hand on top of your right. Your eyes look toward the right front. (fig. 2-136)

Fig. 2-136

Requirements: The action of your two hands crossing in front of your chest occurs at the same time as you draw in your right leg. When you bring your right arm into position, settled in front of your chest, keep the ward-off energy (peng jin) in this arm. Relax your hips, bend your knees, and keep your body vertical and centrally balanced. First inhale and then exhale during this action.

ACTION 2: With your weight on the left, lift your right leg and take a step out (kai bu) toward the right rear. Your right arm leads your energy (yin jin) toward the left as your body turns toward the left. Your eyes look toward the right side. (fig. 2-137)

Fig. 2-137

Requirements: When you take an opening step (kai bu) with your right leg you are in a posture of leading in above while advancing below (shang yin xia jin). Don't lose your vertical and centrally balanced body posture. Inhale during this action.

ACTION 3: Shift your weight to the right, turning your body slightly to the right. Twine your right arm outward (ni chan) as you separate it downward, twining your left hand outward (ni chan) as it wards off (peng) upward. Your eyes look forward. (fig. 2-138)

Fig. 2-138

Requirements: While separating your two arms, the action of your arms is the result of the revolving of your crotch and waist. Keeping your body's vertical and centrally balanced posture and the ward-off energy (peng jin) in your two arms, this posture should be stable enough to withstand a force acting upon it from any direction. Exhale during this action.

ACTION 4: Turning your body to the right, shift your weight to the left. Your right hand twines inward (shun chan) and turns over, warding off (peng) upward on the right side of the body to shoulder level. Your eyes follow the movement of your right hand. (fig. 2-139)

Fig. 2-139

Requirements: As your right hand rotates, turns over outward and wards off (peng) upward, you should open your chest and relax your hips, keeping in mind that within opening (kai) there is the potential for closing (he). Inhale during this action.

ACTION 5: Turn your body toward the right and then toward the left, shifting your weight to your right leg, with the toes of your right foot turned inward. At the same time, your right hand changes to outward twining (ni chan) and circles inward to a position in front of the right side of your chest. Your left hand twines inward (shun chan) and moves inward slightly to a position in front of your body. Your eyes look toward the right front. (fig. 2-140)

Fig. 2-140

Requirements: Drop your waist energy and round your shoulders forward slightly. Relax your hips and bend your knees, with the toes turned inward. All parts of your body should combine in this action. Continue inhaling during this action.

ACTION 6: With your weight on your right leg, continue turning your body to the left. Your left foot draws backward, describing an arc past the inside of your right foot and on to the rear, with just the toes touching the ground. At he same time, drop your elbow and relax your shoulder of your right arm which twines inward (shun chan) and pushes (tui) toward the right side. Your left hand, twining inward (shun chan), draws in to a position in front of your abdomen, at navel level with your palm facing upward. Your eyes look toward the right front. (fig. 2-141, and 141 supplemental)

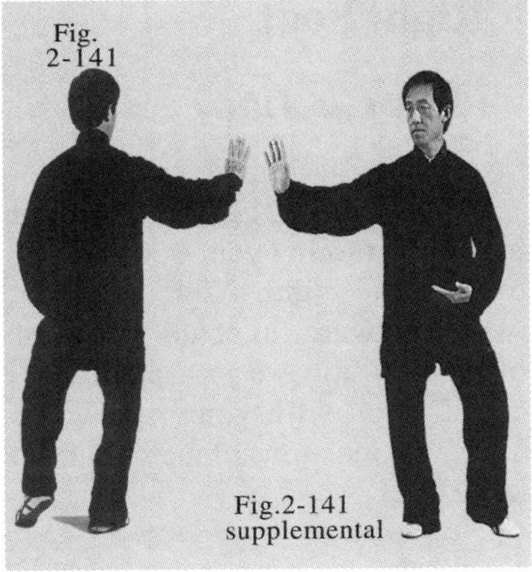
Fig. 2-141

Fig.2-141 supplemental

Requirements: The action of pushing with your right palm depends on the action of your body's turning, with all parts of your body linked together to move as one. Exhale during this action.

Internal Energy: This form makes use of your waist as a hub. The energy first comes together (he) at the center and then moves outward (kai) from the center. Then, dropping your waist, relaxing your hip creases, opening your chest (kai xiong), and turning your arms; your right hand comes in to (he) the right side of your chest. Turning your body, relaxing your shoulder and sinking your elbow, the energy goes through to your right palm.

29. Slapping the Right Foot *(You Ca Jiao)*

ACTION 1: Don't move your feet while turning your body slightly toward the right. Your left hand twines outward (ni chan) and wards off (peng) upward to a position in conjunction with your right hand. Your eyes look toward the right front. (fig.2-142)

Fig. 2-142

Fig.2-142 supplemental

Requirements: When both hands are acting in concert, use the energy of your waist to propel the action of your hands. Turning your left knee slightly inward also helps to support the action of your hands, your two hands are the main focus of this action. Inhale during this action.

ACTION 2: Without moving your feet, turn your body slightly toward the left. Your two hands roll-back (lu) downward to the left, with your left hand twining outward (ni chan) and your right hand twining inward (shun chan). Your eyes look toward the right front. (fig. 2-143, 143 supplemental)

Fig. 2-143

Fig.2-143 supplemental

Requirements: As your two hands roll-back (lu), don't drop their outward ward-off energy (peng jin). The action of your two hands depends on the rotation of your body, which relaxes and sinks lower as it turns. Exhale during this action.

ACTION 3: Your left hand changes from twining outward (ni chan) to twining inward (shun chan) as it describes an upward arc, changing again to outward twining (ni chan) as it comes together with and crosses with the right hand in front of your chest. At the same time, raise your left leg and take a step (gai bu) toward the right of your right leg, stepping in front of and crossing over your right leg. Your weight is on the right and the outside of your left heel is touching the ground. Your eyes look toward the right front. (fig. 2-144, 144 supplemental)

Fig. 2-144

Fig.2-144 supplemental

Requirements: With your weight on your right leg, your hands and your feet both cross at the same time. Your entire body should be relaxed and flexible; you should absolutely avoid being hard and stiff in your movements and you should be absolutely stable in your stance. Inhale during this action.

ACTION 4: Shifting your weight to your left leg, your left foot presses down to the ground. Your right leg is not weighted, with the foot just touching the ground. Your two arms twine outward (ni chan), turn over outward and ward-off (peng) upward. Your body sinks down and your eyes look toward the right side. (fig. 2-145, 145 supplemental)

Fig. 2-145

Fig.2-145 supplemental

Requirements: Your body sinks downward and your two arms ward-off (peng) upward with the intention of balancing the upper and lower parts of your body with each other. The muscles of your rib and abdominal region should relax and sink downward. The center of gravity on your left leg should be stable. Exhale during this action.

ACTION 5: Rapidly raise your right leg upward, with your two hands raising upward and then separating downward. Your right hand slaps downward on the top of your right foot with some force as the result of its downward motion meeting the upward motion of your right foot. Your posture is now a standing on one leg (du li bu) stance with your left leg supporting the entire weight of your body. Your eyes look toward the right front. (fig. 2-146)

Fig. 2-146

Requirements: Your left leg must be stable as it supports the weight of your body. The energy of your two hands, as they rise up, separate and then come downward with combined energy, should be evenly distributed between your two hands, with left and right balanced with each other. The kick upward with your right foot should begin very rapidly, with your upper body and your lower body acting in concert. First inhale and then exhale during this action.

Internal Energy: In this form the energy issues from your waist and twines upward to your left hand, with your two hands in combination. Your two hands roll-back (lu) downward and then cross in front of your chest, with ward-off (peng) upward. Your body sinks lower, with a stable center of gravity. Raising your leg and kicking, your right leg meets your right hand, with your energy reaching to your right foot and right hand.

Self-Defense Application: If an attacker is on your right side, the action of your right hand moving from above to below would pass by his face and obscure his line of sight. Raising your right foot, you can kick his crotch at the lower level and kick his abdomen, chest or lower jaw at a higher level.

30. Slapping the Left Foot (Zuo Ca Jiao)

ACTION 1: Turning your body toward the right, your right foot drops downward and turns a circle clockwise in the air, setting down with the foot turned toward the outside, the outside edge of the heel touching the ground. Your weight is on the left side of your body. At the same time, your two hands cross in front of your chest with your left hand on top and your right hand below. Your eyes look straight ahead. (fig.2-147)

Fig. 2-147

Requirements: Your posture needs to be stable as you twine your right foot inward (shun chan), turn it outward and cross your two hands. At the same time you have to keep your body posture upright and centrally balanced. First inhale and then exhale during this action.

ACTION 2: As you shift your weight to your right leg, continue turning your body toward the right. Your left foot, without weight on it, lightly touches the ground. At the same time, your two arms turn over outward and ward-off (peng) upward. Your eyes look toward the left side. (fig.2-148)

Fig. 2-148

Requirements: Your two arms ward-off (peng) upward and your body sinks lower. Your right leg supports the weight of your body and should be completely stable. First inhale and then exhale during this action.

ACTION 3: With your right leg supporting the weight of your body, kick upward rapidly with your left foot after raising it up off the ground. Your two hands separate downward from above, with your left hand slapping downward on the top of your left foot with some force which is the result of the force of your rising foot and the force of your descending hand meeting. Your eyes look toward the left front. (fig. 2-149)

Fig. 2-149

Requirements: With your right leg supporting your body, your center of gravity must remain stable. The raising of your left foot must be very rapid and combine with the action of your left hand. First inhale and then exhale during this action.

Internal Energy: In this form, the energy twines naturally (shun chan) in your right leg and swings outward. The energy of your two hands comes together. Following the rotation of your body to the right, the energy twines into your right leg. The energy of your two arms reverse twines (ni chan) and wards off (peng) outward. The energy goes through to the tip of your left foot which meets together with your left hand.

Self-Defense Application: Continuing from the previous posture, quickly turning your body in a small space and kick with your left foot. This is a form of advancing with a continuous attack.

31. Kicking with the Left Heel (Zuo Deng Yi Gen)

ACTION 1: After slapping your foot, turn your body 180 degrees toward the left. Your left foot, from behind, turns along with your body as your body turns toward the left and draws inward to a position next to the inside of your right foot in an empty step (xu bu) without weight, your foot just touching the ground. Your two hands come together in front of your abdomen and your eyes look forward. (fig. 2-150, 150 supplemental)

Fig.2-150 supplemental

Fig. 2-150

Requirements: When turning your body, with your weight on your right leg, your right leg must remain stable. Turn smoothly and naturally, concentrating the energy of your entire body and keeping it from dispersing.

ACTION 2: Without moving your feet, turn your body slightly toward the left. Your two hands both twine outward (ni chan), separating downward with each hand moving on an arc to it's respective side. Let your gaze sweep left and right. (fig. 2-151, 151 supplemental)

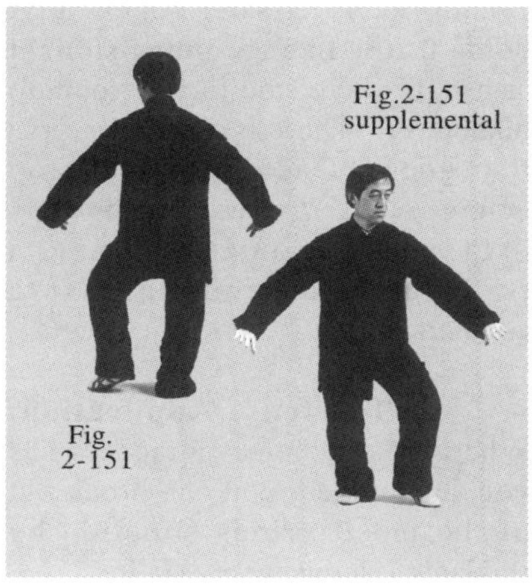
Fig. 2-151
Fig.2-151 supplemental

ACTION 3: Your two hands form fists and come together in front of your abdomen with your palms facing inward. Bend your left knee and raise your left leg, with the foot hanging, toes downward, naturally and relaxed. Your eyes look toward the left front. (fig. 2-152, 152 supplemental)

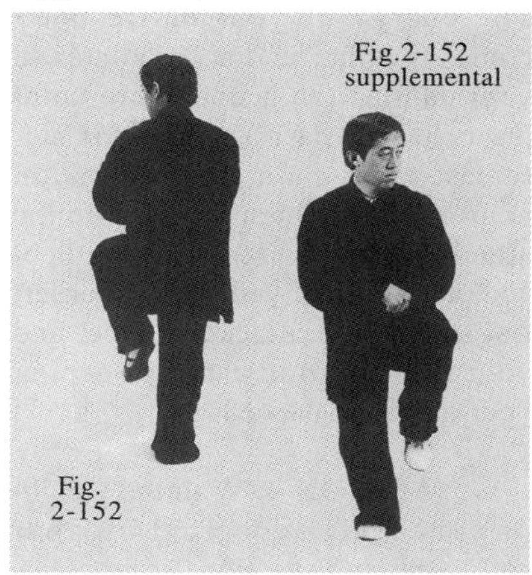
Fig. 2-152
Fig.2-152 supplemental

Requirements: Your body sinks lower as your leg raises, upper and lower combined harmoniously. Relax your hips and bend your knees, your two elbows ward-off (peng) outward, storing energy for later release. Inhale during this action.

Internal Energy: The energy of your whole body unites and gathers in your dantian. A boxing treatise says, in storing up (xu) energy you should pack it in tightly, in releasing (kai) energy you should release it all completely. Storing up energy (xu jin) is like drawing a bow, releasing energy (fa jin) is like letting the arrow fly. Your entire body relaxes and combines into one whole unit; then your energy releases and that simply completes the cycle, totally integrated and all at one go.

Self-Defense Application: The energy of your entire body comes together and accumulates in your dantian (an acupuncture point just below the navel), storing for later release. The main emphasis is on your left foot which thrusts into the attacker's waist area with the heel and outer edge of your foot. Your left fist strikes the attacker's face, and your right hand assists by keeping your posture balanced.

ACTION 4: With the weight of your body supported by your right leg, incline your torso on a diagonal line toward the right. Your left foot, utilizing the elastic strength (tan li) of your waist and crotch, kicks out horizontally toward the left side on a level with your waist and hips. Your two fists separate forcefully (fa jin) out to both sides, with the strength (li) going through to your fist (quan ding). (fig. 2-153)

Fig. 2-153

Requirements: Your right foot holds firmly to the ground, with your left foot and your left and right fists issuing energy (fa jin) simultaneously. Your actions should be like the phrase, contracting your body like a hedgehog, then spitting out qi with boundless energy. Exhale during this action.

Internal Energy: Continuing from the previous form, gather your dantian energy together into a ball. At the same time, the energy goes through to your left foot and your left and right fists. However, you cannot open (kai) out completely; doing that is like becoming straight as a staff: there's no further room to manoeuver. There is a boxing verse that goes, "I advise you to stop before you exert yourself completely to the end, keep thirty percent as a reserve to defend against a counterattack."

Self-Defense Application: When an attacker or attackers has you surrounded, you can break out of the most serious situation by suddenly issuing energy (fa jin).

32. Walking Forward by

Stepping to Both Sides

(Qian Tang Ao Bu)

ACTION 1: Your left foot drops to the ground and your weight shifts to your left leg. Your two fists change into open palms, your left palm describing an arc and pushing forward, and your right palm circling to a position below your right ear. Your eyes look toward the left front.

Fig. 2-154

Requirements: After kicking with your heel, as your body is turning toward the right after drawing back your left foot, step forward again to the left front in coordination with the circling of your left and right hands. Inhale as you draw in your leg and exhale as you lower your foot and step forward.

Internal Energy: After kicking with your heel, the energy draws back into your dantian. The energy is directed by your waist and your body turns toward the left. The energy then goes through to your left leg. Above it combines in the left and right hands.

Self-Defense Application: As you step forward after kicking with your heel, press downward against the attacker's retreating leg with your heel, taking this opportunity to strike the attacker.

ACTION 2: Continue turning your body toward the left, and shift your weight to your left leg, turning the tip of your left foot outward. Raise your right leg and take a step forward. As your body turns toward the left, your left hand describes an arc while pushing downward, and your right hand pushes forward. Shift your weight to your right leg. Your eyes look toward the right front. (fig. 2-155)

Requirements: Taking a step forward while flashing your hands should be perfectly coordinated, with the insubstantial (non-weight bearing leg) and the substantial (weight bearing leg) clearly distinguished. Step forward smoothly and naturally.

Fig. 2-155

Inhale while raising your leg and exhale when setting it down.

Internal Energy: Along with the turning of your body to the left, your energy moves downward from your waist. Relaxing your hip crease and raising your knee, your energy goes through to your right foot. Moving upward through relaxed shoulders and sunken elbows, it goes through to your two hands. Using your waist as hub, your two arms swing in circles on both sides of your body.

Self-Defense Application: The action of your two arms is like a rolling wheel that throws off everything it comes into contact with; thus, protecting your whole body, front and back, left and right.

ACTION 3: With your weight shifting to your right leg, raise your left foot and take a step forward (shang bu) to the front . Your body turns toward the right as a result of taking a step to the front with your left foot. Your right hand twines outward (ni chan) as it describes an arc to the right side of your body where it pushes downward. Your left hand twines inward (shun chan) as it turns over upward and wards off (peng) toward the front. Your eyes look toward the left front. (fig. 2-156)

Fig. 2-156

Requirements: When taking a step forward with your left foot, with your weight shifting toward the right, the tip of your right foot turns outward. Your left hand turning over upward and warding off (peng) forward, and pushing downward with your right hand should all be perfectly coordinated with the rotation of your body toward the right and stepping forward. Inhale during this action.

Internal Energy: The energy drops into your waist and goes through to your hands. The energy of your crown draws upward.

Self-Defense Application: This posture can be used to issue energy (fa jin) with your shoulder or elbow toward the lower left.

Fig. 2-157

33. Punching Toward the Ground *(Ji Di Chui)*

ACTION 1: Lower your body and turn slightly toward the right, shifting your weight toward the left. Change your two hands into fists, the center of the palm of your left fist facing upward and inward. Your right fist raises up to a position level with your right shoulder, with the center of the palm facing inward. Your eyes look downward toward the left front. (fig.2-157)

Requirements: Lower your body, with hips relaxed and knees bent, let your waist energy attenuate and keep ward-off energy (peng jin) on your two arms. Continue inhaling during this action.

Internal Energy: Your crotch energy should be round, dropping your waist energy. The energy goes through to your two fists.

ACTION 2: Turning your body toward the left, shift your weight toward the left. Your left fist twines outward (ni chan), describing an arc downward, passing in front of your left knee and raising up to the left side of your head, level with the top of your head. Your right fist twines outward (ni chan) as it bores forward and downward from a position behind your right ear. Your eyes look forward on a downward angle. (fig. 2-158)

Fig. 2-158

Requirements: When boring downward with your fist, your spine is extended, as if being stretched by a force pulling upward from above. Guard against bending your waist and protruding your buttocks. Exhale during this action.

Internal Energy: Twist your waist and turn your hips. Your left fist reverse twines (ni chan) and raises upward, your right fist reverse twines (ni chan) and carries forward and downward (zai quan).

Self-Defense Application: If an attacker pushes you from behind, you suddenly pivot your back and relax, sinking downward. The attacker's energy slides off harmlessly, causing him to fall. You can fold your back and strike the attacker with your left shoulder.

34. Turning and Kicking Twice in the Air *(Ti Er Qi)*

ACTION 1: Shift your weight toward the right and twine your right fist outward (ni chan) while you ward-off (peng) with your right elbow upward toward the right rear. Your left fist twines outward (ni chan) as it bores downward to the outside of your left leg. Your eyes look toward the right rear. (fig. 2-159)

Requirements: When turning your body around toward the right, you must turn your body, shift your weight, and ward-off (peng) upward simultaneously. Inhale during this action.

Fig. 2-159

Internal Energy: Your energy issues from your waist and turns toward the right, twining upward into your right elbow. Your left fist reverse twines and settles downward.

Self-Defense Application: If an attacker ambushes you from the rear, you can turn your body rapidly and strike his face with your right elbow.

ACTION 2: Continuing from the previous action, keep turning your body toward the right. Shift your weight to your left leg and raise your right leg, drawing your right foot in to a position to the right front of your left foot, your knee bent and the just the toes of your right foot touching the ground. At the same time, your right fist twines inward (shun chan) and turns over outward with the turning of your body, settling to a position at the right side of your body. Your left fist twines inward (shun chan) and shoots upward with the turning of your body to a position in front of the left side of your face. Your eyes look forward. (fig. 2-160)

Fig. 2-160

Requirements: With your waist as the axis, your body turns around 180 degrees, and, your two fists keep ward-off energy (peng jin) as they rotate and turn over. That is why this form is also called Turn the Body and Kick Twice (Fan Shen Ti Er Qi). Exhale during this action.

Internal Energy: Using your waist as a hub, the energy twines into your two fists.

Self-Defense Application: The action of turning your body around is like the spinning of a rolling wheel, taking the attacker's incoming energy and rolling it off in a harmless direction.

ACTION 3: Turning your body slightly toward the right, shift your weight forward to your right leg. Your right fist moves toward the back and your left fist wards off (peng) toward the front while your body inclines forward slightly. Your eyes look forward. (fig. 2-161)

Fig. 2-161

ACTION 4: Dropping your weight onto your right leg, raise your left leg and kick forward with your left foot. Ward-off (peng) with your right fist toward the rear. Your eyes look forward. (fig. 2-162)

Fig. 2-162

ACTION 5: Turn your body slightly toward the left. Your right fist changes into an open palm and circles upward along an arc from behind to a level above your head. Your left fist changes to an open palm and moves downward along an arc at the left side of your body and waves toward the rear, your left palm continuing on an upward trajectory. Your eyes look forward. (fig. 2-163)

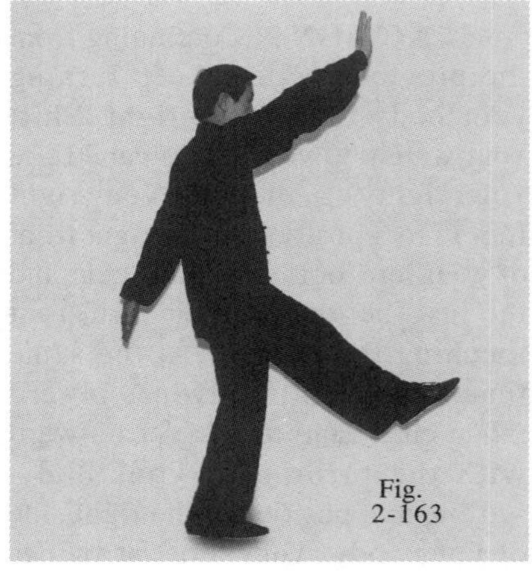
Fig. 2-163

ACTION 6: Your left foot rapidly drops back down to the ground and your right foot rapidly kicks upward. Your right hand slaps downward onto the top of your right foot, with your left hand moving (in a motion like waving) backward and upward. Your eyes look at the palm of your right hand. (fig. 2-164)

Fig. 2-164

Requirements and Explanation (actions four through six): In order for beginners to more clearly observe the changes in the direction of movement, a few illustrations of transitional movements have been added. When you become more proficient, these movements would be performed continuously without stopping. When kicking forward, leap upward vigorously, with the action of your right foot kicking upward and the action of your right hand combined. Your left hand draws energy upward. Exhale when kicking with your foot.

Internal Energy: The energy starts out from your waist. Your left leg starts first, then your right leg pushes against the ground and kicks upward. Your two arms circle on both sides of your body, combining with your right foot.

Self-Defense Application: Kick upward at the attacker's throat or lower jaw. The two legs, one rising and one falling, can also be used in a combination kicking pattern.

35. Protecting the Heart with the Fist *(Hu Xin Quan)*

ACTION 1: After your right hand slaps your right foot, your right foot drops down to the ground next to the instep of your left foot. Your left hand pushes downward to the outside of your left thigh and your right hand pushes downward to the outside of your right thigh. Bend your knees, relax your hips, and stand with an upright, centrally balanced posture. Your eyes look forward. (fig. 2-165)

Fig. 2-165

Requirements: After leaping upward (in the previous action) your body descends downward, with your knees bending and hips relaxed, your two hands settle downward.

Internal Energy: Your right foot drops to the ground. The energy settles to your dantian.

ACTION 2: Shifting your weight to your right leg, raise your left leg and step out (kai bu) toward the left front. At the same time, your two hands describe an arc toward the left, ward-off (peng) upward and then roll-back (lu) downward. Your body turns toward the right. Your eyes look toward the left front. (fig. 2-166)

Fig. 2-166

Requirements: Your body sinks downward, with your weight on the right. When you step out (kai bu) with your left leg, it should be smooth and natural, combining in perfect unison with the roll-back (lu) of your two hands toward the rear. Inhale during this action.

Internal Energy: The energy twines downward from your waist into your left leg, the tip of your left foot turning inward. Your two hands roll-back (lu) toward the upper rear, your left hand twining naturally (shun) and your right hand reverse twining (ni).

ACTION 3: Turn your body, first toward the right, and then toward the left. Shift your weight to your left leg. Raise your right leg and draw your right foot back beside the instep of your left foot, without weight and just touching the ground. At the same time, your two hands first describe an arc toward the right, sinking downward, then ward-off (peng) upward toward the left. Your left hand changes from twining inward (shun chan) to twining outward (ni chan) and your right hand changes from twining outward (ni chan) to twining inward (shun chan). Your eyes look toward the right front. (fig. 2-167)

Requirements: Use your hands to draw or guide your energy. Your right foot draws back naturally, in smooth coordination with your hands. Before your two hands ward-off (peng) upward toward the left,

Fig. 2-167

Fig. 2-168

they first describe an arc toward the right, sinking downward; as in the saying, If you want to go left, first go right. Exhale during this action.

ACTION 4: With your weight on the left, raise your right leg and take a step sideways (kua bu) toward the right side. Your two hands ward-off (peng) upward toward the left. Your eyes look toward the right front. (fig.2-168)

Requirements: Your hand leads and your foot opens a step, drawing in above while advancing below. Your body's posture is upright. Inhale during this action.

ACTION 5: Turn your body toward the right and shift your weight to your right leg while sinking lower. At the same time, your right hand changes to outward twining (ni chan) and moves downward along an arc past a point below your right knee where it rotates outward. Your left hand changes to twining inward (shun chan) as it crosses from the left toward the right to a point in front of your face. Your eyes look forward. (fig.2-169)

Fig. 2-169

Requirements: If you are

practicing the large degree of difficulty style, your right shoulder and right elbow both turn below the level of your right knee, combining with the energy of your waist and the crotch. There is, therefore, the potential to use the seven inch shoulder and elbow strike techniques. Exhale during this action.

ACTION 6: Turning your body slightly toward the right, relax your hips and sink lower. At the same time, your right hand changes to a fist and raises up to a position in front of the right side of your chest. Your left hand changes to a fist and sinks down to a position forward of your lower abdomen. The center of the palms on both your right and left fists face downward. Your eyes look forward. (fig. 2-170)

Fig. 2-170

Requirements: As you raise up your right fist, your left fist descends together with your body's sinking downward, your entire body integrated in action. Inhale during this action.

ACTION 7: Turn your body toward the left, with your weight tending toward your right leg. At the same time, dropping your right elbow and relaxing your right shoulder; your right fist twines inward (shun chan) as it wards off (peng) forward to a position in front of your chest on the centerline of your body. Your left fist twines inward (shun chan) and draws inward to a position in front of your abdomen on the centerline of your body. Your right fist above is on a line drawn upward from your left fist below. Your eyes look forward. (fig. 2-171, 171 supplemental)

Fig.2-171 supplemental
Fig. 2-171

Requirements: With your pelvic girdle as a stable platform, your knees bent and your hips relaxed, the energy of your crotch (dang jin) opens and rounds. Your posture is upright and centrally balanced. The shape formed by each arm should be rounded like the surface of a ball, with ward off (peng). Exhale during this action.

Internal Energy: The form Hu Xin Quan turns to the left and revolves to the right, the emphasis is on turning your waist and the energy of the groin. From turning your waist and revolving your groin, the energy twines into your right elbow and is then driven into your right fist.

Self-Defense Application: The first few actions of this form serve to adjust your body position (shen fa) and your stance (bu fa), and to use your shoulder and elbow to strike an attacker behind you. The last position uses your waist and your crotch to drive the action of your right elbow, enabling you to either strike with energy held in reserve - outwardly soft yet hard internally, or to strike with a forceful explosion of energy (fa jin).

36. Whirlwind Kick

(Xuan Feng Jiao)

ACTION 1: Turn your body first toward the left and then toward the right. At the same time, change your two fists into open palms and first ward-off (peng) upward toward the left and roll-back (lu), and then ward-off (peng) upward toward the right and roll-back (lu). Your eyes look forward. (fig. 2-172)

Fig. 2-172

Requirements: The circling energy (huan rao jin), as you change your two hands from fists into palms; entirely depends on the rotating in folds energy (zhuan zhe jin) of your waist and your crotch, and manifests in small and perfectly round circles. Your waist and crotch rotating in a small circle toward the left and then toward the right drives the action of your fists changing into palms, your left hand twining inward (shun chan) and your right hand twining outward (ni chan) changing into roll-back energy (lu jin). Inhale during this action.

Internal Energy: Your crotch and waist first make a small circle to the left and then to the right, moving your two fists changing into two palms. Your left hand twines naturally and your right hand reverse twines, changing into roll-back (lu) energy.

ACTION 2: Your two hands first roll-back (lu) toward the right and sink down lower. They then rise up, describing an arc upward toward the left, your left hand moving to eye level and your right hand moving to chest level. Your left hand twines outward (ni chan) and your right hand twines inward (shun chan) as they ward-off (peng) upward. At the same time, first turn your body toward the right and then slightly toward the left, with your weight shifting from your right leg to your left leg. Bend your right knee and raise up your right leg. Your eyes look forward. (fig. 2-173)

Fig. 2-173

Requirements: You should perform the actions of shifting your weight, raising your right leg, and warding off (peng) upward with your two hands simultaneously. Your body should be upright and your stance firm, with your entire body concentrated and connected. First exhale and then inhale during this action.

Internal Energy: The energy shifts from your right leg to your left leg. Your two hands ward-off (peng) upward, your left hand reverse twining (ni chan) and your right hand natural twining (shun chan).

ACTION 3: Turning your body slightly toward the right, turn your right foot outward (toward the right) and set it down on the ground, with the outside edge of your right heel touching the ground. Bend your left knee and relax your hip. Your two hands cross in front of the chest. Your eyes look forward. (fig. 2-174)

Requirements: Cross your hands and turn your right foot outward simultaneously, dropping your waist energy and relaxing your hips, with energy (jin) concentrated in your hands. Inhale first, and then exhale during this action.

ACTION 4: Shifting your weight to your right leg, turn your body 90 degrees toward the right,

Fig. 2-174

bending your knees and squatting down. At the same time, your two hands twine outward (ni chan) and ward-off (peng) outward. Your eyes look toward the left front. (fig. 2-175)

Fig. 2-175

Requirements: Your body spirals or corkscrews as it sinks downward, and your two arms continue to ward-off (peng) throughout the action (don't let the ward-off energy drop). Exhale during this action.

Internal Energy: The energy settles to your waist, twines into your leg, and wards off (peng) in your two arms.

ACTION 5: Turning your body toward the right, rapidly raise up your left leg and sweep your left foot around toward the front of your body, at the same time, your two hands open out horizontally to the two sides (left hand toward your left and right hand toward your right), with your left hand slapping the inside of your left foot. Your eyes look toward the left front. (fig. 2-176)

Fig. 2-176

Requirements: You must raise your left leg and sweep it around toward the front very rapidly. You must also open your hands toward your two sides together with the action of your leg, in perfect unison. Exhale during this action.

Internal Energy: The energy drives from your waist. Your left leg raises upward and inward, combining with the outward splitting (lie) of your reverse-twining (ni chan) left hand.

Self-Defense Application: Sweep your left leg toward the front. This action can be performed relatively high or low to strike the attacker's waist or sweep his legs. As you sweep your leg toward the front of your body, your two hands opening outward in the opposite direction can be used to topple the attacker.

ACTION 6: Keep turning your body toward the right, 180 degrees from the previous action. Your left foot sets down near the instep of your right foot without weight and only the toes touching the ground. At the same time, your two hands cross and settle in front of your abdomen. Your eyes look forward. (fig. 2-177)

Requirements: After slapping the inside of your left foot with your left hand, rapidly revolve your body without stopping, turning your body and setting your foot down, with

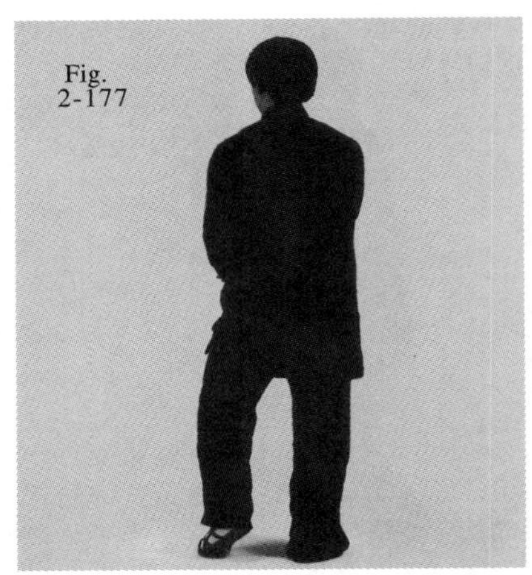
Fig. 2-177

your upper and lower body in harmony, standing firmly with your body in balance. Continue to exhale during this action.

Internal Energy: After the combined striking action of your left hand and foot your energy returns to your dantian. Your whole body is connected (xiang he), without letting up the ward-off energy (peng jin).

37. Kicking with the Right Heel *(You Deng Yi Gen)*

ACTION 1: Take a step sideways toward the left with your left foot. Your two hands, twining outward (ni chan), turn over upward and ward-off (peng) outward. Relax your hips and sink lower. Your eyes look forward. (fig. 2-178)

Fig. 2-178

Requirements: Separate your two hands upward at the same time as you take a step to the left. Round your crotch and stand with upright posture, keeping your head and neck erect as if balancing something on the crown of your head. Inhale during this action.

ACTION 2: Shift your weight to your left leg and draw your right foot in to a position near the instep of your left foot. At the same time, your two hands draw inward to cross in front of your abdomen. Your eyes look toward the right front. (fig. 2-179)

Requirements: The actions of shifting the weight, drawing your right foot in, and bringing your two hands together, should all be

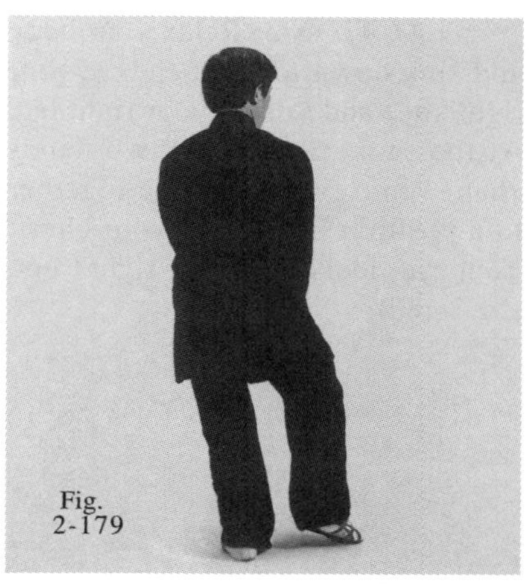
Fig. 2-179

performed quickly and in perfect coordination with each other. Exhale during this action.

Internal Energy: Starting from the above action, the energy issues from your waist. First opening (kai) and then closing (he). The energy gathers in your dantian.

Self-Defense Application: The first and second actions of this form consist of taking a step sideways toward the left rapidly, and then raising your left leg to kick the attacker with the bottom of your foot. If you find yourself too close to the attacker, where it isn't possible to bring your full force to bear, then you may rapidly step out sideways in order to place yourself in an advantageous position at a suitable range for a kick.

ACTION 3: Relax your body and sink down lower, bending your right knee and raising your right leg. At the same time, your two hands change into fists and raise together to a position in front of your chest. Your eyes look toward the right front. (fig.2-180)

Fig. 2-180

Requirements: In raising your leg and bending your knee, the actions of your entire body are coordinated harmoniously. The centers of the palms of your fists face inward toward your body and your elbows don't drop their ward-off energy (peng jin). Inhale during this action.

Internal Energy: The energy collected in your dantian relaxes and gathers in your fist and foot. Gathering tightly and releasing to the maximum; like a paper firecracker, the tighter the paper is rolled, the louder the sound of the explosion.

ACTION 4: With your left leg supporting the entire weight of your body, your right leg thrusts toward the right with the outer edge of the foot leading and your leg parallel to the ground. At the same time, your two fists thrust rapidly toward the two sides in an explosive release of energy (fa jin). Your eyes look toward the right front. (fig. 2-181)

Fig. 2-181

Requirements: When issuing energy with explosive force (fa jin), you must stand firmly so that your body is stable, allowing you to complete the release of energy without breaking it off prematurely. Exhale during this action.

Internal Energy: From your waist, the whip-snapping energy (tan dou jin) penetrates to your right foot and your two fists.

Self-Defense Application: Depending on how close you are to the attacker, you also have the option of not taking a step prior to kicking, as long as you can reach his waist or leg with your foot.

38. Cover Fist and Punch

(Yan Shou Gong Quan)

ACTION 1: Draw your right foot back and let it hang down naturally under your crotch. Your right fist changes into an open palm and drops down, settling to a position inside of your right leg. Your left fist changes into an open palm and comes in to a position at the left side of your body. Your eyes look toward the right front. (fig. 2-182)

Fig. 2-182

Requirements: After kicking, you can set your right leg down or not; the important thing is to train the strength of supporting your body on one leg while keeping your body standing firm and stable, combined with dropping your two hands downward. Inhale during this action.

ACTION 2: Your right hand turns a circle and chops downward toward the right side with some force (fa jin) while your left hand raises up, palm upward, to a position to the left front of your forehead. At the same time, turn your body 45 degrees toward the right, turning your weighted left foot to point inward with your right foot raised. Your eyes look forward. (fig. 2-183)

Fig. 2-183

Requirements: Standing on one leg, issuing energy (fa jin) and turning your body, with your knee raised and hip relaxed, with upper and lower in balance, the entire action is performed with seamless continuity. Exhale during this action.

Internal Energy: After the above kicking action, the internal energy returns to your dantian. Turning your waist and swinging your arms, the energy goes through to your right hand.

Self-Defense Application: This action serves to train issuing energy (fa jin) with your right hand while keeping your lower body stable with your right leg raised, to avoid being kicked in the right leg by an attacker. Raise your right leg to dodge his kick and then chop downward with your right hand against his shin with some force (fa li).

ACTION 3: Your right foot stamps down to the ground and your left foot then steps out one step toward the left front, with your weight on the right. At the same time, your two hands cross in front of your abdomen with your left hand on top and your right hand underneath the left. Your eyes look forward. (fig. 2-184)

Requirements, Internal Energy and **Application:** Same as for the fifth action of the thirteenth form, Ao Bu.

Fig. 2-184

ACTION 4: Turning your body slightly toward the right, shift your weight toward the left. Both hands twine outward (ni chan) and separate downward. Your eyes look forward.(fig.2-185)

Fig. 2-185

Requirements, Internal Energy and **Application:** Same as for the first action of the fourteenth form, Yan Shou Gong Quan.

ACTION 5: Turn your body toward the left and shift your weight toward the right. Your right hand twines inward (shun chan) as it turns over upward and forms into a fist, settling to a position by the right side of your waist with the center of your palm facing upward. At the same time, your left hand first twines outward (ni chan) and then twines inward (shun chan) as it describes a small circle and comes in to a position in front of the left side of your chest. Your eyes look forward. (fig.2-186)

Fig. 2-186

Requirements, Internal Energy and **Application:** Same as for the second action of the fourteenth form, Yan Shou Gong Quan.

ACTION 6: Press down hard with your right foot, rapidly shifting your weight toward the left as you quickly turn your body toward the left. Your right fist twines outward (ni chan) as it shoots toward the front in an explosion of energy (fa jin) as your left elbow shoots backward (fa zhou jin) in the same burst of energy. Your eyes look forward. (fig. 2-187)

Fig. 2-187

Requirements and Application: Same as for the third action of the fourteenth form, Yan Shou Gong Quan.

39. Small Grab and Hit

(Xiao Qin Da)

ACTION 1: With your weight on the left, your right fist changes into an open palm, your shoulders relaxing and your elbows dropping. Your left hand twines outward (ni chan) from beside your ribs on the left side of your body upward to a position inside of your right forearm. At the same time, lift up your right leg and take a half-step forward, with your heel touching down and the toes raised upward. Your eyes look forward. (fig. 2-188)

Fig. 2-188

Requirements: After your fist strike goes out, step forward (shang bu) as your elbow drops and your shoulder relaxes, performing these actions with your entire body moving in a smoothly coordinated way. First inhale and then exhale during this action.

Internal Energy: When your fist goes outward, the energy penetrates to the tip of your fist (quan ding). In an instant, the energy returns to your dantian. The energy makes a slight circuit of your whole body. Relax your shoulders and drop your elbows, warding off (peng) with your forearms.

ACTION 2: Shifting your weight to your right leg, turn your body slightly toward the right. Bend your left knee and raise up your left leg. At the same time, your right hand twines outward (ni chan) and wards off (peng) outward. Your left hand lightly touches the inside of your right forearm and wards off (peng) outward. The actions of your upper body and the lower body should be well-coordinated. Your eyes look toward the left side. (fig. 2-189)

Fig. 2-189

Requirements: When you raise your left leg, the upper and lower parts of your body must be kept in balance. Keep the ward-off energy (peng jin) on your right hand. Inhale during this action.

ACTION 3: Turn your body slightly toward the left and take a large step toward the left front. At the same time, the action of your left hand follows the action of your left leg, your left hand describing an arc toward the left front as it pushes downward to a position above your left knee. Your right hand wards off (peng) upward and your eyes look toward the left front. (fig. 2-190)

Fig. 2-190

Requirements: The actions of taking a step and pushing downward with your left hand toward the left front are to be performed simultaneously. With your weight on your right leg, your right hand wards off (peng) upward, your posture is erect and the energy draws upward toward the top of your head (tou ling jin). Exhale during this action.

ACTION 4: Shift your weight from your right leg to your left leg. Your left hand, twining outward (ni chan), wards off (peng) upward. Your right hand moves downward along an arc to a position in conjunction with your left hand. Your eyes look toward the left front. (fig. 2-191)

Fig. 2-191

Requirements: Your crotch shifts forward along a downward arc and the right and left hands act together in perfect coordination. Inhale during this action.

ACTION 5: Turn your body slightly toward the right and shift your weight a little to the right. At the same time, your left hand twines inward (shun chan) as it moves along an arc upward and draws inward. Your right hand moves along an upward arc and comes in to a position in front of your chest. Your eyes look toward the left front. (fig. 2-192)

Fig. 2-192

Fig. 2-193

Requirements: As your two hands move upward along their respective arcs and settle downward (he jin), your body sinks lower, and, with your weight shifting toward the right, your two hands store energy for later release. Continue inhaling during this action.

ACTION 6: Turning your body toward the left, shift your weight to your left leg. At the same time, as your weight shifts toward the left, your two hands push with combined strength to a position at shoulder level above your left knee, your left hand above sweeping horizontally toward the left and your right hand below with an upright palm pushing toward the left. Your eyes look toward the left side. (fig. 2-193)

Requirements: Your left hand wards off (peng) upward and your right hand pushes forward, combining with the shifting of weight forward and the rotation of your body toward the left, all in perfect coordination. Exhale during this action.

Internal Energy: In the form Xiao Qin Da, the energy turns from your waist. Relax your shoulders and drop your elbows, then take a step forward. Your right hand wards off (peng) upward and then step out (kai bu) with your left foot. Your two hands first open (kai) then close (he), and then push forward with combined force. The energy all comes from the rotation of your crotch and waist, spiraling through to your two hands. Your two hands twine inward (li chan) with combined energy. Your left hand holds up (jia) and your right hand strikes (da).

Self-Defense Application: Taking into consideration the meaning in the name of this form Xiao Qin Da (Small Grab and Hit), it contains a technique for grabbing and twisting (qin na) an attacker's limb and also a technique for striking an attacker's body. Your two hands rolling in a circle as if entwining (gun chan) is a grabbing technique; the action of your left hand warding off (peng) upward and your right hand pushing forward contains a striking technique. When performing this action you have the option to either store the energy (xu jin) without releasing it or to release the energy with explosive force (fa jin).

40. Protecting the Head and Pushing the Mountain *(Bao Tou Tui Shan)*

ACTION 1: Turn your body slightly toward the left and draw your right foot toward the instep of your left foot with the toes just touching the ground. At the same time, your right hand twines inward (shun chan) and moves into a position under your left hand. Your eyes look forward on a downward angle. (fig. 2-194)

Fig. 2-194

Requirements: In this action, the action of your hand directs the turning of your body which in turn drives the action of your leg drawing inward. The actions of each part of your entire body are perfectly coordinated with each other. Inhale during this action.

ACTION 2: Turn your body 90 degrees toward the right, pivoting on the toes of your right foot, with your right foot turning outward. At the same time, your two arms ward-off (peng) outward as they turn with your body toward the right, the centers of the palms facing inward toward your body, and your two arms forming a circular shape as they ward-off (peng) around their outer circumference, like the surface of an overinflated ball. Your eyes look toward the right front. (fig. 2-195)

Fig. 2-195

Fig. 2-196

Requirements: Use the action of your waist to drive the action of your body's rotation toward the right. Your two arms ward-off (peng) forming a circular shape and rotate toward the right along an arc. Exhale during this action.

ACTION 3: Your body sinks downward and your two hands separate downward, with the palms of your two hands facing each other. Your eyes look toward the right front. (fig.2-196)

Requirements: Your two hands drop downward as your body sinks, with your entire body relaxed and your internal heart qi (xin qi) descending. First inhale and then exhale during this action.

ACTION 4: Your body sinks downward, with your weight on your left leg. Raise your right leg and take a step out (kai bu) toward the right front. At the same time, your two hands twine outward (ni chan) as they rise upward, describing an outward arc, with each hand settling to a position below your ear on either side of your body. Your eyes look toward the right front. (fig. 2-197)

Fig. 2-197

Requirements: With your foot opening (kai) and your hands closing (he), and with upper and lower in harmony, drop your waist energy (yao jin) downward, opening and rounding your crotch and your waist. Inhale during this action.

ACTION 5: Turning your body slightly toward the right, shift your weight from your left leg toward your right leg. At the same time as you shift your weight forward, your two hands push forward with combined strength. Your eyes look toward the right front. (fig. 2-198)

Fig. 2-198

Requirements: With your consciousness concentrated, and the energy (jin) combined in your two hands, shift forward as your weight shifts forward; the energy of your crotch, waist, hands and arms all arriving on target at the same time. Exhale during this action.

Note: In the first routine of Chen style Taijiquan, there are the movements Slapping the Left Foot and Slapping the Right Foot, and, Kicking with the Left Heel and Kicking with the Right Heel which are all a way of training left and right in symmetry. This action of pushing toward the right, together with the action of ward-off (peng) and issuing energy (fa jin) toward the left in Small Grab and Hit is also a way to practice both left and right techniques in symmetry.

Internal Energy: In this form the energy starts out from your waist and, following along with the turning of your body to the right, wards off (peng) in your two arms. Separating downward and stepping out then coming together in your two hands, with your crotch and waist energy or action combining with the energy of your two hands.

Self-Defense Application: When you wish to close the distance between yourself and the attacker, you must step past his perimeter. (Shen yu jin ren, bu yao guo ren.) By lightly extending your leg, you can step into (cha bu) the attacker's stance, or, encircle (tao bu) his stance by stepping past behind his forward leg as if to entwine it. Your two hands pushing forward with combined strength can be used to issue whip-snapping energy (tan dou jin) with enough energy potential to push Hua Mountain.

41. Sealing Six Avenues of Attack and Closing Four Sides

(Liu Feng Si Bi)

Requirements, Internal Energy and Self-Defense Application: Same as for the fourth form, Liu Feng Si Bi.

42. Single Whip

(Dan Bian)

ACTIONS 1-4: (Same as actions 1-4 of the fifth form.)

ACTION 5: Turn your body slightly toward the right and shift your weight to your left leg. Your left hand thrusts, fingers pointing in the direction of movement, as in a piercing palm, toward the upper right, turning over outward and warding off (peng) upward. Let your gaze sweep left and right.

ACTION 6: Turning your body slightly toward the left, your left hand twines outward (ni chan) as it opens your left arm out toward the left. With your knees bent and hips relaxed, drop your elbows and relax your shoulders. Rounding your shoulders slightly forward and dropping your waist energy. Your entire body is relaxed with upper and lower in balance, and your posture is upright, with your crotch open and rounded. Your eyes look forward.

Requirements, Internal Energy and Self-Defense Application: Same as for the fifth form, Dan Bian.

43. Forward Technique

(Qian Zhao)

ACTION 1: Turn your body toward the right and shift your weight to your right leg. Raise your left foot and draw it in toward the instep of your right foot, with just the toes of the left foot touching the ground. At the same time, your right hand changes into an open palm and, twining outward (ni chan), wards off (peng) upward; your left hand twines inward (shun chan) and moves downward along an arc toward the right side, warding off (peng) outward. Your eyes look toward the left front. (fig. 2-208)

Requirements: The action of your right hand, leading the

Fig. 2-208

attacker's energy in and warding off (peng) upward, in combination with the action of your left hand below and the action of your left foot drawing inward should all occur at the same time. First inhale and then exhale during this action.

Internal Energy: Using your waist to twine the energy to your right hand, your right hand reverse twines (ni chan) and wards off (peng) upward. Your left hand twines naturally (shun chan) to a position below. Your left leg draws inward to block off the crotch.

Self-Defense Application: Meet the incoming energy (jie jin) and lead it toward the right, protecting your crotch area by drawing your leg inward.

ACTION 2: Your body sinks slightly downward and turns a little toward the right, your two hands warding off (peng) upward. At the same time, raise your left leg and take a step out (kai bu) toward the left front, with the inside of your left heel touching down and the front part of the foot raised up and turned inward. Your eyes look toward the left front. (fig.2-209)

Fig. 2-209

Requirements: Your left leg steps out (kai bu) and your two hands lead the attacker in toward the right, the upper and lower acting in unison. Inhale during this action.

Internal Energy: Your left leg reverse twines and steps out (kai bu). Your waist turns right, sending the energy twining to your left arm. The energy then settles downward to gather at the left side of your waist.

Self-Defense Application:

Leading in above while advancing below, this action can be used for striking the attacker with your left shoulder and applying bursting energy (beng jin) outward with your left arm.

ACTION 3: Turning your body first toward the right and then toward the left, shift your weight to your left leg. Raise your right leg and draw your right foot in to a position at the right front of your left foot, your right foot without weight and just the toes touching the ground. At the same time, your left hand twines outward (ni chan) and wards off (peng) upward along an arc. Your right hand twines inward (shun chan), moving downward along an arc and warding off (peng) toward the left. Your eyes look forward. (fig. 2-210)

Requirements: Combine the energy of your waist with the action of your two hands warding off (peng) toward the left, in unison with drawing your right foot in. This action can be done as a sudden release of explosive energy (fa jin) movement. Exhale during this action.

Fig. 2-210

Internal Energy: Using the rotation of your waist, the energy goes through to your two hands.

Self-Defense Application: Following the above action of leading the energy in, you can strike toward the left side with an application of splitting energy (lie jin).

44. Backward Technique *(Hou Zhao)*

ACTION: Without moving your feet, turn your body toward the right. Your right hand twines outward (ni chan), turning over outward and warding off (peng) upward. Your left hand twines inward (shun chan), moving downward along an arc and warding off (peng) toward the right. Look toward the right front. (fig 2-211)

Requirements: As your body rotates to the left and to the right, use your lower spine as the axis of movement. First inhale and then

Fig. 2-211

exhale during this action.

Internal Energy: Using the right twining of your waist, the energy goes through to your two hands.

Self-Defense Application: Apply splitting energy (lie jin) toward the right side.

45. Parting the Wild Horse's Mane *(Ye Ma Fen Zong)*

ACTION 1: Turning your body toward the left, sink down lower. With your weight on your left leg, raise your right leg and take a step forward (shang bu). At the same time, your right hand twines inward (shun chan) and moves downward, coming in to a position inside your right knee. Your left hand twines outward (ni chan) and wards off (peng) upward. Your eyes look toward the right side. (fig. 2-212)

Fig. 2-212

Requirements: Your left hand warding off (peng) upward and your right hand settling downward, together with your right leg taking a step forward (kai bu), should all combine with the overall movement of your body as your body settles lower. Your crotch energy (dang jin) rounds and opens the crotch, with your posture upright and centrally balanced. First inhale and then exhale during this action.

Internal Energy: Settling downward, the energy combines in your waist and crotch, and wards off (peng) in your two hands. Your right arm uses the form or advantageous position (shi) of moving inward and then entwining outward.

Self-Defense Application: Extending your foot forward, you can step into the attacker's stance (cha) or put your foot down in back of his leg and foot (tao). By dodging and shedding off harmlessly an incoming force from behind, you are in a position to fold your back and strike with your shoulder.

ACTION 2: Shifting your weight from your left leg to your right leg, turn your body toward the right. At the same time, your right hand twines outward (ni chan), describing an arc upward as it wards off (peng) to a position level with your forehead; your left hand twines inward (shun chan), settling to a position to the outside of your left leg. Your eyes look toward the right front. (fig. 2-213)

Fig. 2-213

Requirements: As you ward-off (peng) upward with your right hand, use the movement of your crotch to propel the movement of your waist, and the movement of your waist to propel the movement of your shoulder and your elbow, and, on through to your arm and hand, the energy traveling unimpeded through your body—like water through a garden hose. Inhale during this action.

Internal Energy: Your crotch twists and your waist turns, twining into your right arm which revolves outward with ward-off energy (peng zhu jin). Your left hand moves downward together (he) with the action of your right hand.

Self-Defense Application: From below, your right hand thrusts upward with fingertips forward as in a piercing palm, warding off (peng) outward, with entwining (jiao), corkscrewing (gun), and overturning (fan) energy. If you are subjected to a random attack by a stick, or, by a fist or foot, thrust your right palm upward obliquely. Twisting and turning so that the incoming energy is redirected harmlessly, gradually move up your point of contact on the attacker, putting him in a position where he cannot continue his attack. This action is like separating the tangled mane of a wild horse with your two hands.

ACTION 3: Turn your body toward the right and turn your right foot out toward the right. Lift your left leg and take a large step forward toward the front. Your right hand wards off (peng) to a point in front of your right temple, with your left hand settling to a position at the inside of your left knee. Your eyes look toward the left front. (fig. 2-214)

Fig. 2-214

Requirements: Stepping forward with your left foot should be performed smoothly and naturally, coordinated with the action of your body and the hands. Exhale during this action.

Internal Energy: The energy combines (he) in your waist and crotch, wards off (peng) in your two arms, your right arm moving inward and then entwining outward.

Self-Defense Application: Lead in the attacker's energy and then strike.

ACTION 4: Turning your body toward the left, shift your weight to your left leg. At the same time, your left hand twines outward (ni chan), turns over outward, and wards off (peng) upward to in front of your left temple. Your right hand, twining inward (shun chan), moves downward and comes inward to a position above your right knee. Your eyes look toward the left front. (fig. 2-215)

Fig. 2-215

Requirements: By twisting your crotch and turning your waist, the energy goes to ward-off (peng) on your left arm. Your entire body is coordinated, upper to lower and lower to upper, and, the action of the upper and lower parts of your body is in balance. Inhale during this action.

Internal Energy: The energy rotates from your crotch to your waist and twines to your left arm from your waist. Your right hand moves downward together (he) with the action of your left hand.

Self-Defense Application: Similar to the second action above, where your right palm thrusts and wards off (peng) upward, only, now in a different direction.

46. Sealing Six Avenues of Attack and Closing Four Sides

(Liu Feng Si Bi)

47. Single Whip

(Dan Bian)

48. Jade Maiden Working Her Loom

(Yu Nu Chuan Suo)

ACTION 1: Turning your body slightly toward the left, with your weight on your left, raise your right foot and draw it in toward the instep of your left foot, your right foot without weight and just touching the ground. At the same time, your right hand changes into an open palm, twines inward (shun chan) and descends, crossing with your left hand in front of the left side of yourchest. Your eyes look toward the right front.(fig. 2-228)

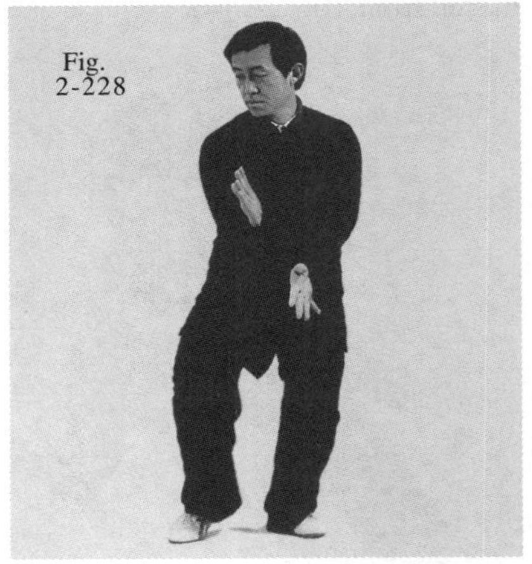
Fig. 2-228

Requirements: The actions of your right hand and your right foot are evenly matched, the intention is to lead an attack in harmlessly and then advance and counterattack. Continuing from the previous action, first inhale and then exhale.

ACTION 2: Turn your body toward the right. As your body turns, your two hands form standing palms (li zhang) and turn to ward-off (peng) in front of your chest, your right hand in front and your left hand behind the right. At the same time, turn your right knee outward, pivoting on the toes of your right foot. The toes of your left foot turn inward along with your body's turning toward the right. Your eyes look forward. (fig. 2-229)

Fig. 2-229

Requirements: When turning your body, you should use your waist to propel your shoulder, your shoulder in turn propelling your elbow, and the resultant force manifesting as ward-off (peng) in your hands. First inhale and then exhale during this action.

ACTION 3: Bending your knees and relaxing your hips, lower your body, with both hands twining outward (ni chan) and settling downward (xia he). Your eyes look forward. (fig. 2-230)

Requirements: As your body sinks down lower and your two

Fig. 2-230

hands push (an) downward, guard against bending your waist and sticking out your buttocks. Continuing from the previous action,exhale as your body sinks lower.

ACTION 4: Both hands twine inward (shun chan) and rapidly lift upward, rapidly leaping upward with both feet leaving the ground as your hands lift upward. Your eyes look forward. (fig. 2-231)

Requirements: Using your hands to draw the energy upward, with the actions of your whole body coordinated, leap upward in a light and nimble fashion. Inhale during this action.

ACTION 5: As both feet stamp down to the ground, both hands twine outward (ni chan) and

Fig. 2-231

push downward (xia an). Your eyes look forward. (fig. 2-232)

Fig. 2-232

Requirements: Stamping your feet downward to the ground and pushing downward with your hands requires that you drop your weight downward with some force, all at once. Your body's posture should be upright and centrally balanced. Exhale during this action.

ACTION 6: As both hands twine outward (ni chan) and ward-off (peng) upward, bend your right knee and raise your right leg. Your eyes look forward. (fig. 2-233)

Fig. 2-233

Requirements: Your hands ward-off (peng) and your leg is raised, requiring a firm and steady stance with all parts of your body united (he yi). The internal energy (nei jin) comes together and is concentrated within your body, and not dispersed. Inhale during this action.

ACTION 7: With your weight on your left leg, rapidly turn your body toward the left. Your right leg moves in toward the centerline and kicks out with the heel. Your right palm twines outward (ni chan) and pushes forward, while your left hand twines outward (ni chan) to a position in front of the left side of your chest with your left elbow issuing energy toward the left rear (fa jin). Your eyes look toward the right front. (fig. 2-234)

Fig. 2-234

Requirements: When the energy of your entire body is concentrated, it rapidly shoots through to your right foot and hand and your left elbow. Your left leg supports your body and must be stable and firm. Exhale during this action.

ACTION 8: Your right foot extends out a step forward and sets down. With your weight shifted to your right leg, turn your body slightly toward the right, lowering your left palm a little. Your eyes look forward. (fig. 2-235)

Requirements: This action is

Fig. 2-235

a rapid transitional movement, your right foot setting down on the ground and taking right off again, using the ball of your foot to spring against the ground while pushing off and leaping forward (like when using a springboard). First inhale and then exhale during this action, the breathing pattern of this action and the following action are linked.

ACTION 9: Your right foot rapidly drops to the ground, the ball of your right foot rapidly pressing down and springing upward with a forward leap. While up in the air, your body revolves 180 degrees toward the right. Your left hand twines outward (ni chan) and pushes forward with a mighty push while your right hand opens out toward the rear. Your eyes look toward the left side. (fig. 2-236)

Fig. 2-236

Fig. 2-237

Requirements: Your right foot presses against the ground and springs upward, your body leaps ahead while in the air, leaping out over two meters or so with the energy going through to your left palm. In connection with the above action, exhale during this action.

ACTION 10: Your left foot drops down to the ground first, your right foot comes from behind your left leg and steps forward behind the left foot, with just the tip of the right foot touching the ground. Your left palm toward the front and your right palm opened out toward the rear. Your eyes look toward the left side. (fig.2-237)

Requirements: This action is a transitional movement with the action below, when practicing, you can perform them continuously. Setting down on the ground should be done with a light touch and stable stance, like a cat, with your posture upright and centrally balanced.

ACTION 11: Turning your body 180 degrees toward the right, shift your weight to your right leg, with your left leg turning inward along with the turning of your body. At the same time, your two hands, the right twining outward (ni chan) and the left twining inward (shun chan), roll-back (lu) from the left toward the right as they turn along with the turning of your body toward the right. Your eyes look toward the left front. (fig. 2-238)

Internal Energy: The energy is directed by your waist, twining into your two arms. It settles downward and is lead upward; stamping your feet and issuing

Fig. 2-238

energy, leaping out, inserting the foot into the attacker's stance and rotating, all originate from your lower spine as hub. Gathering together your dantian internal energy, or moving it to the extremities, or gathering it at the source; use your mind (yi) to guide your internal energy (qi), use your internal energy (qi) to move your body, making a continuous circuit of your body.

Requirements: When turning your body, keep a stable stance and lower your body downward, keeping the ward-off energy (peng jin) on your two hands. Inhale during this action.

Note: This form, Yu Nu Chuan Suo, can be characterized as follows: leaping upward like a swallow darting upward while on the wing, naturally light and nimble; stamping downward with your feet with a sound like a clap of thunder reaching your ear, dropping your weight like dropping a mountain; leaping forward like an arrow leaving the bowstring, accelerating as suddenly as a shooting star; revolving like a whirlwind, with matchless speed. You can practice this form rapidly or slowly, leaping upward or not leaping upward. Use your judgement as to which way is most suitable to the conditions and your own level of skill.

Self-Defense Application: This form contains one method of rousing your spirits, a way of practicing using sound of stamping downward with both feet to boost your morale and to break out of a tight encirclement. The techniques of kicking with the bottom of your foot (deng), pushing with your palms, striking with your elbow and your shoulder are all brought into play against an attacker (or attackers) in this form.

49. Lazily Tying One's Coat *(Lan Za Yi)*

ACTION 1: Your two hands change from both twining outward (ni chan) to both twining inward (shun chan), each hand describing an arc to cross in front of your chest, your left hand settling to a position inside your right arm with the palm facing outward, the palm of your right hand facing upward. Shifting your weight to your left leg, raise your right leg and step sideways out toward the right, with the inside edge of your right heel touching down and the toes raised and turned inward toward the centerline of your body. Your eyes look toward the right side. (fig.2-239)

Fig. 2-240

Fig. 2-239

ACTION 2: Turning your body toward the left, shift your weight toward the right. Your right hand twines inward (shun chan) while warding off (peng) upward. Your eyes look toward the right side. (fig.2-240)

ACTION 3: Your right hand twines outward (ni chan) and turns over outward, while your left hand twines inward (shun chan) and sinks lower, with the palm facing upward, to a position in front of your abdomen. Turning your body toward the right, your right hand twines outward (ni chan) and opens out to a position on a line above your right knee, with your shoulder relaxed and your elbow dropped, your right hand changes to a slight inward twining (shun chan) with the tips of the fingers at eye level. Your left hand twines outward (ni chan) to the left side of your body where it holds the right side of your waist, fingers in front and thumb at the back. Your weight is on the right. Your eyes follow the motion of your right hand to the right side and then look toward the front. (fig. 2-241)

Fig. 2-241

Requirements, Internal Energy and Self-Defense Application: Same as for the third form, Lan Za Yi.

50. Sealing Six Avenues of Attack and Closing Four Sides

(Liu Feng Si Bi)

51. Single Whip

(Dan Bian)

52. Rolling Hands Through the Clouds

(Yun Shou)

Actions, Requirements, Internal Energy and **Self-Defense Application:** See the twenty seventh form, Yun Shou.

53. Swing the Foot and Drop Down

(Bai Jiao Die Cha)

ACTION 1: Turning your body toward the left, shift your weight to your left leg. Your two hands change from the right twining outward (ni chan) and the left twining inward (shun chan), into your left hand twining outward (ni chan) and your right hand twining inward (shun chan). Both hands move downward along an arc and ward off (peng) toward the left. Your eyes look toward the left front. (fig. 2-254)

Requirements: Your two hands move as your body turns and your weight shifts toward the left, these movements all performed in

Fig. 2-254

Fig. 2-255

unison. Exhale during this action.

ACTION 2: Turn your body toward the right and shift your weight to your right leg. Your two hands change from warding off (peng) toward the left to rolling-back (lu) toward the upper right, your left hand twining inward (shun chan) and your right hand twining outward (ni chan). Your eyes look toward the left side. (fig. 2-255)

Requirements: The action of two hands changing from ward-off (peng) toward the left into roll-back (lu) toward the upper right should be performed in perfect unison with shifting your weight toward the right and turning your body toward the right. Use the rotation of your waist to turn your body. Inhale during this action.

Internal Energy: Using your waist to drive the movement, the energy twines from your left leg to your right leg. Your two arms roll-back (lu) upward, the left natural twining (shun) and the right reverse twining (ni). Relaxing your shoulders and dropping your elbows, the energy goes through to your two hands.

ACTION 3: With your body continuing to turn toward the right, change to turning your body slightly toward the left as your weight shifts to your left leg. Your two hands continue to roll-back (lu) toward the right, sinking downward and the left hand changing into twining outward (ni chan) and your right hand twining inward (shun chan), settling to a position at the right side of your body. Your eyes look toward the right front. (fig. 2-256)

Fig. 2-256

Requirements: As your body turns toward the right and your weight shifts toward the left, your two hands settle to a position at the right side of your body. These actions should follow a smooth circular path, with your energy concentrating (he jin) to fullness. Exhale during this action.

Internal Energy: Rotating to the right and dropping your waist, the energy twines to your left leg and combines (he) in your two hands.

ACTION 4: Turning your body toward the left, swing your right leg upward toward the left along an arc, continuing around in an arc toward the right rear. Your two hands move from the right side of your body toward the left side, your hands slapping the top of your right foot as the top of your right foot strikes your hands. Your eyes look at the right foot. (fig. 2-257)

Fig. 2-257

Requirements: Your right foot should swing outward with rapid speed, and, the energy should be integrated with your two hands slapping the top of your foot. Standing on one leg, your left leg should be stable. First inhale and then exhale during this action.

Internal Energy: Swinging your foot, the energy twines from your waist to your outward swinging foot. Your two hands move inward, forming a combined energy of your hands and foot.

ACTION 5: Swing your right foot outward after slapping the top of your foot, then, draw your right leg inward and stamp down to the ground. Shifting your weight to your right leg, bend your left knee and raise your left leg, with just the toes of your left foot touching the ground. At the same time, your two hands form fists, the left fist (palm facing downward) on top of the right fist (palm facing upward), crossing in front of the right side of your chest. (fig.2-258)

Fig. 2-258

Requirements: With your body upright and your stance firm, stamp downward with combined strength (he li), your body's energy completely integrated with the action. First inhale and then exhale during this action.

Internal Energy: After swinging your foot, the energy moves from your dantian down to your right foot and twines upward into your two hands. Your left fist reverse twines and your right fist twines naturally to cross together in front of your body.

Self-Defense Application: Stamping your foot serves to drive the circulation of blood and rouse the spirits. This action can be used to trample on an attacker's toes. Your right fist settles downward and then rushes forward to strike at the attacker's chest or abdomen.

ACTION 6: With your weight on the right, raise your left leg and, with the inside edge of your left heel touching the ground, slide your left foot out, squatting down on your right leg (pu bu), with your crotch about four fingers distance off the ground. At the same time, your two fists separate, the right fist twining outward (ni chan) and the left fist twining inward (shun chan). Your right fist raises up to a position at the right rear of your body, on a level with the top of your head. Your left fist, twining inward (shun chan), moves downward and comes in to a position above your left leg, the center of your left palm and the center of your right palm facing toward each other. Your eyes look forward on an upward angle. (fig. 2-259)

Requirements: In the elementary version of this lowering to the ground stance (pu bu) your two legs are nearly touching the ground. It can also be performed with both legs flat against the ground, not dead or incapable of further

Fig. 2-259

movement however, but, with mobility and torque in the crotch area. Your body's posture should be upright, with your head and neck held erect, as if balancing an object on the top of your head. Inhale during this action.

Internal Energy: The energy twines from your right leg to your left leg which turns inward and slides outward along the ground with the appropriate amount of force, not too light or too heavy, just touching lightly to the ground and going outward. Your two fists combine with your waist energy; your left fist twines naturally and your right fist reverse twines, the two fists separating.

Self-Defense Application: The posture in this form is low to the ground, leading off harmlessly the attacker's energy (coming from above) while striking below at his lower body, keeping the torquing energy (xuan zhuan jin) in your crotch or groin.

54. Golden Rooster Standing on One Leg *(Jin Ji Du Li)*

ACTION 1: Torquing your crotch and waist, turn your body first toward the right and then toward the left, moving your center of gravity downward along an arc to your left leg. As your weight shifts forward, your left fist twines outward (ni chan) and rapidly thrusts upward; your right fist settling to a position at the right side of your body. Your eyes look forward. (fig. 2-260)

Fig. 2-260

Requirements: With your body's posture upright and centrally balanced, keep ward-off energy (peng jin) in your two fists. Your crotch and waist rapidly rotate in an upward thrust, and, as your left fist thrusts upward, keep your left wrist firm. Inhale during this action.

Internal Energy: The energy from your right leg, combining with the torquing energy of your waist and crotch, moves downward along an arc and shifts toward your left leg, going through to your two fists.

Self-Defense Application: Your crotch energy (dang jin) rapidly spirals forward, going through to your left fist. You can hit the attacker's vital points, located along his body's centerline, such as his crotch, belly, chest, and throat, etc..

ACTION 2: Rotate your body 90 degrees toward the left. With your weight on the left, raise your right leg and step forward (shang bu), with your knees bent and hips relaxed, your right foot not weighted and just touching the ground. At the same time, your left fist shoots upward to in front of your chest, to a position level with your lower jaw. As you step forward with your right foot, your right fist shoots up to a position to the inside of your left fist. Your eyes look forward. (fig. 2-261)

Fig. 2-261

Requirements: Stepping forward with your right leg should be done in a light, smooth and relaxed, natural way. The energy (jin) of your right fist thrusting rapidly upward connected with the energy of stepping forward. Exhale during this action, in connection with the previous action.

Internal Energy: Your left fist leads the energy (ling jin), torquing your body and stepping forward drives the forward explosive thrust of your right fist, the two fists coming together (xiang he).

Self-Defense Application: With your right fist as auxiliary you can continue to advance and strike the attacker, and your right fist can also be used to reinforce or backup your left fist.

ACTION 3: Your weight is on the left. With your left leg supporting the weight of your body, your left knee is bent and your left hip relaxed. Bending your right knee, raise your right leg upward, with your right foot hanging down below the crotch. At the same time, your right fist changes into an open palm and lifts, palm upward, revolving as it moves upward to finish with the center of the palm facing the front. Your left fist, changing into an open palm and twining outward (ni chan), pushes downward to the left side of your body. Your eyes look forward. (fig. 2-262)

Fig. 2-262

Requirements: The standing on one leg stance (du li bu) must be completely stable, your body's posture upright and centrally balanced. With upper and lower in harmony, this posture stretches upward to the sky yet is firmly fixed to the ground. Inhale during this action.

Self-Defense Application: Practicing the one-legged stance is useful training for self-defense. Your right palm raises up under the attacker's lower jaw, and raising up the right knee can be used for striking the attacker's crotch area, and can also be used for protecting your own crotch area from an attack.

ACTION 4: Stamping down to the ground with your right foot, your right hand, at the same time, pushes downward. Your body relaxes and sinks down. Your eyes look forward on a downward angle. (fig. 2-263)

Fig. 2-263

Requirements: When you stamp downward with your right foot, your right hand and your right foot come down simultaneously. With your knees bent, hips relaxed and your body sinking downward, guard against bending your waist. Exhale during this action.

ACTION 5: Turning your body slightly toward the left, the weight on your left leg, raise your right leg and take a step sideways toward the right side. At the same time, your two hands describe an arc as they roll-back (lu) from the lower right to the upper left, your left hand twining outward (ni chan) and your right hand twining inward (shun chan). Your eyes look toward the right front side. (fig. 2-264)

Fig. 2-264

Requirements: The actions of shifting your center of gravity, stepping out toward the right, and your two hands describing an arc as they ward-off (peng) and roll-back (lu) upward, should all be performed simultaneously, in perfect unison. The inside edge of your right heel touches the ground in the step out (kai bu) toward the right. Inhale during this action.

ACTION 6: Turn your body slightly toward the right and shift your weight to your right leg. Raise your left foot and draw it in to a position to the front of your right instep, with just the toes of your left foot touching the ground. At the same time, your two hands roll-back (lu) toward the right as they describe a downward arc, sinking downward, with your left hand then lifting palm upward to chest level. Your right hand twines outward (ni chan) and pushes downward to the right side of your body. Your eyes look forward. (fig.2-265)

Fig. 2-265

Requirements: Shifting your weight and drawing your left leg inward, with your left hand turning from roll-back (lu) into lifting with palm upward, the upper and lower parts of your entire body need to be in balance and move together in perfect unison. Exhale during this action.

ACTION 7: Your left hand revolves toward the outside and lifts upward, the center of your left palm facing the front as the action concludes. Bend your left knee and raise your left leg, with your left foot hanging downward below the crotch. Standing on your right foot, relax your hip and bend your right knee slightly, pushing downward with your right hand. Your eyes look forward. (fig. 2-266)

Fig. 2-266

Requirements: The one-legged stance requires a firm foothold and stability as you raise your other knee to hip level. Your energy is concentrated (he jin) inward and not dispersed outward. Inhale during this action.

Internal Energy: After stamping your foot in the left style of standing on the left leg, the energy twines from your waist to your two hands which roll-back (lu) to the left. Then sinking down and settling at your waist, going through to your left hand which reverse twines and raises up, the force reaching the base of your palm (zhang gen).

Self-Defense Application: The application for this action standing on the right leg is the same as for the action standing on the left leg.

55. Stepping Back and Whirling Arms *(Dao Juan Gong)*

(Same as the twentieth form, Dao Juan Gong.)

56. White Goose Spreading Its Wings *(Bai E Liang Chi)*

(Same as the twenty-first form, Bai E Liang Chi.)

57. Diagonal Posture *(Xie Xing)*

(Same as the twenty-second form, Xie Xing.)

58. Turning Back with Arms Twining *(Shan Tong Bei)*

(Same as the twenty-third form, Shan Tong Bei.)

59. Cover Fist and Punch *(Yan Shou Gong Quan)*

(Same as the twenty-fourth form, Yan Shou Gong Quan.)

60. Sealing Six Avenues of Attack and Closing Four Sides *(Liu Feng Si Bi)*

(Same as the twenty-fifth form, Liu Feng Si Bi.)

61. Single Whip *(Dan Bian)*

(Same as the twenty-sixth form, Dan Bian.)

62. Rolling Hands Through the Clouds (Yun Shou)

(Same as the twenty-seventh form, Yun Shou.)

63. Patting the Horse's Back *(Gao Tan Ma)*

(Same as the twenty-eighth form, Gao Tan Ma.)

64. Reverse Sweep with Right Leg *(Shi Zi Jiao)*

ACTION 1: Turning your body slightly toward the right, relax your right shoulder, drop your right elbow, and twine your right arm inward (shun chan) as it draws inward toward the centerline of your body. Your left hand twines outward (ni chan) and describes an arc to a position at the inside of your right forearm. Your eyes look toward the right front. (fig. 2-268, 268 supplemental)

Fig. 2-268 Fig.2-268 supplemental

Requirements: When turning your body with closing energy (he jin) in the hands, don't collapse your arms against your body. Keep the circularity in your movements, turning your body freely with your waist as the axis. Inhale during this action.

ACTION 2: Turn your body toward the right, pivoting on the tip of your left foot, with the heel of your left foot turning outward and setting down on the ground. Shifting your weight to your left leg, your right leg becomes un-weighted and the tip of your right foot turns to point outward. At the same time, your right arm twines outward (ni chan) as it wards off (peng) outward, with your left hand to the inside of your right forearm at the ready. Your eyes look toward the left front on a downward angle. (fig. 2-269)

Fig. 2-269

Requirements: Separate clearly the weighted and the weightless, turning freely with circularity. The ward-off energy (peng jin) is full to overflowing. Exhale during this action.

ACTION 3: Shifting your weight to your right leg, bend your left knee and raise your left leg. With your two hands continuing to ward-off (peng) outward, your body sinks lower, with your upper body and lower body in balance. Your eyes look toward the left on a downward angle.(fig. 2-270)

Requirements: With your

Fig. 2-270

Fig. 2-271

knees bent and your hips relaxed, and, the movements of the upper and lower parts of your body combined harmoniously, don't lose your ward-off energy (peng jin). Inhale during this action.

ACTION 4: Take a large step toward the left front with your left leg. Your left hand, as your left leg steps out, twines outward (ni chan) and your left arm opens out downward, your right hand and arm warding off (peng) upward. As your left leg steps out, your body sinks lower, with upright and centrally balanced posture, and, your head and neck erect as if pushing something upward on the top of your head. Your eyes look toward the left side. (fig. 2-271)

Requirements: Your foot steps out and your arm opens out at the same time, your whole body moving in unison. Your crotch is rounded, your body's posture upright, and your head and neck held erect as if suspended from above. Exhale during this action.

ACTION 5: Turning your body toward the right, shift your weight from your right leg to your left leg. Your left hand, changing from twining outward (ni chan) to twining inward (shun chan) as it moves along an arc, changes again to twining outward (ni chan) as it comes in to in front of your face. Your right hand moves downward along an arc and comes in to a position under your left elbow, the center of the right palm facing downward. Your eyes look toward the right front. (fig. 2-272)

Fig. 2-272

Requirements: Your weight shifts with your crotch circling toward the rear. Rolling your waist and rotating your hips, your hands and feet move together. Inhale during this action.

ACTION 6: Raise your right leg and sweep it along an upward arc toward the left. Your eyes look toward the right front. (fig. 2-273)

Fig. 2-273

ACTION 7: Your right leg, without stopping from the above action, swings down toward the right rear. Your left hand moves downward and slaps the top of your right foot. Your eyes look at the right foot. (fig. 2-274)

Fig. 2-274

Requirements: Your right foot moves upward along a circular arc as it rises up. Relax your hip and let the action of your waist lead the action of your leg and hands, with your hands and leg moving in conjunction. Exhale during this action.

Internal Energy: In the form Shi Zi Jiao (Reverse Sweep), the energy twines from your right leg to your left leg. Your waist turns right and the energy twines to your left hand. Your right leg swings outward and your left hand moves downward, with your hand and your foot hitting together.

Self-Defense Application: If your two hands are crossed and being held by an attacker, use your foot to kick inward and to swing outward. Strike outward with your left hand toward the left, or with your shoulder to release the attacker's hold.

65. Punch Toward the Crotch *(Zhi Dang Chui)*

ACTION 1: After slapping your foot, let your right foot drop and hang downward but not touch the ground. Flick your right hand upward and push downward with your left hand. Your eyes look forward. (fig. 2-275)

Fig. 2-275

Note: This action is a transitional movement to the next action, when practicing it you don't have to stop.

ACTION 2: Chop downward forcefully (fa jin) with the edge of your right hand (zhan shou) and flick your left hand upward. As you chop downward with your right hand, turn your body 90 degrees toward the right, turning on your heel of your left foot, with the toes of your left foot turning to point inward. Raise your right leg upward, with your right foot hanging down below the crotch. Your eyes look forward. (fig. 2-276)

Fig. 2-276

Requirements: The action of your two hands, the left moving upward and the right moving downward with some force (fa jin), and turning your left foot inward and turning your body, should all be performed simultaneously and in perfect unison. Your stance should be completely stable. First inhale and then exhale during this action.

Fig. 2-277

Internal Energy: Use the right rotation of your waist to twine the energy to your right hand and issue energy (fa jin). The left hand matches your right hand's downward movement by raising upward. Hooking your foot and turning your body, the force goes through to your right palm.

Self-Defense Application: If an attacker were to ambush you from the rear, you could rapidly turn your body and chop downward with the edge of your right hand, intercepting the incoming energy.

Fig. 2-278

ACTION 3: Stamp down to the ground with your right foot and take a step with your left foot toward the left front, turning your body 45 degrees toward the right. At the same time, cross your two hands in front of your abdomen. Your eyes look forward. (fig. 2-277)

ACTION 4: Turning your body slightly toward the right, shift your center of gravity a little toward the left. Your two hands, twining outward (ni chan), separate downward. (fig. 2-278)

ACTION 5: Turn your body slightly toward the left and shift your weight to your right leg, relaxing your right hip, bending your knees and sinking downward. At the same time, your right hand changes into a fist and draws inward, settling to a position at the right side, below your ribs; your left hand, as a standing palm (li zhang) settling to a position forward of your chest. Your eyes look forward. (fig. 2-279)

Fig. 2-279

ACTION 6: Turn your body rapidly toward the left, shifting your center of gravity toward the left. Your right fist, twining outward (ni chan), punches forcefully (fa jin) toward the front on a downward angle. Your left hand, half forming into a fist, draws in toward the left side of your ribs, with your left elbow shooting back forcefully (fa jin) toward the rear. Your eyes look forward on a downward angle. (fig. 2-280)

Requirements: The first part of this form, Zhi Dang Chui, is like the action, Yan Shou Gong Quan (Cover Fist and Punch), but the direction of the final release of energy (fa jin) here is forward on a downward angle.

Fig. 2-280

Self-Defense Application: Strike the attacker in the lower abdomen or crotch.

66. Ape Picking Fruit *(Yuan Hou Tan Guo)*

ACTION 1: Bend your knees and lower your body. Your right fist, first twines outward (ni chan) and then twines inward (shun chan), with your right wrist rotating into folds upward. Your left fist, at the same time, also changes to twining inward (shun chan), both fists ending up with the centers of your palms facing upward. Your eyes look toward the right front. (fig. 2-281)

Requirements: Combine the rotation of your fists and the rotation of your waist as your body sinks

Fig. 2-281

down lower, with your whole body acting in concert. First inhale and then exhale during this action.

Internal Energy: Using an undulating movement of your torso and waist, rotate your hands into folds (zhe). Start out by thrusting your fist downward to the front, then, by turning a circle according to the principle of not breaking off the energy, rotate into an upward thrust with your fist.

Self-Defense Application: Revolving your wrists into folds is a way of shaking off an attacker's grip when he grabs your wrists, and, is a way of changing the direction of your counterattack by rotating into folds after your last strike, and lashing out at the attacker in a new direction.

ACTION 2: Turning your body toward the left, turn your left foot so that your left toes point outward. At the same time, your right fist thrusts rapidly upward toward the upper right, and your right leg raises upward. Your eyes look toward the right front. (fig. 2-282)

Fig. 2-282

Requirements: The actions of turning your body, thrusting rapidly with your fist, and raising your leg upward, are all performed simultaneously and in perfect unison, with the energy and force of your body blended in. Inhale during this action.

Internal Energy: Using your internal energy (qi) combined in your dantian to drive the rotation of your waist. Relaxing your shoulders and dropping your elbows, the energy goes through to your right fist and your right knee.

Self-Defense Application: Your right fist thrusts rapidly upward under the attacker's lower jaw and your right knee strikes against his crotch area.

ACTION 3: Turn your body slightly toward the left and take a step toward the right front with your right foot, setting it down with the heel touching the ground. Your two fists circle around and change into open palms, settling to a position below your two ears. Your eyes look toward the right front. (fig. 2-283)

Fig. 2-283

Requirements: The actions of turning your foot and your body, setting your foot down and changing your two fists into open palms, should all be performed in perfect unison, with the actions of the upper and lower parts of the body blended harmoniously. Continue to inhale during this action.

ACTION 4: Turning your body slightly toward the right, shift your center of gravity from the left toward the right, drawing your left foot in toward the instep of your right foot. At the same time, your two hands push (an) downward with combined strength. Your eyes look toward the right front on a downward angle. (fig. 2-284)

Fig. 2-284

67. Single Whip *(Dan Bian)*

ACTION 1: Turn your body toward the right, with your weight on the right. Your two hands twine inward (shun chan), your right hand drawing inward toward your body and your left hand revolving around toward the outside away from your body. Your eyes look toward the right front. (fig. 2-285)

Fig. 2-285

ACTION 2: The five fingers of your right hand come together to form a hook hand, twining outward (ni chan) with the right wrist relaxed and raising upward toward the upper right, your right wrist drawing energy upward. Turn your body toward the left, with your left leg in an empty step (xu bu - without weight), your left knee turning outward as your body turns toward the left. Your left hand draws inward to a position in front of your abdomen with the center of your palm facing upward. Your eyes look toward the right front. (fig.2-286)

Fig. 2-286

ACTION 3: With your right wrist drawing energy upward, turn your body toward the right. Bending your left knee and raising up your left leg, your left hand sinks slightly downward, with the upper and lower parts of your body combined in action. Your eyes look toward the left side. (fig. 2-287)

Fig. 2-287

ACTION 4: With your weight on the right leg, slide your left foot along the ground toward the left side with the inside edge of your left heel touching the ground, the toes of your left foot raised and turned inward. Your eyes look toward the left front. (fig. 2-288)

Fig. 2-288

Fig. 2-289

ACTION 5: Turn your body slightly toward the right and shift your center of gravity toward the left. Your eyes look toward the left front. (fig.2-289)

ACTION 6: Your left hand thrusts, fingertips forward, toward the upper right and turns over outward. Your eyes look toward the right front. (fig. 2-290)

Fig. 2-290

ACTION 7: Turning your body toward the left, your left hand describes an outward arc as it pulls open toward the left. With your entire body relaxed, your hand and foot in harmony, your shoulder and hip in harmony and your entire body, upper and lower, reunited and not dispersed. Your eyes look forward.

(fig.2-291)

Fig. 2-291

Requirements, Internal Energy and Self-Defense Application: Same as the fifth form, Dan Bian.

68. Dragon Rolling Downward *(Que Di Long)*

ACTION 1: Turn your body toward the left and continue to shift your center of gravity toward the left, with both hands forming into fists. Your right fist twines inward (shun chan) as it moves downward along an arc toward the left into conjunction with your left fist. Your left fist, twining outward (ni chan) comes in to a position on top of your right forearm, the center of your left palm facing downward and the center of your right palm facing upward. Your eyes look forward. (fig. 2-292)

Fig. 2-292

Requirements: The form (xing) and the internal energy (qi) of your whole body come together in perfect unison. Exhale during this action.

Internal Energy: Continuing from the previous form, Dan Bian, after the qi returns to your dantian in that form the qi again starts out from the dantian. Your waist turns left and your two arms come together, the energy spiraling into your two arms; your left arm reverse twining (ni) and your right arm twining naturally (shun).

ACTION 2: Turning your body toward the right, shift your weight from your left leg to your right leg while bending your knees and squatting down lower. Your left leg has become stretched out straight (by shifting your weight and turning toward the right) with your left foot turned inward, you are now in a lowering to the ground stance (pu bu). At the same time, your right fist twines outward (ni chan) and raises upward to a position level with your head; your left fist twining inward (shun chan) and settling to a position just above your left knee. Your eyes look toward the left front. (fig. 2-293)

Fig. 2-293

Requirements: Keep your head and your neck erect, your body's posture upright, and the energy of your crotch (dang jin) flowing in a circular path, with your two arms rounded with ward-off (peng) energy. Exhale during this action.

Internal Energy: The energy twines from your left leg to your right leg. Your waist turns right, your two arms open outward into two fists with your left arm twining naturally and your right arm reverse twining. Your energy is drawn to the tips of your fists (quan ding).

Self-Defense Application: This action is similar to a low-level leg sweep (die cha). In the low-level leg sweep, your right foot stamps down on the attacker's toes and your left heel kicks his shin bone.

In this action, assume a lowering to the ground stance, as you sit back downward toward the right. You can press down on the attacker's leg and knee, or you can turn your body and sweep with your leg, pushing down against the ground with your hands for support. Because this form contains three methods for hitting the attacker in the lower body, it is called Que Di Long (Dragon Rolling Downward), or Pu Di Jin (Spreading Brocade on the Ground).

69. Stepping Forward into Seven Stars Stance *(Shang Bu Qi Xing)*

ACTION 1: Turn your body slightly toward the right and rotate your center of gravity from the right leg toward the left, forming a left bow stance (gong bu). At the same time, your left fist thrusts rapidly upward as the weight shifts forward, and your right fist twines inward (shun chan), moving downward and inward to a position at the right side of your waist. Your eyes look toward the left front. (fig. 2-294)

Fig. 2-294

Requirements: When you thrust your fist rapidly upward, combine your crotch and your waist's rotational force, your right foot pressing against the ground - driving your body forward, and your body standing upright, pushing up with your head and neck. This combined action uses the internal to drive the external, and, the movement of your lower body to drive the movement of your upper body, in one continuous action. Exhale during this action.

Internal Energy: Directed by your waist, it starts out from your right foot,twines into your left leg and, moving upward it goes through to your left fist.

Self-Defense Application: Thrusting your fist rapidly upward can be used to strike an attacker in the chest or throat. Raising your right leg, can be used to strike the attacker with your knee or kick him in the crotch or shin with your foot. Your two feet, knees,two and your head, are seven in number like the Seven Stars of the Big Dipper, and each has it's self defense application.

ACTION 2: Turning your body 90 degrees toward the left, raise your right leg and take a forward step (shang bu), with just the toes of your right foot touching the ground to the right front of your left foot.Relax your hips and bend your knees.At the same time, your right fist thrusts rapidly to a position at the inside of your left fist, with your two fists oriented in the same general direction and close to each other.Your eyes look forward.(fig.2-295)

Requirements: In this action, you should complete both thrusting your fist rapidly forward, and, taking a step forward, at the same time. Inhale during this action.

Another way of practicing

this action is to rapidly thrust your right fist to a position at the front outside of your left fist instead of inside and roll it around in a circle together with the left fist.

Internal Energy: These two moves are both carried out while not moving your feet. They utilize the moving into folds of your torso and waist to drive the motion of your wrists and arms in a complete circle going upward and then downward. After that, your energy sinks downward, dropping your waist, and going through to your palms.

ACTION 3: Sinking your body slightly downward, relax your shoulders and ward-off (peng) upward just a little with your two elbows. Your two fists twine outward (ni chan) and sink downward. Your eyes look forward on a downward angle. (fig. 2-296)

Requirements: Relaxing your hips and your shoulders, use the moving in folds energy (zhe die jin) of your torso and waist to rotate your two wrists. Inhale during this action.

ACTION 4: Your two elbows sink downward and draw in towards your centerline. Changing your two fists into open palms, lower your palms downward. Your eyes look forward. (fig. 2-297)

Requirements: When changing your two fists into open palms, you should lower your waist and relax your hips, relaxing your shoulders and sinking your elbows, with the energy (jin) going all the way through to the outer edge of your palms. In this action, in connection with the previous action, exhale as you lower your body.

Fig. 2-297

Fig. 2-298

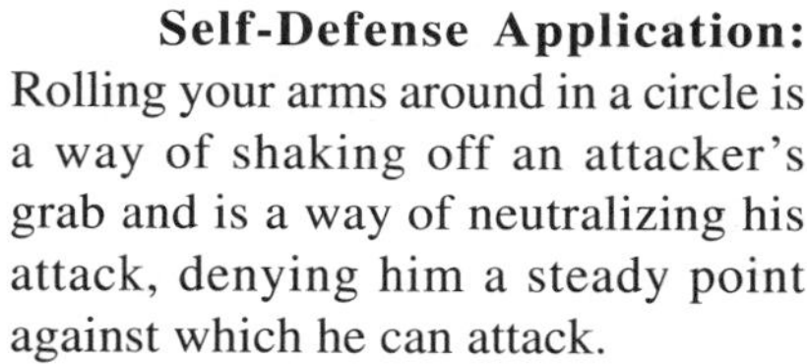

Self-Defense Application: Rolling your arms around in a circle is a way of shaking off an attacker's grab and is a way of neutralizing his attack, denying him a steady point against which he can attack.

70. Stepping Backward into Riding Stance *(Xia Bu Kua Gong)*

ACTION 1: Turn your body slightly toward the left, warding off (peng) slightly upward with your two hands. Raise your right leg and take a step sideways (kua bu) toward the right rear. Your eyes look toward the right rear. (fig. 2-298)

Requirements: Your step sideways should be light and nimble, with your movements showing clearly which side of your body carries weight and which side is emptied of weight. The upper part of your body leads an attacker in while the lower part advances, the movement of any one part of your body setting your whole body into motion. Inhale during this action.

ACTION 2: Turning your body toward the right, shift your weight to your right leg. Your right hand twines outward (ni chan) and separates downward toward the right, your left hand twining outward (ni chan) and opening out toward the front. Your eyes look forward. (fig. 2-299)

Requirements: Use the movement of your body to lead the movement of your hands, rotating your body freely in a perfectly

Fig. 2-299

Fig. 2-300

circular way, with your body's posture erect and centrally balanced, your head and neck held erect. Exhale during this action.

ACTION 3: Turn your body 45 degrees toward the right, turning the toes of your right foot to point outward. Raise your left leg and take a step forward toward the right front, with just the toes of the left foot touching the ground. At the same time, twine both hands inward (shun chan), bringing the edges of your two palms into conjunction with each other in front of your chest (with the edges of the palms mutually opposed as if holding something vertically between them), your right hand above and your left hand below, the fingers of both palms pointing forward. Your eyes look forward. (fig. 2-300)

Requirements: The energy (jin) spirals down your right leg from your dantian (acupuncture point below your navel) as your right leg steps sideways toward the rear; then, with your waist turning, shift your weight and turn your body, your energy again combining in your two hands.

Self-Defense Application: Stepping sideways toward the rear and turning your body is a way of training shifting your weight from one leg to the other and changing your center of gravity from the weighted (shi) to the weightless (xu) side. This form combines the techniques of leading in above while advancing below, and striking with both hands.

71. Turning Around and Sweeping with Both Legs *(Zhuan Shen Shuang Bai Lian)*

ACTION 1: Continue turning your body toward the right. With your weight on your right leg, turn your left heel toward the outside, pivoting on the toes of your left foot. At the same time, both hands twine outward (ni chan), your right hand warding off (peng) upward and your left hand pushing downward. Your eyes look toward the lower left. (fig. 2-301)

Fig. 2-301

Requirements: As you ward-off (peng) above and settle or close (he) below, separate clearly the weighted (shi) and the weightless (xu), rotating and shifting your center of gravity back and forth naturally, with your foothold firm and stable. Exhale during this action.

ACTION 2: The heel of your left foot drops to the ground and your weight shifts to your left leg. Turning the toes of your right foot outward, continue to turn your body toward the right, your right hand warding off (peng) toward the right and your left hand pushing downward. Your eyes look forward. (fig.2-302)

Fig. 2-302

Requirements: While shifting your center of gravity from one side to the other and turning your body naturally, continue to exhale during this action.

ACTION 3: Shifting your weight to your right leg, turn your body toward the right. At the same time, your left hand twines inward (shun chan) and wards off (peng) toward the front, the action of the left hand leading your left leg forward as your left leg takes a step toward the front, your right hand warding off (peng) upward. Your eyes look forward. (fig. 2-303)

Fig. 2-303

Requirements: With the action of your hands leading the rotation of your body, and the movement of your body leading the movement of your legs, the actions of your whole body should be well-integrated. Inhale during this action.

ACTION 4: Drop your left foot to the ground, bending your knees and lowering your body. With your weight on your right leg, your two hands roll-back (lu) toward the right rear. Your eyes look toward the left front. (fig. 2-304)

Fig. 2-304

Requirements: Your foot drops to the ground and your body sinks downward, with your posture upright and centrally balanced, keeping ward-off (peng) and roll-back (lu) energy in your two hands. Continue to inhale during this action.

ACTION 5: Turning your body toward the right, shift your center of gravity toward the left. Your two hands change from rolling-back (lu) toward the rear to moving forward along a downward arc toward the front with closing energy (he jin), settling to a position at the right side of your waist. Your eyes look forward. (fig. 2-305)

Requirements: Drop your waist energy and relax your hips, with all parts of your body combined harmoniously. Exhale during this action.

Fig. 2-305

ACTION 6: With your weight on your left leg, raise your right leg and swing it around in an arc toward the left, upward to downward, changing direction and swinging around toward the right rear. Your two hands move forward and meet with your right foot, slapping your foot. Your eyes look forward. (fig. 2-306)

Fig. 2-306

Requirements: Swinging your foot into your hands while slapping your foot with your hands should occur at high speed, bringing your energy into play in one continuous action. First inhale and then exhale during this action.

Internal Energy: The turning energy (pan xuan jin) of your waist and crotch falls into your hips and combines in your hands at the same time that they meet your outward sweeping right leg.

Self-Defense Application: This is a way of training the technique of turning your body freely while keeping your footwork stable, and integrating the combined force (of your foot swinging outward and your hands moving inward). You can turn your body either 180 degrees or 360 degrees.

72. Cannon Right Overhead (Dang Tou Pao)

ACTION 1: After slapping your foot, your right foot withdraws a step toward the right rear. Your two hands continue to ward-off (peng) upward, with your weight on your left leg. Your eyes look forward. (fig.

2-307)

Fig. 2-307

Requirements: Slapping your foot and stepping back, your footwork should be stable, combining harmoniously with the upper part of your body leading the attacker's energy inward while the lower part advances at the same time. Inhale during this action.

ACTION 2: Turn your body slightly toward the right and shift your weight to your right leg. At the same time,your two hands roll-back (lu) downward toward the rear as your weight shifts toward the rear, your left hand twining inward (shun chan) and your right hand twining outward (ni chan).Your eyes look toward the left front.(fig. 2-308, 308supplemental)

Requirements: Your two hands roll-back (lu) in unison with

Fig. 2-308

Fig.2-308 supplemental

the shifting of your center of gravity and the turning of your body. Guard against bending your waist and settling your body downward. Exhale during this action.

ACTION 3: Lowering your body slightly, your two hands change into fists and settle to a position beside the right side of your chest. Your eyes look forward. (fig. 2-309, 309 supplemental)

Requirements: Your two hands form into fists and raise upward, in accord with the situation of the lower body. With your weight settling on your right leg and your crotch rounded, your body should store energy like a bow pulled all the way back - ready to release with a single touch. Inhale during this action.

Fig. 2-309

Fig.2-309 supplemental

Fig. 2-310

Fig.2-310 supplemental

ACTION 4: Press your right foot into the ground, shifting your weight rapidly from your right leg to your left leg, with your body turning toward the left as your weight shifts. At the same time, your two fists thrust rapidly forward with combined strength, issuing the stored energy (fa jin). The eye of your fists (circular shape formed by the thumb and forefinger) faces upward. Your eyes look forward. (fig. 2-310, 310 supplemental)

Requirements: With the rise of your intention, suddenly snap out a strike, like a lion shaking his mane, or a fierce tiger descending a mountain. This strike comes completely from the elastic vibrational energy (tan dou jin) of your crotch and waist, the energy going through to the tip of your fist (quan ding). There is a spring-like force within the crotch, once it is set into motion, even a bird would have difficulty escaping. Exhale during this action.

Internal Energy: The energy follows the downward roll-back (lu) of your two hands and settles to your dantian. Gathering up (xu) in your right leg, in an impulse it turns; pressing down with your foot, rotate your crotch. Turning your waist, the energy goes through to the tip of your fist.

Self-Defense Application: After slapping your foot, rapidly set your foot down a step backward (dao bu), grabbing the attacker and rolling-back (lu) downward. If the attacker tries to pull back, then you can adjust accordingly by suddenly and rapidly thrusting forward with your fists, sending the attacker flying.

73. Pounding the Mortar (Jin Gang Dao Dui)

ACTION 1: Your two fists change into open palms and roll-back (lu) toward the upper right rear as your body turns slightly toward the right, your left hand twining inward (shun chan) and your right hand twining outward (ni chan). At the same time, shift your weight from the left to your right foot. Your eyes look toward the left front. (fig. 2-311, 311 supplemental)

Fig. 2-311

Fig.2-311 supplemental

ACTION 2: Shifting your weight from your right leg to your left leg, turn the toes of your left foot outward and set your left foot down putting weight on the foot. As your weight shifts, your body turns along with the shift, 45 degrees toward the left. Your two hands move downward along an arc, your left hand twining outward (ni chan) and your right hand twining inward (shun chan), to ward-off (peng) toward the front. Your left hand warding off (peng) in front of your chest with the center of the palm facing downward, and, your right hand sinking down to a position above and to the inside of your right knee, the center of the palm facing outward and the fingers pointing toward the rear. Your eyes look forward. (fig. 2-312)

Fig. 2-312

ACTION 3: Your left palm faces toward the front and flicks upward, circling upward and then inward, settling to a position in front of your chest at the inside of your right forearm. At the same time, your right hand draws your right foot forward as it describes an arc forward, your palm lifting upward to a position in front of the right side of your chest, in conjunction with your left hand, with the center of your right palm facing upward and the center of your left palm facing downward. Your right foot passing by the instep of your left foot as it takes a step forward, with just the toes of your right foot touching down. Your weight is on your left leg, and, your eyes look forward. (fig. 2-313, 2-313 supplemental)

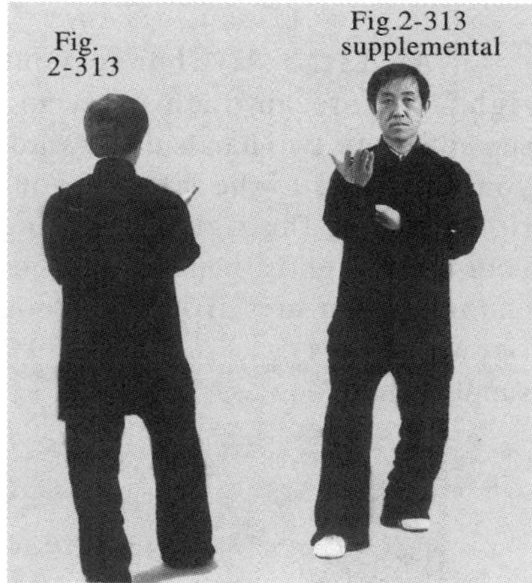
Fig. 2-313 Fig.2-313 supplemental

ACTION 4: Twining inward (shun chan), your left hand turns over outward and sinks down to a position in front of your abdomen, the palm facing upward. Your right hand forms into a fist and sinks downward, dropping into the center of the left palm, the center of the right palm (fist) facing upward. Your eyes look forward. (fig. 2-314, 314 supplemental)

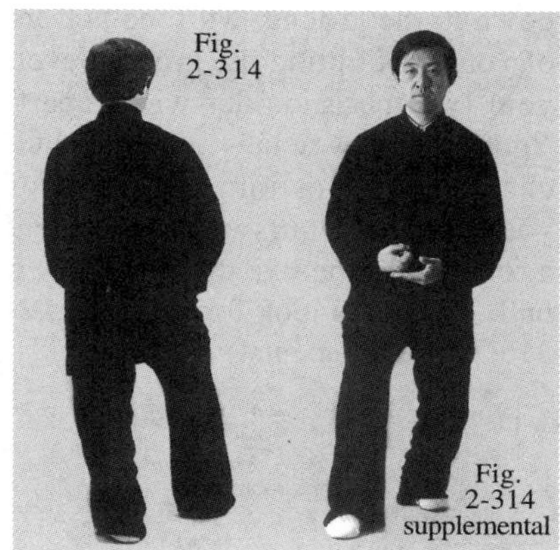
Fig. 2-314 Fig. 2-314 supplemental

ACTION 5: Your right fist twines outward (ni chan) and raises up level with your right shoulder. Bending your right knee and relaxing your right hip, raise your right leg upward, with your right foot hanging down naturally below your crotch. Your eyes look forward. (fig. 2-315, 315 supplemental)

Fig. 2-315 Fig.2-315 supplemental

ACTION 6: Your right foot stamps down to the ground, with the bottom of your foot hitting the ground level, your two feet shoulder-width apart. Your right fist twines inward (shun chan) as it drops into the center of your left palm, your two arms forming a rounded shape like the surface of a ball. Your eyes look forward. (fig. 2-316, 316 supplemental)

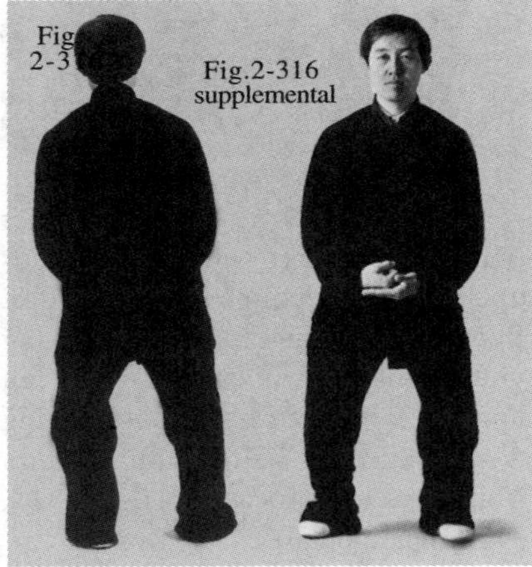
Fig. 2-316
Fig.2-316 supplemental

Note: It is said of this action, with your foot stamping downward to the ground, "one appears as a scholar at the beginning, and, as a warrior at the end.Some people also say, Starting as Yang, finishing as Yin."In other words, when starting out the movement is slow and gentle, elegant and well poised; the movement at the very end, one foot stamping downward and one hand (fist) dropping into the other (palm) has the meaning of seeming both martial and refined (wen wu liang xiang). You face south during the Beginning Posture of Taijiquan and north during the Closing Posture of Taijiquan in accord with the principle of combining Yin and Yang (Yin Yang xiang he).

74. Closing Posture of Taiji *(Shou Shi)*

ACTION 1: Change your right fist into an open palm and separate your two hands downward, your left hand to the left and your right hand to the right. Lowering your body slightly, bend your knees and relax your hips. Your eyes look forward. (fig. 2-317, 317 supplemental)

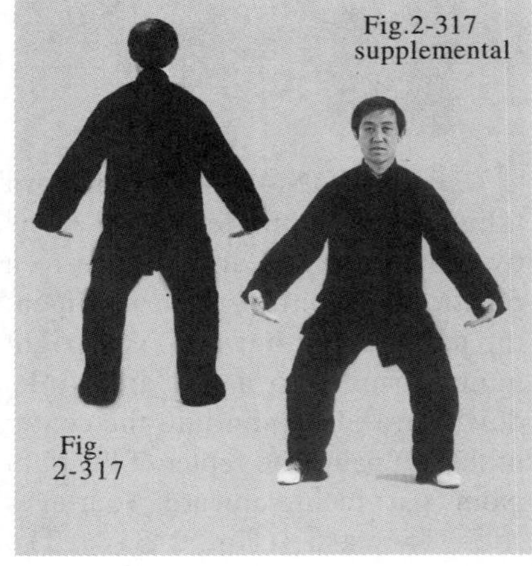
Fig.2-317 supplemental
Fig. 2-317

Requirements: In separating your two hands, lowering your body, relaxing your hips and bending your knees, guard against bending your waist. First inhale and then exhale during this action.

ACTION 2: Your two hands simultaneously move upward, each describing an outward arc to a position in front of its respective shoulder. Your eyes look forward. (fig. 2-318, 318 supplemental)

Fig. 2-318 Fig.2-318 supplemental

Requirements: Your two hands raise upward, with your shoulders relaxed and your elbows sinking downward. Relax the muscles of your chest, abdomen, and back. Inhale during this action.

ACTION 3: Push downward slowly along the sides of your body with both hands, each hand pushing downward to a position beside it's respective thigh. Your eyes look forward. (fig. 2-319, 319 supplemental)

Fig.2-319 supplemental Fig. 2-319

Requirements: Exhale as your two hands push downward, relaxing your whole body. The qi (your body's intrinsic energy) returns to your dantian (acupuncture point just below the navel), and your mind's activity returns to the original state of meditative calm, as in the beginning of Taijiquan. Practicing the entire routine, your mind is calm and your qi harmonized, from beginning to end there is a continuous and unbroken stream of energy within your body. Within each form the qi issues forth from your dantian, circuiting your five internal organs and passing through the one hundred joints internally, and moving along the surface of your skin and the fine hair on it's surface externally, making a circuit of your body and then returning to your dantian. It is like the mighty Changjiang (Yangtze River) unstoppably rushing along its course; having a source and a destination, it circulates endlessly like an unbroken ring. This is expressed well in the verse:

"Open and close, hard and soft change naturally, one to the other, Raising up then pressing down in accord with the internal circuit of energy. One foot draws in to close as the qi returns to the dantian. Movement and stillness, from form to formless, that's Taijiquan".

ACTION 4: Raise your body slowly upward, returning to a posture of standing naturally upright again. Bring both feet together, your right foot drawing in to beside the instep of your left foot. Your two hands both settle to a position hanging down naturally at their respective sides, your palms facing inward beside each thigh. With your body upright in a centrally balanced posture, your eyes look forward. (fig. 2-320, 320 supplemental)

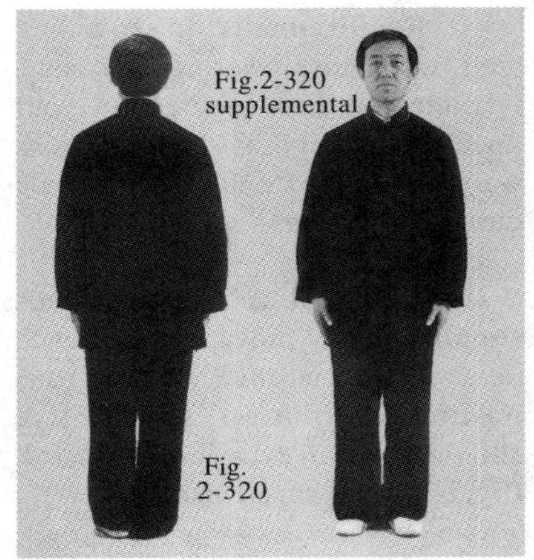

Fig.2-320 supplemental

Fig. 2-320

Chen-style Taiji Single Sword Routine

I. The Synopsis of the Chen-style Taiji Single Sword Routine

The Chen-style Taiji Single Sword Play is a kind of the Chen-style Taiji short weapons. In the several hundreds years, it is spread far and wide in the Chenjiagou Village, and it is the oldest one of the Taiji weapons routines.

There are forty-nine forms in the Chen-style Taiji Single Sword routine, the distribution of it is rational, the joins of movements are compact, the skills of sword are clear. It consists of the techniques of the thrusting, cutting, scooping, hanging, pointing, wiping, supporting, propping, sweeping, intercepting, pricking, pushing, transforming, and combine with the unfolded body work and skilful footwork of the Chen-style Taijiquan, so it can produce the changes of hardness and softness, concealing and appearing, dodges and transfers. It really reflects the Chen-style Taiji Single Sword characteristics, using the body to transport the sword, flowing movements, combining hardness and softness, equaling stress the quickness and slowness, changing the crook and the stretch. The practical applications of the sword are diverse.

Pay attention to that the Chen-style Taijiquan serves as the base to practice the Chen-style Taiji Single Sword, so use the mind to guide the "Qi", use the "Qi" to initiate the body, the force is focused at the tip of the sword, body and weapon become into one, movements circular and natural. It is said in the boxing proverbs: "the broadsword play like a fierce tiger, the sword play like an undulating dragon". So exercising the Taiji sword such as exercising the Taijiquan, the movements like flying clouds and flowing water, movements flowing, an integral whole, to release the force like the gold lion shaking its hairs, to vary from minute to minute. To practice Taijiquan sword, not only can get the effect of health building, but also enjoy the aesthetics of art, so that feeling carefree and joyous. The famous Taijiquan master Chen Zhaopi wrote the poetry for it:

Pricking, pointing, wiping, cutting and thrusting;
Twining force cause attacking comes to nothing.
Scooping like moving plough is the right way;
Pushing and supporting are orthodox school.
Defending all remains skills,
Attacking appears the cold light.
Shrinking the body likes a hedgehog,
Extending the body as a rainbow.
Rays of sun shine in all directions,
Boundless radiances are too wonderful.
After practicing Taiji sword for a long time,
Constant effort yields sure success.

II. Names of the Chen-style Taiji Single Sword Routine

Form 1 Starting Form of Taiji Sword

Form 2 Face-the-sun sword

Form 3 The Celestial Points a Way Out

Form 4 Green Dragon Rises from the Water

Form 5 The Guarding Knee Sword

Form 6 Closing Door Form

Form 7 Green Dragon Rises from the Water

Form 8 Turn Body Over to Hack Sword

Form 9 Green Dragon Turns Its Body

Form 10 Oblique Flying

Form 11 Spread Wing and Nod Head

Form 12 Beat Grasses to Look for the Snake

Form 13 Golden Cock Stands on One Leg

Form 14 The Celestial Points a Way Out

Form 15 Covering and Intercepting Form

Form 16 An Ancient Tree with Twisted Roots

Form 17 Tiger Pounces On Prey

Form 18 Green Dragon Swings Its Tail

Form 19 Step Backward and Whirl Arms

Form 20 Wild Horse Jumps over a Gully

Form 21 White Snake Spits Its Tongue

Form 22 Black Dragon Swings Its Tail

Form 23 Zhongkui Raises the Sword

Form 24 The Arhat Tame the Dragon

Form 25 Black Bear Turns Back

Form 26 The Swallow Pecks at the Mud

Form 27 White Snake Spits Its Tongue

Form 28 Flying Oblique

Form 29 Battle of Wits between the Eagle and the Bear

Form 30 The Swallow Pecks at the Mud

Form 31 Pluck the Star to Exchange the Plough

Form 32 Scoop Up the Moon from the Bottom of the Sea

Form 33 The Celestial Pointing a Way Out

Form 34 The Phoenix Nods Its Head

Form 35 The Swallow Pecks at the Mud

Form 36 White Snake Spits Its Tongue

Form 37 Flying Oblique

Form 38 Hold the Weighty Leftward

Form 39 Hold the Weighty Rightward

Form 40 The Swallow Pecks at the Mud

Form 41 White Ape Presents Fruit

Form42 Flowers Falling Form

Form 43 Thrusting Up and Down

Form 44 Oblique Flying

Form 45 Nezha Searches the Sea

Form 46 Python Turns Over Its Body

Form 47 Weituo Presents a Pestle

Form 48 The Mill Stone Sword

Form49 Finishing Form

III. The Diagram of the Chen-style Taiji Single Sword Routine

Form 1 Starting Form of Taiji Sword

ACTION 1: Stand upright with the feet together. Hold the handle of the sword in the left hand with the center of hand facing backward, put the side of the sword against the inside of forearm, hanging the arm to the left side of body and the tip of the sword pointing upward. Hanging the right hand by the right side of body with the right hand forming sword-fingers. Eyes look forward (Fig.3-1).

Key to the movement: Keep the head and neck upright and natural, the top of head is raised lightly in the mind. The tip of the tongue resting on the hard palate, breathe naturally, "Qi" flows to "Dantian". Keep the body upright, the shoulders are lowered, the hips relaxed. The soles of feet are flat and the "Yongquan" are empty.

Fig. 3-1

ACTION 2: The left foot takes a half step leftward until feet are shoulder-width apart, the knees bent slightly. Eyes look forward (Fig.3-2).

Key to the movements: The knees bent and relaxed, the "Qi" flows downward. The weight is moved first to the right leg, and then the left leg is lifted and taken a half step to the left, the step is light and natural and slowly.

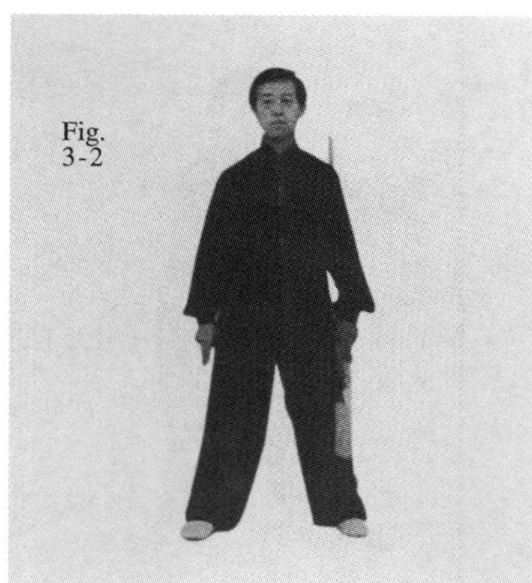
Fig. 3-2

ACTION 3: Raise both arms slowly upward form the sides to the front of body to shoulder level, the handle of sword pointing forward and tip pointing backward. Eyes look forward(Fig.3-3).

Fig. 3-3

Key to the movement: Raise the arms slowly upward and lower down the body. Have your knees bent and elbows lowered, with the chest extending and the abdomen solid.

ACTION 4: Lower the hands downward to the sides of the abdomen. At the same time, the both legs squat slowly downward. The tip of the sword is pointing the upper-rear, the sword-fingers pointing forward. Eyes look forward (3-4).

Fig. 3-4

Key to the movement: Keep the body upright and natural, the knees bent and the hips relaxed. Do not protrude the buttocks out and bow the torso forward.

ACTION 5: Ward the both arms off to the upper-left, the center of right sword-fingers facing upward and the tip pointing forward. The left hand holds the sword with the center of hand facing downward and the tip of sword pointing backward. The body turns leftward slightly, the weight moving to the right leg. Eyes look to the forward-left (Fig.3-5).

Key to the movement: Turning the body to left should be natural and smooth. The main weight is on the right leg.

Fig. 3-5

ACTION 6: Turn the toes of the right foot outward. The upper body turns to the right 90 degrees, the main weight being on the left leg. Following the turning of body, the both arms moving rightward in horizontal arcs in the front of body, the right sword-fingers pointing right and the center of hand facing outward, the tip of sword pointing left. Eyes look forward (Fig.3-6).

Key to the movement: Moving the weight leftward, turning the toes of right foot outward, moving the both arms with the turning of body

Fig. 3-6

must be well coordinated, the upper and lower limbs well-coordinated, the turning of body natural and smooth. Eyes look forward over the left shoulder.

ACTION 7: Move the weight to the right leg and squat down with right knee bent. At the same time, lift the left leg with the knee bent and the toes pointing downward. The body lowers down and ward off both arms slightly upper-right. Eyes look forward(Fig.3-7).

Key to the movement: When lifting the left knee, the hips must be relaxed, the upper and lower limbs well-coordinated, the ward-off force is remain, the “Qi” flows to hands and feet.

Usage: Ward off the opponent’s attack, and lift the left leg

Fig. 3-7

Fig. 3-8

to return.

ACTION 8: The weight move onto the right leg, the left foot takes a step forward with the inside of the heel on the floor and the toes turned inward, the knees bent and hips relaxed. When taking the step, the body turns rightward and lowers slightly, the both arms warding off to the upper-right. Eyes look forward (Fig.3-8).

Key to the movement: Concentrate on the movements, the whole body coordinates into one, do not bend the head and bow the torso.

Usage: The form is skill of the upper pulling and lower striking. Take a step with the left foot to lock the opponent's foot.

ACTION 9: Move the weight onto the left foot with the whole sole of the foot touching on the floor, and then the upper body turns leftward about 75 degrees, the right foot takes a little step with the toes touching the floor. At the same time, the left hand holds the sword and moves in a rightward, downward, forward arc in the side of body, and then moves upward in the front of body. The right sword-fingers arcs forward and upward to the front of body, the center of hand facing upward and the sword-fingers pointing forward, both elbows bent, the left sword-fingers is pressing on the handle of sword in the right hand, the tip of the sword pointing leftward. Eyes look forward (Fig.3-9).

Key to the movement: The top of head is raised slightly in the mind, keep the body upright and natural, the shoulders and elbows lowered,

chest held slightly inward and the waist relaxed, the knees bent and hips relaxed, the upper and lower parts of the body are well coordinated.

ACTION 10: Take a step rightward with the right foot, the toes pointing forward. At the same time, turn the body rightward slightly, move the right sword-fingers with the twining adversely to the lower-right in the outside of the right leg, the center facing downward and the sword-fingers pointing forward. Swing the left hand leftward with the sword in it, the tip of sword pointing backward. Eyes follow the turning of body and then look forward (Fig.3-10).

Key to the movement: Taking the step, turning the body, swing both hands must be combined with the force of the waist.

ACTION 11: Move the weight to the right leg, bend the right knee and relax the hips, and turn the body leftward about 90 degrees, follow the turning of body, draw a half step rightward with the left foot and bend the left knee, the toes touching the floor. At the same time, move the right sword-fingers rightward, backward, upward in an arc, and then push it passing to the lower side of the right ear at the shoulder level, the sword-fingers pointing upward. Move the sword in the left hand downward and backward in an arc to the rear-left of body, the tip of sword pointing upward(Fig.3-11).

Key to the movement: When moving the weight rightward and swinging and pushing the right hand,

Fig. 3-11

the right leg bent and right hip relaxed, the right toes of foot turned inward. The whole body weight being on the right leg, the emptiness and solidness is clear.

Usage: Left hand swing the sword in the front of the opponent's face, and push your right fingers to thrust the opponent's eyes, it is called "two dragons play with the pearls".

ACTION 12: Move the weight onto the left leg, the whole sole touching on the floor. Take a step forward with the right foot passing to the inside of left foot. Both legs form a right bow stance. At the same time, swing the right sword-fingers outward, backward and draw it to beside the right leg, when the weight moving forward, ward both hands off to in the front of the chest, the tip of sword pointing backward and the centers of both hands facing upward. Eyes look forward (Fig.3-12).

Fig. 3-12

Key to the movement: When taking a step forward, the force of the groin and waist follows to the sword-fingers and the handle of the sword.

Usage: Use the handle of the sword and the sword-fingers attack opponent's groin or abdomen.

ACTION 13: Move the weight to the left, bent the left leg and straighten the right leg, the toes turned outward, the body turns rightward slightly. At the same time, move the right hand to beside the waist with twining adversely, the center of the right sword-fingers facing downward, move the left hand leftward slightly with twining smoothly. Eyes look forward (Fig.3-13).

Key to the movement: The weight being on the left leg, the toes of right foot turned outward. The right leg remains the force of twining smoothly, and the both hands remain the force of twining adversely.

Form 2 Face-the-sun Sword

ACTION 1: Continuing from previous movement. The toes of left foot fall to ground, the weight moves onto the right leg, left leg bends to squat half. Move the left foot in an arc to the inside of the left foot with the toes touching the floor and the heel raised. At the same time, turn the body rightward 90 degrees. At the same time, close the both hands in the front of chest, elbows bent, hold the handle of the sword with the right hand and left hand loosens it. Eyes lookforward(Fig.3-14).

Key to the movement: The shoulders relaxed and elbows lowered, the knees bent and hips relaxed, the upper and lower movements are combined, save force to prepare for applying.

Usage: The left foot moving in an arc, can sweep the opponent's foot.

ACTION 2: The weight being on the right leg, lift the left leg with the knee bent and the toes pointing naturally downward under the groin. At the same time, both hands hold the sword upward to above the head, support the sword in right hand above the head with the tip pointing leftward, the left hand forms a sword-fingers, put it above the left shoulder, the center of the left sword-fingers facing the upper-front. Eyes look forward(Fig.3-15).

Fig. 3-15

Key to the movement: The weight being on the right leg, the knee bent and hip relaxed, draw the abdomen and anus in. The both arms curve, the force is focused at the tip of the sword.

Usage: Using the sword to support the weapon of the opponent, protect own head

Form 3 The Celestial Points a Way Out

ACTION 1: Continuing from previous movement. Lower the body down and turn the body rightward 45 degrees and incline forward slightly, the lower part of body doesn't change. Move the sword in the right hand to forward, rightward, downward in and arc, and then draw it to in the front of chest. At the same time, move the left sword-fingers downward passing to the face, close it with the right hand. Eyes look to the forward right (Fig.3-16).

Fig. 3-16

Key to the movement: The whole body combined and steady, the movements of the lower limbs aren't changed, it is said: "the body shrink like a hedgehog, the body extend like a rainbow".

Usage: Swing the sword to ward off the opponent's weapon.

ACTION 2: The right hand holds and thrusts the sword to the lower-front in the right of body with the center of hand facing upward, the body leaning to the forward-right. At the same time, swing the left hand to the upper-left, the left sword-fingers pointing forward and the center of hand facing upward, both hands remain the symmetry. Eyes look at the tip of the sword of the right hand (Fig.3-17).

Fig. 3-17

Key to the movement: Support the weight with the right leg. Lift the left knee to protect the groin, the knee bent and hips relaxed. Thrusting the sword, extend upward and thrust downward, the whole body coordinated, thrusting the sword must be swift and powerful, the force focused at the tip of the sword.

Usage: Thrust the sword to the opponent's leg.

Form 4 Green Dragon Rises from the Water

ACTION 1: Continue from previous movement. Take a step to the forward-left with the left foot, the heel landing the floor and the toes hooked up. The weight being on the right leg, the knee bent and hips relaxed. At the same time, turn the body leftward 45 degrees, bend the right elbow and twist the right wrist inward, draw the sword in an arc to beside the right side of waist, the center of right hand facing upward and the tip of the sword pointing to forward-left. At the same time, swing the left sword-fingers downward with the arm straight and the sword-fingers pointing upward. Eyes look forward-left (Fig.3-18).

Fig. 3-18

Key to the movement: The footwork is light. Bending the right elbow, twining the right wrist, turning the sword and the whole movement must be coordinated. The left shoulder is relaxed and left elbow is lowered, the force is focused at the forefinger and middle finger.

Usage: Swinging the sword to slice horizontally and thrust forward.

ACTION 2: Place the tiptoes of the left foot on the floor. Shift the weight onto the left leg to form a left bow step. At the same time, turn the body leftward 90 degrees, thrust the sword in the right hand forward with the tip of sword pointing forward and the center of hand facing upward. Move the left sword-fingers downward passing to the chest in an arc and then to above the left forehead with the arm rotating inward, the sword-fingers pointing upper-right, the center of hand turning outward and facing upper-left. Eyes look the tip of sword (Fig.3-19).

Fig. 3-19

Key to the movement: When thrusting the sword, the waist rotating and groin turning, the whole body is coordinated. The force is rooted at the foot, walked throughout leg, commanded by the waist, expressed at fingers and ultimately concentrated at the tip of the sword.

Form 5 The Guarding Knee Sword

ACTION 1: Turn the toes of the left foot and shift the weight onto the left leg, the knee bent and left hip relaxed. Take a step forward passing to the inside of left foot with the right foot, the inside of right heel touching on the floor and the toes turned inward. At the same time, turn the body leftward 30 degrees, and then swing sword in the right hand to cut upward in an arc, the right arm and wrist turning inward and the center of hand facing inward, the tip of the sword pointing upper-front. Move the left sword-fingers to close the inside of the right wrist. Eyes look the tip of the sword (Fig.3-20).

Fig. 3-20

Key to the movement: Turning the toes of left foot outward, swinging the sword upward, turning the body and taking a step with the right foot must be coordinated.

Usage: Swinging the sword in circles in the both sides of body must be coordinated with body technique, footwork and twining force. It is a kind of the sword technique to guard the head and body.

ACTION 2: Continuing from previous movement. Land the right foot with the toes turned outward, shift the weight onto the right leg, take a step forward with the left foot passing to the inside of the right foot, the body turning rightward 180 degrees. Following the turning of body, swing the sword in the right hand and the left sword-fingers closing the right wrist to upward, backward, downward in an arc passing to the outside of the left leg, and then to the upper-front, above the right side of head, the center of hand facing outward and the tip of the sword pointing leftward. Eyes look to forward-left (Fig.3-21).

Key to the movement: When swinging the sword in a circle in the left side of body passing to the outside of left leg, the weight being on the right leg. Taking step forward, turning body and cutting sword upward must be well coordinated.

Fig. 3-21

ACTION 3: Continuing from previous movement. Turn the toes of left foot outward and land on the floor, shift the weight onto the left leg. Take a step forward with the right foot passing to the inside of the left foot, the right heel landing on the floor, the toes of foot hooked upward. At the same time, turn the body leftward 90 degrees. Swing the sword in the hand and the left sword-fingers closing the right wrist upward, backward and downward in a circle. Follow taking the step with the right foot, cut the sword to the upper-front, the center of right hand facing inward and the tip of the sword pointing forward. Eyes look forward right (Fig.3-22).

Key to the movement: Swinging the sword, the body turning and the groin twining, the

Fig. 3-22

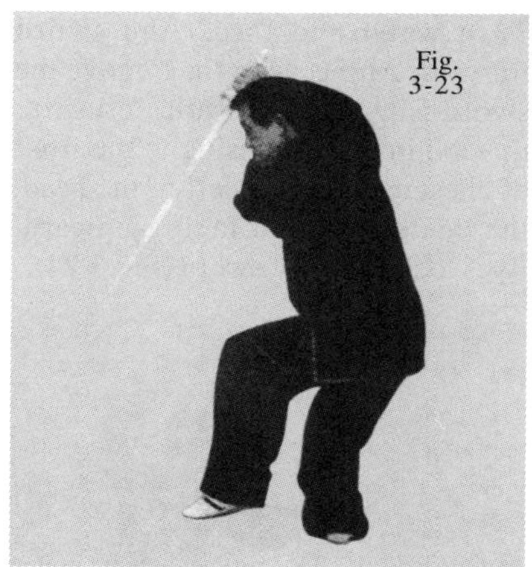
Fig. 3-23

force is focused at the body of the sword.

Form 6 Closing Door Form

ACTION: Move the weight onto the right leg, the knee bent and the hips relaxed. Take a half step rightward with the left foot, the knee bent and toes touching the floor. And then raise the sword in hand upward to the upper-front of the head, the center of the hand facing outward and the tip of the sword pointing the lower front, the left sword-fingers closing on the right wrist. Eyes look the tip of sword (Fig.3-23).

Key to the movement: When raising the sword upward, the body is lowered, the knees bent and the hips relaxed, the "Qi" settling to "Dantian". The upper and lower limps are coordinated.

Usage: Raising the sword to parry the opponent's weapon for guarding the body and knee.

Form 7 Green Dragon Raise from the Water

ACTION: Continuing from previous movement. Take a big step with the left foot and withdraw the sword in an arc to the side of waist with the right arm turned inward, the center of right hand facing upward. And then move the weight leftward, turn the body leftward 45 degrees.

Turn waist and thrust the sword forward. At the same time, move the sword-fingers downward, leftward, upward in an arc passing to the front of chest to the upper-left of the head, the center of hand facing upward. Eyes look the tip of sword (Fig.3-24).

Fig. 3-24

Key to the movement: The force raise from the foot, turn the waist and twist the groin, turn and thrust the sword forward, so the force is focused at the tip of the sword.

Usage: Support the opponent's weapon with the left hand and thrust the sword at the opponent's chest or abdomen.

Form 8 Turn Body Over to Hack Sword

ACTION 1: Lift the right knee with the toes pointing downward naturally and turn the body rightward 90 degrees. At the same time, raise the sword upward to the front of head with the arm turning outward, the tip of sword in the left side of waist, move the left sword-fingers to close the right wrist (Fig.3-25).

Fig. 3-25

Key to the movement: Lifting the knee, turning the body and raising the sword must be coordinated and quick.

ACTION 2: Take a step to the right with the right foot, stamp the right foot with entire sole flat on the floor, shift the weight rightward, the right leg form a right bow step with the knee bent and hips relaxed. At the same time, hack with the sword in the right hand to the lower right, the tip of sword pointing the lower right. Swing the sword-fingers upward to the upper-left, they pointing rightward and the center of hand facing upward. Eyes look the tip of sword(Fig.3-26).

Fig. 3-26

Key to the movement: Striding the step, turning the body, stamping foot and hacking the sword must be coordinated. The left and right hands must be coordinated each other.

Usage: If the opponent sneak attacks in the rear, you can turn the body quickly and stride the step rightward, and hack the sword to return.

Form 9 Green Dragon Turn Its Body

ACTION 1: Move the weight onto the left leg, turn the body left 90 degrees, lift the right knee with the knee bent and the toes pointing downward naturally. At the same time, swing the left hand downward in an arc to the side of the waist with the center of hand facing upward. Sweep the sword horizontally in front of the abdomen, the arm twining smooth and the wrist turned inward, the center of hand facing upward and the tip of sword pointing forward. Eyes look forward (Fig.3-27).

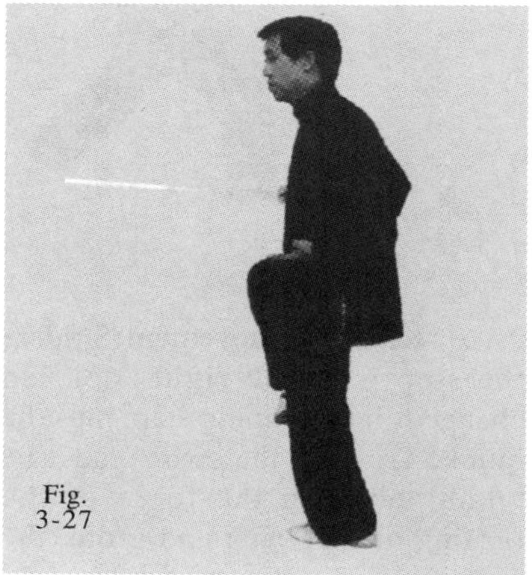

Fig. 3-27

Key to the movement: Turning body and lifting the right knee must be coordinated. Withdrawing and sweeping the sword, the force is focused at the edge of the sword.

ACTION 2: Stride a half step and stamp with the right foot, at the same time, take a step with the left foot passing to the inside of the right foot, shift the weight onto the left leg, bend the knee and relax the hips, and thrust the sword in the right hand forward, the center of right hand facing upward, the tip of the sword pointing forward. Eyes look forward(Fig.3-28).

Fig. 3-28

Key to the movement: Striding the step with the right foot can change it into jumping step, must be quick. Trusting the sword must be combined with the force of the turning of the waist and groin, the force focused at the tip of the sword.

Usage: Continuing from previous movement. After hacking the sword rightward, the opponent comes from the left side of body. You must turn the body leftward quickly and sweep the sword to slice his waist. If he moves backward, you can thrust the sword at his chest or abdomen in the jump step.

Form 10 Oblique Flying

ACTION 1: Lower the sword in the hand, continue move the weight rightward, lean the body forward slightly and turn it rightward 15 degrees. Close the left sword-fingers downward on the right forearm, the fingers pointing forward, the center of hand facing upward. Eyes look to the lower front over the tip of sword (Fig.3-29).

Fig. 3-29

ACTION 2: Shift the weight in a downward arc to the right leg, bent and squat the right knee, the left leg bent slightly. Lower the left hand to the outside of the left leg with the arm twining smoothly, the sword-fingers pointing lower-left and the center of hand facing upward. At the same time, following the shifting the weight and turning the waist rightward, slice the sword forward, rightward and upward in an arc, the right hand is higher than the shoulder, the tip of the sword pointing upper-right. Following the slicing the sword, the body turns rightward 75 degrees. Eyes look at the tip of the sword (Fig.3-30).

Fig. 3-30

Key to the movement: Slicing the sword must be combined with the force of the groin and the waist. The force is focused at the edge of the sword.

Usage: According to the attack and defend situation to slice the opponent's waist, groin or neck.

Form 11 Spread Wing and Nod Head

ACTION 1: Shift the weight leftward and turn the body leftward slightly. At the same time, swing the sword in the hand upward and leftward in an arc to in the left of the forehead, the center of the hand facing inward, the tip of the sword pointing upper-right. Swing the left sword-fingers upward in an arc to close the right wrist. Eyes look to the front right (Fig.3-31).

Fig. 3-31

Key to the movement: Swinging the sword and shifting the weight must be completed in unison.

ACTION 2: Shift the weight onto the right leg. The left foot inserts a step to the rear-right behind the right foot, the both legs squat down to form cross-legged sitting stance. At the same time, cut upward with the sword from lower-left to the upper-right in an arc with the arm twining adversely, the center of hand facing upper-rear. Move he left sword-fingers downward, leftward and upward to above the head, the body leans forward. Eyes look at the tip of sword (Fig.3-32 and attached Fig.3-32).

Fig. 3-32

Key to the movement: Cutting up with the sword must be completed with leaning the body forward, eyes looking at the tip of the sword like the beauty looking at the moon.

Usage: When the opponent swinging the weapon to attack me, I should move the weight, parry and stick his weapon, lower the body quickly and swing the sword upward to cut his groin or throat.

ACTION 3: Land the heel on the floor; move the weight onto the left leg, the left knee bent and hips relaxed. Take a step passing to the front of the left foot with the right foot, at the same time, swing the sword downward, leftward and upward with arm twining smoothly, the tip of sword pointing upper-right, the left sword-fingers holding the handle of sword. Eyes look to forward right (Fig.3-33).

Fig. 3-33

Key to the movement: Swinging the sword in an arc, closing the left hand and taking a step with the right foot must be coordinated.

ACTION 4: Shift the weight onto the right leg, bend the right knee and straighten the left leg. At the same time, turn the body 90 degrees, swing the sword to point downward-right passing to the front of the forehead, the both hands are placed in front of chest, the tip of sword pointing to the forward-right. Eyes look at the tip of sword (Fig.3-34).

Fig. 3-34

Key to the movement: Pointing the sword, turning the waist and shifting weight must be coordinated.

Usage: Parry the opponent's weapon, and then point the opponent's wrist or rib with the sword.

Form 12 Beat Grasses to Look for the Snake

ACTION 1: Move the weight onto the left leg, bend the left knee and relax the hips, straighten the right leg naturally, turn the body leftward slightly. Both hands swing the sword upward and leftward to above the left shoulder, the tip of sword pointing to upward-right, the left sword-fingers touching on the right wrist. Eyes look to forward-right (Fig.3-35).

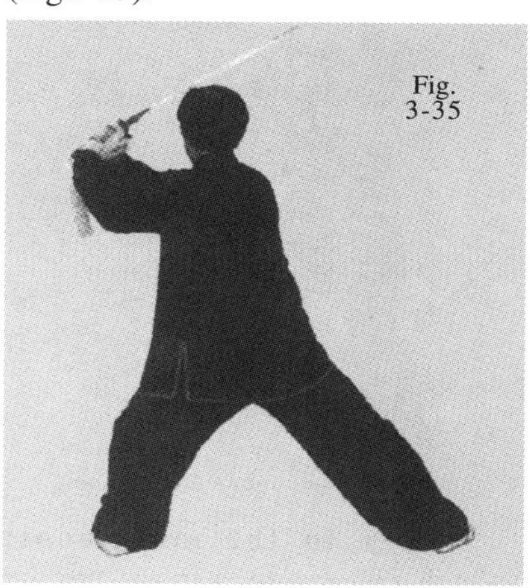
Fig. 3-35

Key to the movement: Swinging the sword upward, shifting weight and turning the body leftward 75 degrees must be combined with the force of waist, the force is focused at the both hands.

ACTION 2: Turn the tiptoes of the right foot outward, move the weight to the right leg, bend the right knee and relax the hips, take a step passing to the inside of right foot with left foot heel landing on the floor, the tiptoes hook upward, the left knee bent slightly. Following stepping forward, turning the upper body rightward 180 degrees, the right hand holds the sword, both hands cut the sword to leftward, downward, rightward and upward to the upward-front of head. Eyes look to the forward-left(Fig.3-36).

Fig. 3-36

Fig. 3-37

Key to the movement: Swinging the sword in an arc, turning the body and taking step forward must be coordinated.

Usage: Following the turning of body, swing the sword in both sides of the body to cut the opponent or guard own body.

ACTION 3: Land the left tiptoes on the floor, turn the body rightward slightly. Bend both leg and squat downward. At the same time, right hand swings the sword upward, rightward and downward in an arc, the sword at the knee level and the center of right hand facing upward, the tip of the sword pointing rightward. Eyes look at the tip of the sword(Fig.3-37).

Key to the movement: Lowering the sword and squatting downward, both knees must be bent and remain the close force. Keep the body upright and natural, do not bow the spine and protrude the buttocks out.

ACTION 4: Turn the tiptoes of left foot outward, move the weight to the left leg. Turn the body leftward 180 degrees, take a step forward with the right foot heel landing on the floor, tiptoes of right foot hooked upward. The weight remain on the left leg, the left leg bent and squatted. At the same time, following the turning of the body, sweep sword horizontally 180 degrees, the sword at the knee level, the tip of sword pointing leftward. Eyes look at the tip of sword (Fig.3-38).

Key to the movement: Keep the body lowered and upright and natural, sweeping the sword, turning

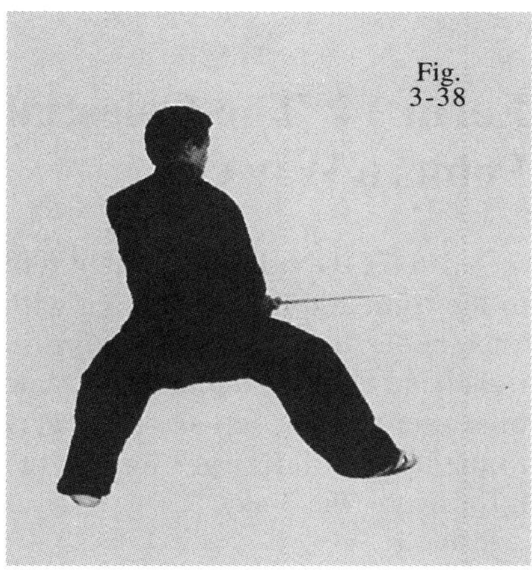
Fig. 3-38

the body and step forward with right foot must be coordinated.

Usage: When you are surrounding by opponents, you can sweep their legs with the sword.

Form 13 Golden Cock Stands on One Leg

ACTION 1: Shift the weight rightward, turn the body leftward and then rightward, land the tiptoes of right foot, bend right leg and relax the hips. The right hand swing the sword leftward, backward, upward and rightward in an arc to in the front head, turn the wrist inward so the center of right hand facing outward and tip of sword pointing leftward, the left sword-fingers touching on the right wrist. Eyes look forward (Fig.3-39).

Fig. 3-39

Key to the movement: During the processing of shifting the weight, turning the waist and turning the wrist, the force is continuous.

ACTION 2: Lower the body and move the weight leftward, turn the right arm inward and lower it to in the front of the right side of chest, swing the tip of sword from upward-left to forward-right of head at the right shoulder level. At the same time, turn the body leftward slightly. Eyes look to forward-right (Fig.3-40).

Key to the movement: Holding and lowering the sword in hands must be combined with the closed force of waist.

ACTION 3: Shift the weight onto the left leg, straighten the left knee, stand up on left leg and lift the right leg with the knee bent. Raise the

Fig. 3-40

sword in the hand to above the head, the tip of sword pointing rightward, the left sword-fingers touching on the right wrist. Eyes look to forward-right(Fig.3-41).

Fig. 3-41

Form 14 The Celestial Points a Way Out

ACTION: Drop the right foot to the right and lift the left leg with knee bent, thrust with the sword in right hand to lower right. At the same time, ward off the left sword-fingers to the upward-left. Eyes look at the tip of sword (Fig.3-42).

Fig. 3-42

Key to the movement: Taking the right step, lifting the left knee and thrusting the sword quickly must be coordinated, the body leaning forward slightly.

Usage: Continuing from previous movement. Ward off the opponent's weapon and then thrust unawares to his lower limbs with the sword.

Form 15 Covering and Intercepting Form

ACTION 1: Drop the left foot backward with tiptoes landing on the floor. Bend the right knee and squat downward, the weight remain on the right leg, and then turn the upper body rightward 45 degrees. At the same time, lower the left sword-fingers to close the right hand, raise and draw the sword slightly in the lowered arc to in the front of chest. Eyes look forward (Fig.3-43).

Fig. 3-43

Key to the movement: The weight is remained on the right leg, the left leg is solid and right leg is empty, both hands closed.

ACTION 2: Move the weight quickly to the left and withdraw the right foot a half step backward, stamp the right foot, release the force at heel. At the same time, separate the sword in right hand and left hand to the rear sides of the left and the right, release the forces focused at both elbows, the arms are lowered than the shoulders, the tip of sword pointing forward. Eyes look forward (Fig.3-44).

Fig. 3-44

Key to the movement: Stepping backward, stamping the right foot and releasing force at both arms must be well coordinated.

Usage: If you can't turn the body, or the opponent embraces you from back, you can use this skill. Step backward and stamp on the tiptoes of the opponent with your right foot heel, and use the back of body, elbows or the handle of sword to attack the opponent.

Form 16 An Ancient Tree with Twisted Roots

ACTION: Move the weight rightward and turn the body rightward 90 degrees. Bend both knees and sit down on the legs. Follow the turning of the body, support the sword upward to upper-front of head, the tip of sword pointing leftward, at the same time, close the left sword-fingers on the right wrist. Eyes look to forward-left (Fig.3-45).

Fig. 3-45

Key to the movement: Turn the body rightward by using the right heel and the ball of left foot as the pivots, the body rotating and lowering. Turning body and squatting downward and support the sword upward must be coordinated.

Usage: The body is rotating rightward and lowering downward, the sword is support and turned quickly to neutralize the force of the weapon, and prepare to return.

Form 17 Tiger Pounces on Prey

ACTION 1: Take a step passing to the inside of right foot to the left, the heel landing on the floor and the tiptoes hooked. Turn the right wrist inward and lower the sword to beside the right side of waist, the tip of sword pointing forward-left and at the waist level. Eyes look at the tip of sword (Fig.3-46).

Fig. 3-46

Key to the movement: Taking

step forward with left foot, the footwork is light and natural, collect the force to ready for releasing.

ACTION 2: Shift the weight to the left, relax the left hip to form a left bow step, turn the body leftward 75 degrees. At the same time, horizontal thrust the sword forward in both hands, the center of hand facing upward. Eyes look forward (Fig.3-47).

Fig. 3-47

Key to the movement: Trusting the sword forward, the force is originated in the feet, released from the legs, commanded by the waist, flows through shoulders and elbows and reaches the tip of sword, the movements of the whole body must be coordinated.

Usage: Continuing from previous movement. Turn the sword downward to touch the weapon of the opponent, cede the form to thrust the sword forward at the opponent's chest or abdomen.

Form 18 Green Dragon Swings Its Tail

ACTION 1: Continuing from previous movement. Turn the body rightward and shift the weight to the right, the right knee bent and hips relaxed. Following the turning of body, swing the sword rightward in a lowered arc passing to outside of left leg and then raise it to the outside of head, the center of right hand facing outward, the tip of sword pointing the lower-left, the left sword-fingers touching on the right wrist. Eyes look to the forward-left (Fig.3-48).

Fig. 3-48

Key to the movement: The swinging of the sword must follows the turning of the body, the line of the sword must be near to the outside of left leg.

ACTION 2: Move the weight to the left and turn the body first rightward and then leftward, the feet don't move. At the same time, swing the sword from the upper-front of head to upward, rightward and downward, passing to the right side of body and then cut upward to the shoulder level, the tip of sword pointing rightward. Eyes following the tip of sword and then look to the right(Fig.3-49).

Fig. 3-49

Key to the movement: Swinging of the sword must follows turning of body and moving of the weight, the line of the sword must be near to the outside of left leg.

Usage: The feet don't move. Follow the turning of body and moving of weight to swing the sword in the both sides of body, like "Black Dragon Swings Its Tail", it can guard the head and body.

Form 19 Step Backward and Whirl Arms

ACTION 1: Take a step backward passing to the inside of the left foot with right foot. The left sword-fingers touching on the right wrist, the right hand swings the sword upward, backward, downward and forward in a vertical circle in the left side of body, and then cut to the upper-right of body. At the same time, turn the body rightward 180 degrees. Eyes look to forward-left (Fig.3-50).

Fig. 3-50

Key to the movement: Swinging the sword in a vertical circle in the left side of body. After cutting the sword upward from the lower to the upper-front, step backward with right foot, so the body and the sword can be coordinated.

ACTION 2: Take a step backward passing to the inside of right foot with left foot. Swing the sword with right hand in a vertical to the upper-left of head in right side of body, the right arm twining smoothly, the left sword-fingers touching on the right wrist. At the same time, turn the body leftward 180 degrees. Eyes look to forward-right (Fig.3-51).

Fig. 3-51

Key to the movement: When swinging the sword 180 degrees in a vertical in right side of body, take a step backward with the left foot.

ACTION 3: Shift the weight to the right, bend the right knee and relax the hips. Turn the body first left and then right. Follow the turning of body, swing the sword passing to the front of head in a vertical in the left side of body, the tip of sword pointing downward, both hands twining smoothly to the right side of head, above the shoulder level. Eyes follow the sword and then look to the left(Fig.3-52).

Fig. 3-52

Key to the movement: The feet don't move. Swinging the sword in a vertical in the front of body and then raise it to front of head, moving the weight and turning of the waist must be coordinated.

Usage: It is a defend skill sword with step backward, can win in the lose game.

Form 20 Wild House Jumps over a Gully

ACTION 1: Move the weight onto the left leg, straighten the left leg and lift the right leg with knee bent. At the same time, separate the sword in the hand and left hand in downward arcs and then close them to the front of chest, the tip of sword pointing forward. The body turns rightward 15 degrees. Eyes look forward(Fig.3-53).

Fig. 3-53

Key to the movement: Stand steadily on the left leg, lift the right leg with the knee bent and tip of foot hooked in. Keep the chest slightly inward and waist relaxed, the shoulders relaxed and elbows lowered, the "Qi" settles at "Dantian".

ACTION 2: Drop the right foot forward with heel landing the floor and tiptoes hooked upward. Bend the left leg and squat half downward. The movements of upper limbs don't change. Eyes look forward(Fig.3-54).

Fig. 3-54

ACTION 3: Press the left foot against the floor forcefully and then lift it with the knee bent, following it, land the right foot against the floor forcefully and then jump up to the front. The movements of upper limbs don't change. Eyes look forward (Fig.3-55).

Fig. 3-55

ACTION 4: Drop the left foot and lift right foot with the knee bent. The movements don't change. Eyes look forward(Fig.3-56).

Fig. 3-56

ACTION 5: Drop the right foot forward, bend the right knee and straighten the left leg to form a right bow step. Thrust the sword forward horizontally by both hands, the sword at the waist level. Eyes look forward(Fig.3-57).

Key to the movement: The exercises from movement one to five are whole form of "Wild House Jump Over A Gully". Lifting right leg, striding step, jumping up, landing forward and thrusting must be continued and coordinated. The footwork is slight and quick, the force point of sword is accurate.

Usage: It is a kind skill of the breaking out of encirclement or to

Fig. 3-57

attack in distant distance.

Form 21 White Snake Spits Its Tongue

ACTION 1: Turn the body leftward and move the weight to the left, bend the left knee and squat half downward to form a left bow step. Both hands sweep the sword from right to the rear-left passing to the front of body. At the same time, turn the body leftward 180 degrees. Eyes look forward(Fig.3-58).

Key to the movement: Sweeping with the sword must be combined with the turning of body and the force of waist, the force of sword is focused at the edge of sword, the tip is sweeping horizontally 180 degrees.

Fig. 3-58

ACTION 2: Shift the weight rightward, bend right knee and squat fully down, straighten the left leg with toes of left foot hooked upward and turned inward. Both hands withdraw the sword to in the front of abdomen, the centers of hands facing upward. Follow the moving of weight, the body is turning rightward 45 degrees. Eyes look forward-left (Fig.3-59).

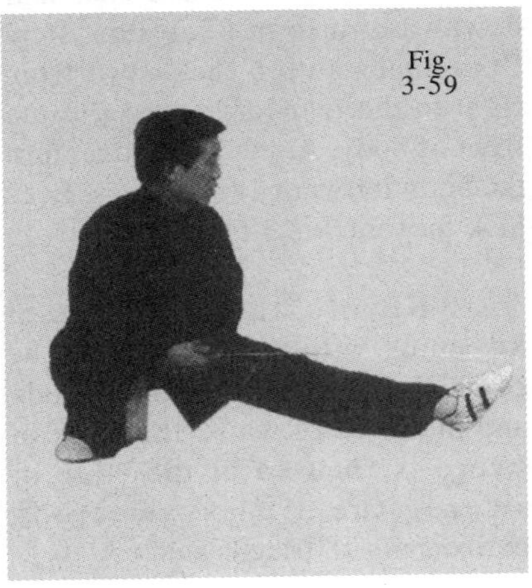

Fig. 3-59

Key to the movement: Moving the weight rightward must be combined with rotating force of the groin, don't sit backward in a straight line, it require exhibiting the elastic force. Lowering the body, the top of head is raised and the upper body is upright.

ACTION 3: Move the weight leftward, step forward with right foot so the feet together, the both knees bent slightly. And then step forward with right foot and turn the body leftward 45 degrees. At the same time, both hands thrust the sword from the side of waist to the forward. Eyes look forward (Fig.3-60).

Fig. 3-60

Key to the movement: Shifting the weight, stepping forward and thrusting with sword must be coordinated.

Usage: The posture 1 is

turning to sweep sword horizontally, it can sweep the waist of the opponent. In the posture 2, lowering the body to space out and neutralize the attack of the opponent. In the posture 3, combining with the force of groin and waist to thrust forward at the opponent's abdomen.

Form 22 Black Dragon Swings Its Tail

ACTION 1: Lift the left leg with the knee bent, turn the body to the right. At the same time, swing the sword with both hands in a downward, backward and upward arc passing to the right side to the back of body, to the shoulder level. Eyes look forward (Fig.3-61).

Fig. 3-61

Key to the movement: Swinging the sword in an arc in right side of body and then raising it, turning the body and lifting the left knee must be completed simultaneously. Lifting the leg, the knee bent and hips relaxed, the "Qi" flows downward. The upper and lower parts of body must be coordinated.

ACTION 2: Drop the left foot forward, the outside of left foot heel touching on floor and tiptoes hooked upward. At the same time, both hands hack the sword to the lower front. Eyes look forward (Fig.3-62).

Fig. 3-62

Key to the movement: Hacking the sword and dropping the foot must be completed at the same time. The force of waist is lowered and the wrist is relaxed the force is focused at the tip of the sword.

Usage: When the opponent thrusting to my left knee with the spear or sword, I lift my left knee quickly and point to his wrist with my sword.

ACTION 3: Lift the right leg with knee bent and stand up with left leg with left knee bent slightly. Turn the body to the left. At the same time, swing the sword with both hands in a downward, backward and upward arc passing to the left side to the back of body, to the shoulder level. Eyes look forward(Fig.3-63).

Fig. 3-63

Key to the movement: Swinging the sword in an arc in left side of body and raising it must be completed with turning the body at the same time. The upper and lower parts of body must be coordinated.

ACTION 4: Drop the right foot forward with the heel touching on the floor and tiptoes hooked upward, the left knee bent slightly, at the same time, hack to the lower front with the sword. Eyes look forward (Fig.3-64).

Fig. 3-64

Key to the movement: Hacking the sword and dropping the right foot must be coordinated, the wrist relaxed, the force is focused at the tip of sword.

Usage: When the opponent thrusting to my right knee with the spear or sword, I lift my right knee quickly and point to his wrist with my sword.

Form 23 Zhongkui Raises the Sword

ACTION 1: Shift the weight to the right, land the right tiptoes on the floor. Take a step forward passing to the inside of right foot with left foot. At the same time, turn the right wrist outward so the center of hand facing outward, swing the sword rightward passing to the front of right leg, the tip of sword pointing downward, while the body turning rightward 130 degrees. Eyes follow the sword (Fig.3-65)

Fig. 3-65

Key to the movement: Taking the left step naturally, the right knee bent and hip relaxed. Following the turning of body, the sword in both hands is swinging rightward and the wrists turning outward.

ACTION 2: Move the weight leftward, the left knee bent slightly, lift the right foot and withdraw a little step backward, the heel touching the floor and toes hooked upward. At the same time, cut upward with sword, the right arm twining smoothly, the left sword-fingers following the right hand to the front of the head. Eyes follow the tip of sword (Fig.3-66).

Fig. 3-66

Key to the movement: Taking a step backward and cutting upward must be coordinated.

Usage: If the opponent attacks from rear, I should take a step backward, turn the right wrist and cut upward sword to the abdomen of opponent.

ACTION 3: Land the toes on the floor, raise both hands to above head and turn wrist to lower-left, the center of hand facing outward and the tip of sword pointing lower-left. Eyes look at the tip of sword (Fig.3-67).

Fig. 3-67

Fig. 3-68

ACTION 4: Move the weight rightward, turn the body rightward 15degrees. Withdraw a half step with the left foot, the tiptoes touching on the floor. Raise the sword in right hand to the upper-right of head, the center of hand facing outward. Push the left sword-fingers forward with arm twining adverse so it is symmetry with the tip of sword. Eyes look forward(Fig.3-68).

Key to the movement: Raising the sword upward, the shoulders relaxed and waist lowered, the knees bent and hips relaxed. Keep the body upright and natural, pay attention to the forward-left.

Usage: Raising the sword upward to guard head, or use the handle of sword to attack the opponent's head.

Form 24 The Arhat Tame the Dragon

ACTION: Take a step forward with the sole of the left foot landing on the floor. Move the weight to the left leg, the left knee bent and hips relaxed. Turn the body leftward 15 degrees. Thrust the sword in right hand to the lower-left, swing the left hand to close the right hand and support the sword-handle. Eyes look at the tip of sword (Fig.3-69).

Key to the movement: Moving the weight, taking step, turning the body and thrusting the sword must be completed at the same time.

Usage: Continuing from previous movement, after supporting

Fig. 3-69

the opponent's weapon, stride quickly forward and thrust to the chest or ribs of opponent with the sword.

Form 25 Black Bear Turns Back

ACTION: Turn the body quickly rightward 90 degrees, lift the right foot and stride a step to the rear-left, drop and stamp the right foot, move the weight to the right leg. At the same time, both hands swing the sword upward passing to the upside of head and then hack to lower right, the force is focused at the tip of sword. Eyes look at the tip of the sword (Fig.3-70).

Key to the movement: Turning the body, striding step, stamping right foot and hacking sword must be

Fig. 3-70

completed at the same time.

Usage: If the opponent attacks from the rear, you can turn the body quickly and hack him with the sword.

Form 26 The Swallow Peck at the Mud

ACTION 1: Turn the body leftward 180 degrees, lift left leg with knee bent. Separate both hands downward in arcs to respective sides, the left to the lower-left with the sword-fingers pointing lower-left and the center of hand facing forward; the right hand to the outside of the right leg, the tip of sword pointing the lower-right. Eyes look forward (Fig.3-71).

Key to the movement: Turning body, lifting knee and separating hands downward must be completed at the same time. Stand up with the right leg, the weight must be steady, the whole body relaxed and lowered.

ACTION 2: Take a step with the left foot. Swing the both hands upward from respective sides and close them to in the front of chest, the tip of sword pointing downward. And then take a step passing to the inside of the left foot with the right foot, the weight moves to the right leg. At the same time, both hand point the sword to the lower-front, the tip of sword pointing the lower front. Eyes look the tip of sword (Fig.3-72).

Key to the movement: Taking the right and left foot, separating and closing hands, and pointing sword must be coordinated.

Usage: If the opponent attacks from the rear, when the distance is far, you should turn body and take a step forward, use the sword point the knee or groin of opponent.

Form 27 White Snake Spits Its Tongue

ACTION: Take a step forward with left foot so the feet together. The both hands hold the sword and thrust it horizontally forward, the centers of hands facing upward. Eyes look forward (Fig.3-73).

Key to the movement: Placing feet together and thrusting sword must be combined with the force of

Fig. 3-73

the waist, the force is focused at the tip of sword.

Usage: When the opponent retreat, you can step forward and thrust horizontally to opponent's waist or abdomen with the sword.

Form 28 Flying Oblique

ACTION 1: Move the weight on the left leg, turn the body leftward slightly, take a step to the rear-right with right foot, bend both legs at the knees and squat down slightly. The right hand holds the sword, the left sword-fingers touches on the right wrist, close them above the left knee, the tip of sword pointing to lower-forward. Eyes look rear-right (Fig.3-74).

Fig. 3-74

Key to the movement: Moving weight leftward, taking a step to rear-right, turning body leftward slightly and closing the sword downward must be coordinated. The footwork must be light and natural.

Usage: If the opponent attacks from the rear, you should turn body leftward shun the coming force, and take the right step and use the right foot to restrain his left foot.

ACTION 2: Turn the body rightward 45 degrees, move the weight to the right leg. The right hand hold the sword and slice it passing to the front of abdomen to upper-right, the tip pointing to upper-right, separate the left hand downward to beside outside of left knee, the sword-fingers pointing leftward and the center of hand facing upper-front. Eyes look forward-left (Fig.3-75).

Fig. 3-75

Key to the movement: Slicing the sword must be combined with the force of the groin and waist, the force focused at the out edge of the sword.

Usage: Swing the sword to slice the neck of the opponent.

Form 29 Battle of Wits between the Eagle and the Bear

ACTION 1: Move the weight to the left leg, turn the body leftward 45 degrees. The right hand holds and cuts the sword to upward-left, the sword-fingers touching on the right wrist, the tip of sword pointing to upward-right. Eyes look to the right (Fig.3-76).

Key to the movement: Moving the weight to the left, turning the body leftward and cutting upward with sword must be coordinated.

Fig. 3-76

ACTION 2: Move the weight to right leg, lift left leg with knee bent. Turn the body rightward 45 degrees. Right hand swings the sword above head to left, passing to the outside of left leg, and then raises it with tip pointing downward, both hands above the right shoulder. Eyes look to the lower-left (Fig.3-77).

Key to the movement: When moving the weight to the outside of left leg, shift the weight rightward and lift the left leg, the right knee bent and hip relaxed. The upper and lower parts of body must be coordinated.

Fig. 3-77

must be coordinated.

Fig. 3-78

Form 30 The Swallow Pecks at the Mud

ACTION 1: Turn the body leftward and lower it, drop the left foot forward, bend both legs to form a cross-legged sitting stance, the main weight remain on the right leg, the right heel raised. The right hand holds sword, the left hand presses on the right wrist. The force is focused at the tip of sword. Right hand pierces the sword downward, backward and upward in an arc with the tip of sword pointing upward. Eyes follows tip of sword and then look forward (Fig.3-78).

Key to the movement: The sword follows the body to lower, piercing the sword and body form must be coordinated.

ACTION 2: Turn the body rightward, move the weight onto the left leg and take a step forward with right foot. Both hand hold and pierce the sword upward, forward passing to the upper side of head, and then to rightward and downward in an arc. Following taking forward and piercing sword, the body turns from left to the right 90 degrees. Eyes look to the lower right (Fig.3-79).

Key to the movement: Piercing the sword in the left and right sides of body must be combined with the body form and footwork. They must be coordinated.

Usage: It is the skill of piercing and thrusting of the sword. It can be used to guard the body.

Fig. 3-79

Key to the movement: Separating the both hands, the shoulders relaxed and elbows lowered, the force of waist is held downward.

ACTION 3: Move the weight onto the right leg and take a step forward with left foot. At the same time, right hand holds sword, separate both hands from the front of abdomen to respective sides to the shoulder level. Eyes look forward (Fig.3-80).

Fig. 3-80

ACTION 4: Move the weight onto the left leg and take a big step with right foot. At the same time, swing both hands upward and close them above the head, and then point sword to lower front, the weight moving to the right leg. Eyes look to downward-front(Fig.3-81).

Fig. 3-81

Key to the movement: Both hands pointing with sword, the hips relaxed and waist lowered. Relax the wrist and use the force of wrist to point sword, the force is focused at the tip of sword.

Usage: Swinging the sword to point the wrist of opponent.

Form 31 Pluck the Star to Exchange the Plough

ACTION 1: Move the weight to leftward and take a step rear-right with right foot. Move the weight rightward. Following taking the step backward, turn the body from left to right 90 degrees. At the same time, both hands hold and sweep the sword from left to rightward-front at the chest level. Eyes look forward (Fig.3-82).

Fig. 3-82

ACTION 2: Turn the body to the left, bend both knees and relax hips to form a horse-stance. Both hands hold and swing the sword to in the front of chest, the tip of sword pointing upward. Eyes look forward (Fig.3-83).

Fig. 3-83

Key to the movement: Moving the weight, bending the knees and squatting down and swinging the sword to in the front of chest must be completed, collecting force to get ready for releasing.

ACTION 3: Turn the body leftward slightly and move the weight rightward slightly. The right hand holds the sword and left hand form sword-fingers. At the same time, push both hands forcefully and quickly to the respective sides of body at the shoulder level, the tip of sword pointing upward. Eyes look to forward-right(Fig.3-84).

Key to the movement: Releasing the force to the left and right must be completed, the waist lowered and hips relaxed, the "Qi" doesn't float.

Usage: If the opponent holds you in his arms from rear or attack to you from left or right side, you can push hands forcefully and quickly to extricate yourself.

Form 32 Scoop up the Moon from the Bottom of the Sea

ACTION 1: Turn the body leftward and move the weight to the left. Take a step forward-left with right foot. Bend the right knee and relax the hips to form a bow step. Following the taking the step, right hand holds and parries the sword from the right to the lower-left, the center of hand facing upward. Raise the left sword-fingers to above the head. Following the taking the step, turn the body leftward 135 degrees and lean it forward slightly. Eyes look to the lower front (Fig.3-85).

Key to the movement: Turning the body, taking the step and parrying the sword must be going on at the same time.

Usage: Take a big step forward, swing the sword to attack the opponent's groin.

ACTION 2: Shift the weight onto the left leg and lift the right leg with knee bent. The right hand holds and cut the sword forward and upward to head level, the force is focused at the edge of the sword. The left sword-fingers are pressing on the inside of right wrist. Eyes look to forward-right (Fig.3-86).

Key to the movement: Cutting upward with the sword, the force is

focused at the edge of the sword.

Usage: Cutting upward with sword from the opponent's groin.

Form 33 The Celestial Points a Way Out

ACTION: Take a step to forward-right with right foot and lift left leg with knee bent. The right hand holds and thrusts the sword from upside to the lower-right, swing the left sword-fingers to the upper-left. Eyes look downward right (Fig.3-87).

Key to the movement: Thrusting to downward-front with the sword, the body leans forward slightly. Use the left leg and left hand to keep the balance. Thrusting sword

can release the force.

Usage: Thrusting with the sword to the opponent's groin, knee or foot.

Form 34 The Phoenix Nods Its Head

ACTION 1: Turn the body leftward slightly and drop the left foot to the left with heel landing on the floor and tiptoes hooked upward. Right hand holds the sword and turns it inward, the tip of sword pointing downward. The left sword-fingers drops to the shoulder level. Eyes look to the rear-right (Fig.3-88).

Key to the movement: Turning the body, dropping left foot and turning sword inward must be

Fig. 3-88

Fig. 3-89

coordinated.

Usage: Thrusting forward with the sword, and then quickly turning the body and walking backward to feign defeat.

ACTION 2: Turn the body leftward slightly and move weight onto the left leg. Take a half step forward with the ball of right foot landing on the floor, the heel raised, the knee bent and hips relaxed. Swing the sword forward in an arc passing to the right side of body and then point backward, close the left hand with right hand. Eyes look to rear-right(Fig.3-89).

Key to the movement: Moving the weight leftward, taking the right step and turning wrist and pointing the sword must be continuous and coordinated, the knee bent and hips relaxed, the force of waist lowered.

Usage: Turning body to feign defeat, and then suddenly return to opponent.

Form 35 The Swallow Pecks at the Mud

ACTION 1: Skip a little step with right foot, and then lift left leg with knee bent. Right hand holds the sword, separate the both hands from upside passing to the front of body to respective lower, the tip of sword pointing downward right. Eyes look to the forward (Fig.3-90).

Key to the movement: Separating both hands downward and lifting left knee must be coordinated. The upper and lower

parts must be coordinated.

ACTION 2: Take a step to forward-left with left foot. And then take a step passing to the inside of left foot to the forward-left, move the weight to the right leg, both legs form a right bow step. At the same time, right hand holds the sword and swings it backward, upward, forward and point it downward. Swing the left hand upward and forward to close the right hand so the sword in both hands. Eyes look to downward-front (Fig.3-91).

Key to the movement: Pointing the sword with step forward, the force is focused at the tip of the sword.

Form 36 White Snake Spits Its Tongue

ACTION 1: Take a step forward with left foot so the feet together, the both legs bent slightly. Both hands hold the sword and thrust it horizontally forward at the waist level. Eyes look forward (Fig.3-92).

Key to the movement: Placing the feet together, the waist lowered. Both hands hold the sword, withdraw and lower it slightly, and then thrust it forward with combined force.

Usage: Combined with the force of waist to thrust to the opponent's chest or abdomen with sword.

Fig. 3-92

Fig. 3-93

Form 37 Flying Oblique

ACTION 1: Turn the body left and move the weight to the left. Take a step to the rear-right with right foot, both legs bent slightly. Right hand holding sword, both hands is closed to above the left knee, the tip of sword pointing to downward-front. Eyes look to downward-front(Fig.3-93).

Key to the movement: The hips relaxed and waist lowered, the force is focused at the left leg.

Usage: If the opponent attacks from the rear, you should turn body leftward shun the coming force, and take the right step and use the right foot to restrain his left foot.

ACTION 2: Turn the body rightward and move the weight in a lower arc to right leg. Bend the right leg and squat downward. The right hand hold the sword and slice it passing to the front of abdomen to upper-right, the tip pointing to upper-right, separate the left hand downward to beside outside of left knee, the sword-fingers pointing left and the center of hand facing upper-front. Eyes look forward-left (Fig.3-94).

Key to the movement: Slicing the sword, the body turning, the waist lowered. Following of the weight moving, the force is focused at the out edge of the sword.

Usage: continuing from previous movement. After shunning the coming force, quickly slice to

Fig. 3-94

rear-right with the sword.

Form 38 Hold the Weighty Leftward

ACTION 1: Turn the body rightward and move weight to the left, lift the right leg with knee bent. At the same time, right hand holds and withdraws the sword in the lower arc to the front of chest. Swing the left hand to close the right hand, both hands holding the handle of sword, the tip of sword pointing right. Eyes look forward (Fig.3-95).

Key to the movement: Shifting the weight, lifting knee, holding the sword, the shoulders and elbows relaxed, knee bent and hips relaxed. The "Qi" flows downward and the footwork is steady.

Fig. 3-95

ACTION 2: Take a step to forward-right with right foot and lift left leg with knee bent. The right leg bent slightly, the upper body lowered. Eyes look forward (Fig.3-96).

Fig. 3-96

Key to the movement: The footwork light and steady, the whole body coordinated. Save the force to prepare for applying.

ACTION 3: Take a step forward with the left foot, move the weight to the left leg to form a left bow step. At the same time, push the sword forward at the chest level, the tip of sword pointing right. Eyes look forward(Fig.3-97).

Fig. 3-97

Key to the movement: Take a big step with left foot, the right leg straight, the waist lowered and hips relaxed. Use the combined force of both arms to push the sword forward.

Usage: Pushing the sword leftward to parry the weapon of opponent, it can release the force.

Form 39 Hold the Weighty Rightward

ACTION 1: Turn the body rightward and move weight to the right. Lift left leg with knee bent slightly and bend the right leg slightly. Both hands swing the sword upward and leftward in an arc to the front of chest, tip of sword pointing leftward. Eyes look to forward-right (Fig.3-98).

Fig. 3-98

Key to the movement: Moving the weight, lifting left leg and turning the wrist to swing the sword must be coordinated.

ACTION 2: Drop the left foot forward and take a step forward with right foot passing to the inside of left foot. Move the weight to the right leg to form a bow step. At the same time, both hands push the sword horizontally to forward right, the tip of sword pointing right and lower the shoulder level (Fig.3-99).

Key to the movement: Take a big step with right foot, the left leg

straight, the waist lowered and hips relaxed. Use the combined force of both arms to push the sword forward.

Usage: Pushing the sword rightward to parry the weapon of opponent, it can release the shaking force.

Form 40 The Swallow Peck at the Mud

ACTION 1: Take a step forward passing to the inside of right foot with left foot toes touching on the floor and heel raised. Separate both hands downward to the respective side, the center of right hand facing the upper-front, the tip of sword pointing to downward right, the center of left sword-fingers facing forward. Eyes look forward (Fig. 3-100).

Key to the movement: Footwork is light, separating both hands downward to respective side in arcs.

ACTION 2: Move the weight leftward, take a big step forward with right foot.Move the weight to the right leg to form a right bow step. At the same time, swing both hands from respective side to above head and hold the sword to point forward. Eyes look at the tip of sword (Fig.3-101).

Key to the movement: Pointing forward with the sword and taking the right step must be advance, the hips relaxed and waist lowered.

Usage: Use the sword to point at the knee of the opponent.

Fig. 3-101

Fig. 3-102

Form 41 White Ape Presents Fruit

ACTION 1: Move the weight backward, and upper body leans backward. Swing both hands upward passing to the front of chest and then separate them to respective side in arcs, the sword passing to upside of the face. Eyes look the tip of sword(Fig.3-102).

Key to the movement: When the upper body leans backward, the hips relaxed and lowered, the weight steady. Right hand holds the sword and swings it outward.

Usage: If the opponent thrust with spear at my chest or throat, I lean the upper body backward quickly and swing the sword to parry it.

ACTION 2: Move the weight forward to form a bow step, lean the body forward. At the same time, right hand holds the sword and swings it over the head, and then slices horizontally to the forward right in an arc, the center of hand facing upward. Swing the left hand from left to right to close the right hand. Eyes look forward(Fig.3-103).

Fig. 3-103

Key to the movement: Leaning the body backward and slicing horizontally forward must be quick.

Usage: Continuing from previous movement. After supporting the spear of opponent, he still doesn't withdraw the spear, you should turn waist quickly and lean body forward, and swing the sword to slice the opponent's neck or head.

Form 42 Flowers FallingForm

ACTION 1: Move the weight leftward and turn the body to the left 80 degrees. Both hands hold the sword and cut it upward, the tip of sword pointing to upward-right over the shoulder. Eyes look rightward (Fig.3-104).

Fig. 3-104

Key to the movement: Cutting upward with the sword, turning the wrist and moving the weight must be combined with the turning of body. The movement is circular and natural.

ACTION 2: Both hands hold and swing the sword backward, downward passing to the left side of body, and then cut it to the upper-front in an arc. At the same time, take a step backward with right foot, move the weight to the right leg, turn the body rightward 180 degrees. Eyes follow the sword to move (Fig.3-105).

Fig. 3-105

Key to the movement: When cutting the sword to the upper-front, take the right step backward and turn the body, so the movements are smooth and natural.

ACTION 3: Both hands swing the sword backward, downward passing to the right side of the body, and then cut it upper-front in an arc. At the same time, take a step backward with left foot. Move weight leftward and turn the body left 150 degrees. Eyes look at the tip of sword (Fig3-106).

Fig. 3-106

Key to the movement: When the sword is arced to the upper-front of head, to take the step. Taking steps backward is such as in the "Step Backward and Whirl Arms".

Usage: These movements are done in stepping backward. Both hands hold and swing the sword upper-front in both sides of the body. It can protect body and prevent the opponent's attack. It can guard the head in the upper and protect the body in the lower.

Form 43 Thrusting Up and Down

ACTION 1: Turn the body first left and then right, move the weight to right leg, bend the right leg and relax hips. At the same time, both hands hold and swing it backward, downward passing to left side of body and raise it to the right-front of head, the tip of sword pointing to lower-left, center of right hand facing outward. Eyes follow the tip of sword to move (Fig.3-107).

Fig. 3-107

Key to the movement: When swinging the sword in left side of body and then raising it upward, the hips relaxed and waist lowered, the shoulders relaxed and the elbows held downward, the "Qi" follows to heels of feet.

ACTION 2: Turn the body rightward slightly. Move weight to left leg and lift right leg with knee bent, the foot in the front of groin. At the same time, both hands hold the handle of sword and move it forward in an arc, and then lower and draw it to front of abdomen, the tip of sword pointing upper-right. Eyes look to forward-right(Fig.3-108).

Fig. 3-108

Key to the movement: When holding and lowering the sword, the knee bent and hips relaxed, the upper and lower parts of body are combined, collecting force to get ready for releasing.

ACTION 3: Lower the body first£¬then raise it. Jump to forward-right with left foot with sole landing on the floor. The upper body doesn't change. Eyes look to forward-right (Fig.3-109).

Fig. 3-109

Key to the movement: Jumping forward, the footwork is light.

Usage: If the distance to opponent is far, it needs jumping forward to thrust with the sword.

ACTION 4: Take a big step rightward with right foot. Move the weight to right leg to form a bow step. Both hands hold and thrust the sword to the upper-right, tip of sword pointing the upper-right. Eyes look at the tip of sword (Fig.3-110).

Key to the movement: Taking the big step must be continued with moving weight forward quickly. The hips relaxed, waist lowered, the shoulders relaxed and elbows held down, the force is focused at the tip of the sword.

Usage: Take a big step

Fig. 3-110

forward and thrust the throat of the opponent with the sword.

ACTION 5: Turn the body leftward and move the weight to the right leg. Bend the wrists and swing the sword to the lower-left so it in the front of right chest, the tip pointing to the lower-left. Eyes follow the tip of sword and then look to the lower-left(Fig.3-111).

Fig. 3-111

Key to the movement: Turn the waist and twist hips quickly, rotate the arms and bend the wrists so the tip of sword pointing lower-left.

ACTION 6: Turn the body leftward slightly, move the weight to left leg, to form a bow step. At the same time, both hands hold the sword, following the moving of weight, thrust forward to the lower-left, the tip of sword pointing the lower front. Eyes look at the tip of the sword (Fig.3-112).

Fig. 3-112

Key to the movement: Following the moving of weight, thrust forward with sword, the waist lowered and hips relaxed, the force is focused at the tip of sword.

Usage: If the opponent attacks from the rear, you can turn and lower body quickly to avoid and then return in the lower.

Form 44 Oblique Flying

ACTION: Move the weight to the right leg, bend the right knee and squat down, the tiptoes of left foot turned inward. Turn the body rightward 45 degrees. At the same time, separate both hands respective side, the left sword-fingers to beside outside of the left leg, the fingers pointing left and center of hand facing forward. The right hand holds and slices the sword passing to front of the abdomen to the upper-right above the shoulder level, the tip of sword pointing to upper-right, the force is focused at the outer edge of the sword. Eyes look at the tip of sword(Fig.3-113).

Fig. 3-113

Keys to the movement: Slicing the sword to the upper-right and moving the weight must be coordinated, the waist lowered and the force is focused at the edge of sword.

Usage: Turn the body to the rear and swing the sword to slice the neck of opponent.

Form 45 Nezha Searches the Sea

ACTION 1: Turn the body to the right, move the weight onto the left leg and lift the right leg with the knee bent, the right foot is placed in the front of groin. At the same time, close both hands to in the front of abdomen, both hands holding the handle of sword, the tip of sword pointing forward at the waist level. Eyes look to forward-right (Fig.3-114).

Fig. 3-114

Key to the movement: When lifting the right leg, the knee bent and hips relaxed, waist lowered and elbows held down, the left leg straight, standing steadily like the Tai Mountain.

ACTION 2: Drop the right foot forward with the heel landing on the floor, the toes hooked upward. The left leg bent, the weight remaining on left leg. The upper body form doesn't change (Fig.3-115).

Fig. 3-115

Key to the movement: Dropping the right foot forward, lower the body to ready for jumping.

ACTION 3: Move the weight quickly to the right leg, the ball of right foot presses on the floor and bounce, lift the left foot and stride a step forward with the toes landing on the floor and lift the right foot in the front of groin. Both hands hold the sword. Eyes look forward (Fig.3-116).

Fig. 3-116

Key to the movement: It is the front movement of the skipping step, use the ball of the foot landing on the floor and have support from the elastic force of arch of foot to jump forward. It must be combined with the body technique.

Usage: It can be used to attack in the far distance or jump out from the surround.

ACTION 4: Stride forward with right foot. After landing, move the weight to the right leg to form a bow step. At the same time, both hands hold the sword and point it to the lower front, the tip pointing the lower front. Eyes look at the tip of sword(Fig.3-117).

Key to the movement: Striding the step and pointing sword must be

Fig. 3-117

advanced at the same time. When pointing the sword, shake the wrist to apply the force.

Form 46 Python Turns Over Its Body

ACTION 1: Turn the body leftward 40 degrees move the weight from right leg to the left leg. At the same time, right hand holds the sword and swings it to cut upward, the wrist rotating inward, the left sword-fingers is pressing on the inside of right wrist. Eyes look to forward-right (Fig.3-118).

Key to the movement: Turning of body, moving of weight and cutting upward with the sword must be coordinated.

Fig. 3-118

ACTION 2: Move the weight to the right leg and take a step forward passing to the inside of right foot with left foot. Turn the body from the left to the right 180 degrees. At the same time, both hands hold the sword and cut it upward passing to the left side of body. Eyes look at the tip of sword (Fig.3-119).

Fig. 3-119

Key to the movement: Stepping forward and turning of body must be coordinated.

ACTION 3: Turn the body rightward and move the weight to right leg to form a bow stance. The right hand holds the sword and swings it past the upper side of head, and then hack to the lower right, the tip of sword pointing to lower right. Separate the left sword-fingers to the upper-left above the shoulder level. Eyes look at the tip of sword (Fig.3-120).

Fig. 3-120

Key to the movement: Turning of the body and swinging arm to hack sword must be coordinated.

Usage: The movements 1-3 must be continuous. If the opponent attacks you from the rear, you can take a step forward, turn the body and swing arm to hack him with the sword.

Form 47 Weituo Presents a Pestle

ACTION 1: Turn the body leftward, rotate and turn the right wrist inward and withdraw the sword to the waist, the tip of sword pointing forward-left. Lower the left hand to the shoulder level. At the same time, turn the toes of left outward slightly. Eyes look to the forward-left (Fig.3-121).

Fig. 3-121

Key to the movement: Swinging the sword, turning of the wrist and turning of the body must be coordinated.

ACTION 2: Move the weight leftward and take a step passing to the inside of left foot with right foot.

Move the weight to right leg to form a bow step. Following stepping forward, turn the body leftward 180 degrees. At the same time, right hand holds the sword and thrust it horizontally forward with the center of hand facing upward. Withdraw the left sword-fingers to beside the left side of waist. Eyes look at the tip of sword(Fig.3-122).

Fig. 3-122

Key to the movement: Stepping forward, turning of body and thrusting sword forward must be coordinated.

Usage: If the opponent attacks from the rear, you can turn body quickly and thrust the sword forward.

Form 48 The Mill Stone Sword

ACTION 1: Move the weight to the left leg, the left knee bent. Lift and turn the toes of right foot outward, with the outside of the heel of right foot, the toes of right foot hooked upward. Right hand holds the sword and swings the sword from the upper to the left, the wrist rotating inward, the center of hand facing downward and the tip of sword pointing to the left. At the same time, turn the body rightward 75 degrees. Push the left sword-fingers forward to press on the right wrist. Eyes look at the tip of sword (Fig.3-123).

Fig. 3-123

Key to the movement: Moving the weight leftward, lift the toes of right foot and swing the sword to the left must be coordinated.

ACTION 2: Continue to turn the body rightward, drop the toes of right foot on the floor, move the weight to the right leg. Take a big step passing to the inside of right foot with left foot, the toes turned inward. At the same time, following the turning of body, right hand holds and sweeps the sword in a horizontal arc, the tip of sword pointing the left, the body turning rightward 90 degrees. Eyes look at the tip of sword (Fig.3-124).

Fig. 3-124

Key to the movement: Taking the step forward can change into a jump step, following the turning of body, using the force of waist to transport the sword.

ACTION 3: Continue to turn the body rightward. Move the weight to left leg, take a step passing to the rear of left foot to the rear-left with the right foot. Move the weight to the right leg, the right leg bent. Right hand holds and sweeps the sword in a horizontal arc, the tip of sword pointing the rear. At the same time, turn the body rightward 90 degrees. The eyes follow the tip of sword (Fig.3-125).

Fig. 3-125

Key to the movement: Continuing from previous movement. After taking the jump step and dropping the left foot on the floor, inserting backward with right foot and turning of body must be advancing at the same time and coordinated.

ACTION 4: Continuing from previous movement. Continue to turn the body rightward and move the weight to the right leg, the toes of left turned inward, the knee bent and hips relaxed. At the same time, right hand holds the sword and sweeps it passing to the front of chest to the right, the tip of sword pointing forward. Separate the left hand to the left the sword-fingers pointing upward and center of hand facing leftward. Eyes look forward (Fig.3-126).

Fig. 3-126

Usage: the meaning of "Millstone Sword" is sweeping the sword such as pushing the millstone round. If you are surrounded, you can sweep the sword round to brake out of their encirclement.

ACTION 5: Move the weight onto the right leg and lift the left leg. At the same time, both hands hold the sword to in the front of abdomen, the tip of sword pointing forward. Eyes look forward (Fig.3-127).

Key to the movement: When lifting the left leg and holding the sword, the knee bent and hips relaxed, the upper and lower parts of body must be coordinated.

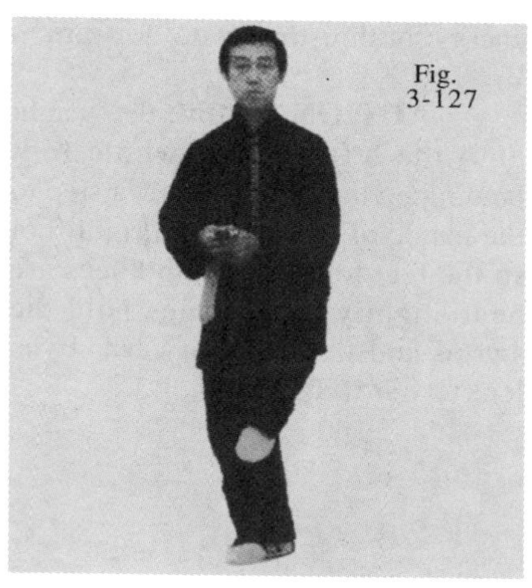
Fig. 3-127

ACTION 6: Bend the right knee and lower the body, take a step forward, the heel landing on the floor and the toes of foot hooked upward. The movements of upper limbs don't change(Fig.3-128).

Fig. 3-128

Key to the movement: Lowering the body to save the

energy for thrusting sword forward.

ACTION 7: Move the weight onto the left leg, the whole foot landing on the floor. Follow a step to the inside of left foot with right foot so the feet together. Both knees are bent slightly. Both hands hold the sword and thrust it forward. Eyes look forward (Fig.3-129).

Fig. 3-129

Key to the movement: Thrusting forward with the sword, the waist lowered and the shoulders relaxed, the force is focused at the tip of the sword.

Usage: The movement 5—7 must be continued from previous movement. After sweeping the sword round and then, thrust forward with the sword to brake out of opponent's encirclement.

Form 49 Finishing Form

ACTION 1: Turn the body leftward slightly, both hands swing sword to upper-left in an arc. Change the left hand into a palm and hold the handle of sword, the tip of sword pointing upward. The right hand is touching the handle of sword. Eyes look forward (Fig.3-130).

Fig. 3-130

ACTION 2: Both hands hold and lower the sword to beside the outside of left leg, the tip of sword pointing upward. The sword is parallel and leaning on the inside of left arm. Eyes look forward (Fig.3-131).

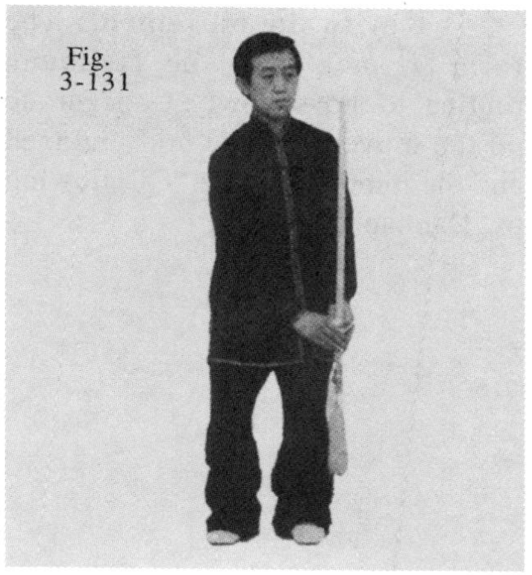
Fig. 3-131

ACTION 4: The body doesn't move. Separate both hands downward, outward and upward in the respective side of body with arms reverse twining. And then close the both hands to the upper-front of both shoulders, the centers of hands facing the lower front. The sword is parallel and touching the inside of left arm, the tip of sword pointing to the lower rear. Eyes look forward (Fig.3-133).

Fig. 3-133

ACTION 3: Separate the right sword-fingers passing to the front of abdomen beside the outside of the right leg, the tip of sword pointing upward. The left hand doesn't move. Eyes look forward (Fig.3-132).

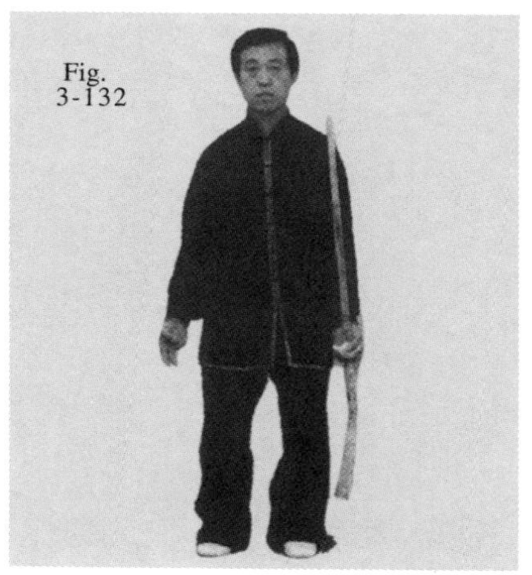
Fig. 3-132

ACTION 5: Press both hands downward at the same time and lower the body, both knees bent and hips relaxed, the "Qi" flows downward. Eyes look forward (Fig.3-134).

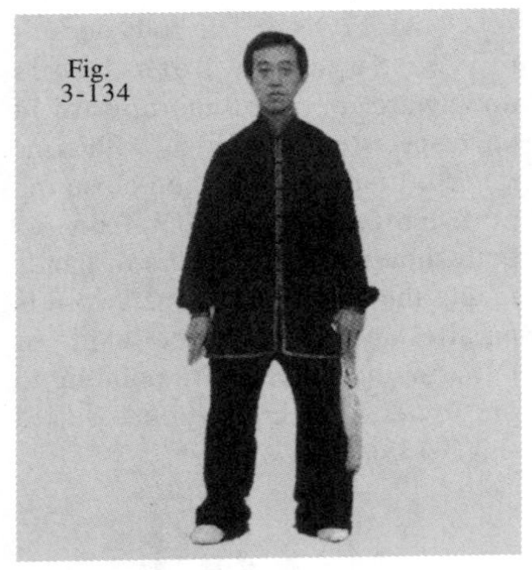

Key to the movement: The form is, such as in the Taijiquan routine, to move slowly. Concentrate on the movement, the body relaxed and the mind quiet, the "Qi" flowing to "Dantian".

ACTION 6: Drop both hands down to sides of body, the right hand touching the outer side of right leg, the sword-fingers pointing downward, the left hand holding the sword touching the outside of left leg. The body is upright, stand at attention with feet together (Fig.3-135).

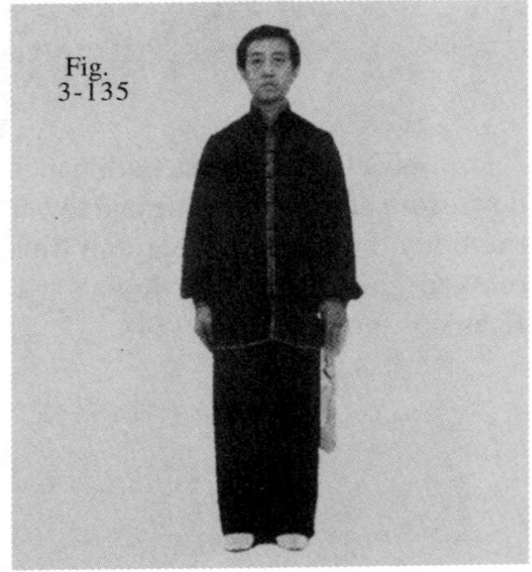

Chen-Style Taiji Single Broadsword Routine

I.The Synopsis of the Chen-style Taiji Single Broadsword Routine

The Chen-style Taiji Single Broadsword Routine is a kind of the Chen-style Taiji short weapons.There are thirteen movements in the routine, so it is called "the thirteen broadswords".

From 1930 to 1938,the famous Taijiquan master,the Chen-Family descendent of the eighteenth generation,Chen Zhaopi had added nine movements at the basic of original routine during teaching Taijiquan in Nanjing city.So it became the popular Taiji Single Broadsword routine in Chenjiagou village.

The Chen-style Taiji Single Broadsword routine is short and refined,the usages of the forms areclear.There are thirteen kinds of rolling,closing, pricking,blocking, cutting, hacking, scooping,cross-cutting, twisting,shaking,supporting, slicing and tilting.They really reflect the characteristics of the Chen-style Taiji Single Broadsword,combining hardness and softness in harmony,equaling stress the quickness and slowness,dodging and transfers,relaxing and nimble, springing and shaking,sticking to each other without being separated,twine to neutralize the force.It remains the momentum of liking a fierce tiger and cutting forcefully to the Hua Mountain. It's short weapon,but it can be used as long weapon.

When practising the Chen-style Taiji Single Broadsword, hands,eyes,body form and footwork must be well coordinated.The force is continuous and uninterrupted.The broadsword techniques are accurate,usages are clear,movements suit to the normal rules.To exercise Taiji broadsword,must use the "Chan-tou-guo-nao"(twining head and wrapping head),widely cutting and hacking with great momentum.It is said in the boxing proverbs: "when playing single broadsword,watch one's hand;when playing double-broadsword,watch one's footwork". So in the process of exercising,one must pay attention to that the hand combines with the broadsword.The right hand holds the broadsword,the left hand forms a palm,following the changes of broadsword techniques, sometimes swing left palm to support the broadsword upward,sometimes press on the back of broadsword to roll leftward or rightward,sometimes move it above the head to guard the head.Sometimes hack downward with broadsword and arc upward with left palm,sometimes prick forward with broadsword and push the left palm backward,in a word,the palm must be well coordinated with body form.

Practising the Chen-Style Taiji Single Broadsword, needs the skilled Taijiquan serving as the base, so the force released can reach the tips of limbs,and then returns to "Dantian".After the routine is skilled,the body transfers the broadsword to move,the broadsword leads the body to turn,so all movements serve the waist as a pivot and shake to release the force,they are majestic-looking.

II.Names of the Chen-style Taiji Single Broadsword Routine

Form 1 Starting Form

Form 2 Heart-protecting Broadsword

Form 3 Green Dragon Comes out of Water

Form 4 The Wind Scattering the Broken Flowers

Form 5 The White Cloud Right over Head

Form 6 Black Tiger Searches the Mountain

Form 7 Suqin Carries the Sword on His Back

Form 8 Golden Cock Stands on One Leg

Form 9 Roll and Close to the Coming Force

Form 10 Horizontally Cut the White Snake's Waist

Form 11 Three Rings Surrounding the Sun

Form 12 Dispel the Clouds and See the Sun

Form 13 Beat Grass to Look for the Snake on the Left

Form 14 Beat Grass to Look for the Snake on the Right

Form 15 Green Dragon Comes out of Water

Form 16 The Wind Scattering the Broken Flowers

Form 17 The Wild Goose Inserts

Golden Wings

Form 18 Yecha Searches the Sea

Form 19 Turn Over Body Leftward to Cut

Form 20 Turn Over Body Rightward to Cut

Form 21 White Snake Spits Out Its Tongue

Form 22 Holding the Moon in the Arms

Form 23 Finishing Form

III.The Diagram of the Chen-style Taiji Single Broadsword Play

Form 1 Starting Form

ACTION 1: Stand upright with feet together. The left hand grasps the guard of the broadsword,hanging the left arm to the left side of body,the left hand holding the handle,the tiger's mouth facing downward,the edge of broadsword facing forward and tip of broadsword pointing upward and the back of broadsword touching on the forearm.Hanging the right hand by the right side of body with the fingers closed naturally. Eyes look forward (Fig.4-1).

Key to the movement: Keep the body and head upright and natural, the entire body relaxed,the tip of the tongue resting on the hard palate and breathe naturally.The hips relaxed,the balls of feet,tiptoes,outside of feet and heels must grasp on the floor. The "Yongquan" is empty. The "Qi" flows to "Dantian".Concentrate on the movement.

Fig. 4-1

ACTION 2: Take a step with the left foot so the feet are shoulder-width apart.The knees bent and hips relaxed(Fig.4-2).

Key to the movement: Eyes look forward,concentrate on the movement, the hips relaxed,knees bent,the "Qi" settle downward.

Usage: Relax the whole body so the "Qi" settles to the tips of body,and get ready to meet an approaching enemy.

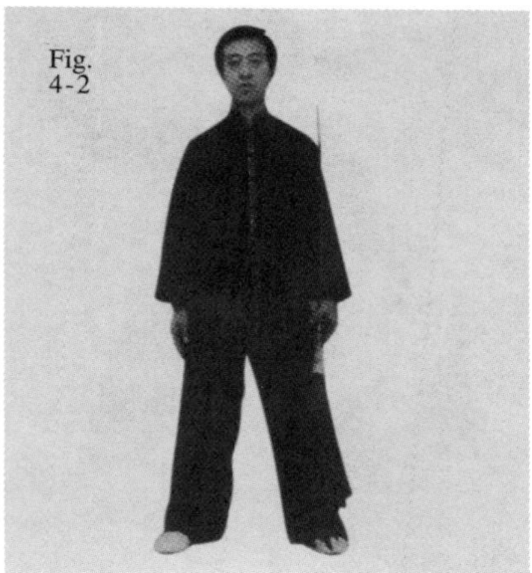
Fig. 4-2

Fig. 4-3

ACTION 3: Continuing from previous movement.Turn the toes of right foot,bend the knee and relax the hips.Take a half step to forward-left with left foot,the inside of heel landing on the floor,the toes hooked upward and turned inward.At the same time,ward both hands to the upper-right to the shoulder level,the left hand in front and the right hand in rear(Fig.4-3).

Key to the movement:the entire body remains the twining force,the Qi flows to the feet and hands.Turning the body,the waist serves as an axis.The footwork must be light and natural.

Usage: Warding the opponent's fist or weapon off,and then lift the left foot to kick at the leg or waist of the opponent.

ACTION 4: Continuing from previous movement.Move the weight forward,take a step forward with right foot passing to the inside of left foot,the tiptoes of right foot landing on the floor and heel raised.The left leg bent and hip relaxed.At the same time,swing the both hands downward and forward in arcs to the front of chest,extend the right hand to hold the handle of broadsword(Fig.4-4).

Key to the movement: Taking the right foot forward,the footwork must be light and natural.The movements of hands and feet must be coordinated.

Usage: Taking the right step forward,can use the right foot to kick at the opponent's leg,groin or abdomen.

Fig. 4-4

Fig. 4-5

Form 2 Heart-protecting Broadsword

ACTION 1: Continuing from previous movement.Withdraw a half step with the right foot,the knee bent and hip relaxed.At the same time,right hand withdraws the broadsword backward and hides it in the rear-right of body,tip of broadsword pointing forward and edge of broadsword facing downward.At the same time,push the left palm forward at the eyes level. While withdrawing broadsword,pushing left palm forward,the upper body turns leftward 15 degrees.Eyes look forward over the left palm(Fig.4-5).

ACTION 2: Continuing from previous movement.The right hand holds and swings the broadsword backward,upward,forward and downward in an arc to the front of left side of chest,the edge of broadsword facing outward.Left palm swings leftward,upward,rightward and downward in an arc to press on the back of broadsword.At the same time,withdraw a half step backward with left foot tiptoes touching on the floor and heel raised.Following withdrawing the step backward,the body turns leftward 60 degrees.Eyes look forward(Fig.4-6).

Key to the movement: The previous movements must be continuous.The emptiness and solid must be clear.The "Qi" settles to "Dantian",the force is focused at the palm.

Fig. 4-6

Usage: It is a defense movement,is used to "wait for movement with stillness",to guard the main entrance of body.The left foot is empty step, so it can move nimbly and the body turn swiftly.It's ready at all time to defense the attack of the opponent in the all directions.If the opponent thrusting the spear at the main entrance of your body,you can roll and close to neutralize opponent's attack with broadsword.

Form 3 Green Dragon Comes out of Water

ACTION 1: Continuing from previous movement.Lift the left leg with the knee bent.The upper body turns leftward 15 degrees.Following of turning of body,rotate the right hand inward and push the broadsword to the upper-left,the left arm rotating outward,the left palm pressing on the back of broadsword,the edge of broadsword facing left.Eyes look forward(Fig.4-7,the reverse side of Fig.4-7).

Fig. 4-7

Fig.4-7 supplemental

Key to the movement: Pushing the broadsword,turning body and lifting left leg must be coordinated and quick.

Usage: If the opponent thrust to my chest with the spear,I turn body quickly and swing the broadsword to stick the spear so cause his attack to be ineffective,and thrust to the wrist or abdomen of the opponent.

ACTION 2: Continuing from previous movement.Land and stamp the left foot on the floor,and lift the right leg with knee bent.The body turns leftward 90 degrees,continue to rotate the right arm inward so the edge of broadsword facing forward.The left palm is pressing on the back of broadsword.Eyes look to forward-right(Fig.4-8,the reverse side of Fig.4-8).

Key to the movement: Bend the right knee,lower the body and lift

Fig. 4-8

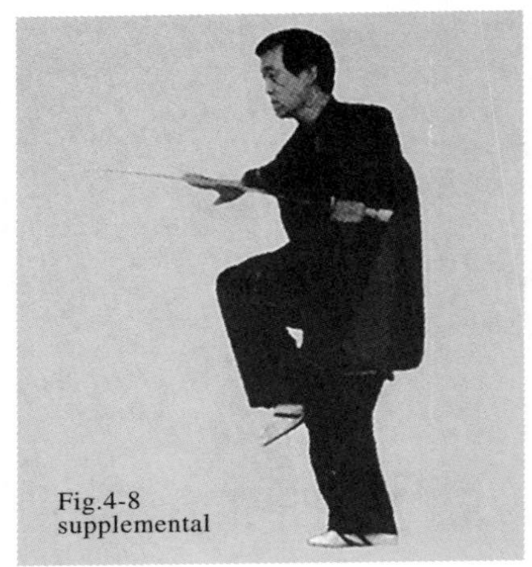

Fig.4-8 supplemental

right leg,collect the force for releasing.

ACTION 3: Continuing from previous movement.Take a big step to the right,move weight rightward,both legs form a right bow step.At the same time,right hand holds and thrusts the broadsword rightward to the shoulder level,the edge of broadsword facing forward.Swing the left palm leftward in an arc to the shoulder level.Eyes look to forward right(Fig.-4-9).

Key to the movement: Taking the right step,thrusting forward with broadsword and pushing left palm must be completed at the same time.The speed is quick and the force must be smooth.

Usage: It is same as the previous movement.

Fig. 4-9

Fig. 4-10

Fig.4-10 supplemental

Form 4 The Wind Scattering the Broken Flowers

ACTION 1: Continuing from previous movement.Lift the left knee to in the front of right knee.At the same time,right hand holds and swings the broadsword rightward,backward and forward in an arc to the upside of forehead,the right arm rotating outward so the tip of broadsword pointing downward. Withdraw the left palm to in the front of chest(Fig.4-10,the reverse side of Fig.4-10).

Key to the movement: Swinging the broadsword around the head,the back of broadsword must be near the body,the edge of broadsword facing outward.

Usage: Swing the broadsword to parry the opponent's weapon.

ACTION 2: Continuing from previous movement.Drop the left foot to the outside of right foot,and then take a step rightward with right foot,move the weight rightward to form a right bow step.At the same time,cut horizontally to the right with broadsword,passing to the front of chest,the edge of broadsword facing rightward and tip of broadsword pointing forward,is a little lowered than the shoulder.Eyes look at the tip ofbroadsword(Fig.4-11).

Fig. 4-11

Key to the movement: Cutting horizontally with broadsword and pushing left palm,pay attention that the waist serves an axis to initiate the movements of the arms,the force through the shoulder and elbow,ultimately concentrated at the edge of the broadsword.The lower section must be steady.

Form 5 The White Cloud Right over Head

ACTION: Continuing from previous movement.Withdraw a half step with the left foot tiptoes landing on the floor and heel raised.At the same time,rotate the right hand inward so the tip of broadsword points downward,and swing it downward,leftward to in the front of abdomen.Left hand moves to the front of abdomen from leftward and press the back of broadsword.Both hands support the broadsword to upper-front of forehead,the edge of broadsword facing upward,the tip of broadsword pointing leftward.Eyes look to the upper-front(Fig.4-12).

Fig. 4-12

Key to the movement: Both hands must be moved in the front of abdomen,the left palm presses on the back of broadsword,and then the body lowered slightly,the hips relaxed,the wrists bent upward,turn the broadsword so the edge of broadsword faces upward.Supporting the broadsword upward must use the force of waist and legs.

Usage: If the opponent thrust to my face or throat,I swing broadsword to support it.

Form 6 Black Tiger Searches the Mountain

ACTION 1: Continuing from previous movement. Lift left leg with knee bent and turn the body leftward 90 degrees.At the same time,both hands swing the broadsword forward, downward to the outside of left shank,the left hand pressing on the back of the broadsword.Eyes look at the back of broadsword(Fig.4-13).

Fig. 4-13

Key to the movement: Left hand holds and lowers the broadsword.Right hand pushes the broadsword.Turning the body and lifting the left leg must be completed at the same time.

Usage: Continuing from previous movement.After supporting the opponent's weapon,pushes the broadsword forcefully with right hand,left hand holds and lowers the broadsword,and then turn the body and lift the left leg to neutralize opponent's attack to be ineffective. And take a step forward and thrust to the throat or chest of the opponent with broadsword.

ACTION 2: Land and stamp the left foot and lift right foot with knee bent.Turn the body leftward 90 degrees.At the same time,both hands swing the broadsword downward, backward,upward and rightward in an arc so the tip of broadsword points rightward,the edge of broadsword facing forward,at the shoulder level,the left palm pressing on the broadsword.Eyes look forward(Fig.4-14).

Key to the movement: Upper and lower limbs must be coordinated,both hands collect the force to get ready for releasing.

Fig. 4-14

Fig. 4-15

ACTION 3: Take a step rightward with right foot,the tiptoes turn outward.Move the weight to the right to form a right bow step.At the same time,thrust the broadsword passing to the front of chest to the right at the shoulder level,the elbow bent slightly,the tip of broadsword pointing rightward and edge of broadsword facing upward. Push the left palm passing to the front of chest to the left at the shoulder level.Eyes look foraward(Fig.4-15).

Key to the movement: The body and the broadsword must be coordinated. Thrusting broadsword with the elastic-shaking force,it must be coordinated with the left hand.

Usage: It can be used to thrust and cut upward with broadsword in the short distance,not counting the first usage in the action 1.

Form 7 Suqin Carries the Sword on His Back

ACTION: Continuing from previous movement.Turn the toes of left foot outward, move the weight to left leg.Turn the body leftward 90 degrees.Take a step passing to the inside of left foot with right foot toes landing on the floor and heel raised.At the same time,drag the broadsword touching on the right shoulder,the tip of broadsword pointing backward and edge of broadsword facing upward,left hand pressing on the handle of broadsword.Eyes look forward(Fig.4-16).

Key to the movement: The

Fig. 4-16

upper and lower parts movments must be coordinated,the shoulders relaxed and elbows lowered,the knees bent and hips relaxed,the emptiness and solidness are clearly demarcated.

Usage: It is a defense movement,stillness controlling the movement.

Form 8 Golden Cock Stands on One Leg

ACTION: Continuing from previous movement.Withdraw a step backward with right foot passing to the inside of left foot,move the weight to the right leg.At the same time,loosen left hand.Right hand swings the broadsword backward, downward,forward and upward to in the front of chest,edge of broadsword facing forward and tip pointing upward,left hand presses on the back of broadsword.Eyes look forward(Fig.4-17).

Fig. 4-17

Key to the movement: Changing steps must be nimble and steady.Right hand swinging the broadsword,the wrist must nimble,and combined with the force of waist.

Usage: If the opponent thrusting at my chest with broadsword,I step backward and swing the broadsword to stick it,roll and parry out,and then thrust forward.

Form 9 Roll and Close to the Coming Force

ACTION: Continuing from

previous movement.Turn the body leftward about 10 degrees.Right hand holds and rolls the broadsword inward so the edge of broadsword faces leftward,the left hand pressing on the back of broadsword.Eyes look forward(Fig.4-18).

Fig. 4-18

Key to the movement: The weight must be steady.The force is focused at the edge of broadsword.

Usage: If the opponent thrust to left side of my chest with the spear,I swing the broadsword to parry,roll and close leftward to neutralize opponent's attack,and then thrust at him.If the opponent thrust to right side of my chest with the spear,I swing the broadsword to parry,roll and close rightward to neutralize opponent's attack,and then thrust at him.

Form 10 Horizontally Cut the White Snake's Waist

ACTION 1: Continuing from previous movement.Turn the heel of left outward,the ball of left foot serving as a pivot.The right foot inserts a step to the rear-left behind the left leg.And then turn the body rightward 180 degrees.At the same time,following the turning of body,right hand holds and slices the broadsword from left to right,left hand pressing on the back of broadsword.Eyes look to forward-left(Fig.4-19).

Fig. 4-19

Key to the movement: Inserting the step and turning body must be quick.The bodywork must be steady.

Usage: If the opponent thrusts to the right side of my chest with the spear, I swing broadsword to parry, roll and close it rightward to neutralize his attack, and then insert step and turn body, swing broadsword to cut his waist.

ACTION 2: Continuing from previous movement. Continue to turn the body rightward 135 degrees,, move the weight to right leg to form a right bow step. At the same time, following the turning of body, right hand swings the broadsword passing to the front of chest to cut rightward, tip of broadsword pointing forward and edge of broadsword facing backward, at the shoulder level. Push the left palm leftward. Eyes look to forward-right(Fig.4-20).

Fig. 4-20

Key to the movement: The bodywork must be steady, the left and right hands must be coordinated.

Usage: Continuing from previous movement. Left hand grips the spear of opponent, and drags and presses it to cause the opponent near me, and swing the broadsword to cut forcefully at his waist.

Form 11 Three Rings Surrounding the Sun (I)

ACTION 1: Right hand rotates inward and sweeps the broadsword horizontally passing to the front of chest to the left, the edge of broadsword facing leftward, the tip of broadsword pointing forward at the knee level. Withdraw and press the left palm on the right forearm. Following the sweeping of broadsword, turn the body leftward 90 degrees, the weight moving to the left leg (Fig.4-21).

Fig. 4-21

Key to the movement: Sweeping broadsword must be quick,the body lowered.

Usage: If you are surrounded,you can sweep his lower section with broadsword,and cut in jump step and cross-legged sitting stance.Sweep three around and cut three times with broadsword to break through encirclement.

ACTION 2: Continuing from previous movement.Take a step forward with right foot passing to the inside of left foot.Following stepping forward,turn the body leftward 90 degrees,knees bent and hips relaxed,the weight is mainly on the left leg (Fig.4-22).

Fig. 4-22

Key to the movement: When taking the right step you can jump.The body must be upright, doesn't lean forward or backward.

ACTION 3: Continuing from previous movement.Left foot inserts to the rear-right behind right leg,bend knees to form a cross-legged resting stance.At the same time,right hand rotates outward and swings the broadsword downward,leftward and upward to the outside of left shoulder,the edge of broadsword facing upward,the tip of broadsword pointing leftward.Left palm is pressing on the right arm in the front of right shoulder.Eyes look to forward-right(Fig.4-23).

Fig. 4-23

Key to the movement: Forming the cross-legged resting stance,the both hands crossed,the shoulders relaxed,both arms warding outward,the "Qi"flowing downward.

ACTION 4: Continuing from previous movement.Both hands continue to ward the broadsword upward to the upper-front of head,the edge of broadsword facing upward,the tip of broadsword pointing to the lower-left,the left palm pressing on the back of right hand.Eyes look forawrd(Fig.4-24).

Fig. 4-24

Key to the movement: Lower the body and ward the both arms upward,to collect the form for releasing.

ACTION 5: Continuing from previous movement.Right hand holds and swing the broadsword to downward right,the edge of broadsword facing downward,tip of broadsword pointing the upper-right.At the same time,press the left palm to the lower-left,it is lowered than the shoulder.Eyes look to forward-right(Fig.4-25).

Fig. 4-25

Key to the movement: Cutting broadsword and pressing palm must be quick,the body lowered.

Three Rings Surrounding the Sun (II)

ACTION 1: Continuing from previous movement.Right hand rotates inward and sweeps the broadsword horizontally passing to the front of body to the left.Swing the left palm to press on the right hand.Following the sweeping of broadsword,turn the body leftward 90 degrees.Move the weight to the right leg,the left leg bent and kneel half down,the ball of left foot landing on the floor and heel raised.Eyes look forward(Fig.4-26).

Fig. 4-26

Fig. 4-27

Key to the movement: The body must be lowered.The speed of sweeping with broadsword must be quick.

Usage: The same as the previous "Three Rings Surrounding the Sun(I)".

ACTION 2: Continuing from previous movement.Continue to sweep the broadsword leftward, backward,turn the body to the left 180 degrees,move the weight to the left leg,right leg bent and the heel of right foot raised, left palm pressing on the right hand.Eyes look forward(Fig.4-27).

ACTION 3: Continuing from previous movement. Take a step forward passing to the inside of left foot with right foot. Following taking the step with right foot, turn the body leftward 90 degrees, both legs form a semi-horse stance, the weight is main on the left leg. Eyes look to forward-right(Fig.4-28).

Fig. 4-28

Key to the movement: Keep the body upright, the shoulders relaxed and elbows lowered, the waist lowered and groin round and empty. Both arms remain the warding-off force. The "Qi" follows to the tips of body.

ACTION 4: Continuing from previous movement. Left foot inserts a step behind the right leg, both legs bent. At the same time, right hand rotates outward and swings broadsword leftward passing to the front of body to the outside of left shoulder, the edge of broadsword facing upward. Move the left palm to press on the right arm in the front of right shoulder. Eyes look to forward-right (Fig.4-29).

Fig. 4-29

Key to the movement: Forming the cross-legged resting stance, the both hands crossed, the shoulders relaxed, both arms warding outward, the "Qi" flowing downward.

ACTION 5: Continuing from previous movement. Continue to ward off both hands upward to the upside of head, the left palm pressing on the back of right hand, the edge of broadsword facing upward. Eyes look forward (Fig.4-30).

Fig. 4-30

Key to the movement: Lowering the body, the both arms are warded off to form a circle form, to collect the energy for releasing.

ACTION 6: Continuing from previous movement. Right hand swings the broadsword upward, rightward passing to the upside of head and cut to downward-right, the edge of broadsword facing downward and tip of broadsword pointing to upward-right. At the same time, press the left palm passing to the upside of head to downward-left, it's lowered slightly than the shoulder. Eyes look to forward-right(Fig.4-31).

Fig. 4-31

Key to the movement: Cutting with the broadsword and pressing the palm must be coordinated, the body is lowered and the speed is quick.

Explain: The previous 1-6 movements must be continued.

Three Rings Surrounding the Sun (III)

ACTION 1: Continuing from previous movement. Right hand rotates inward and sweeps the broadsword horizontally passing to the front of body to the left. Swing the left palm to press on the right hand. Following the sweeping of broadsword, turn the body leftward 90 degrees. Move the weight to the right leg,the left leg bent and kneel half down,the ball of left foot landing on the floor and heel raised. Eyes look forward(Fig.4-32).

Fig. 4-32

Key to the movement: The body must be lowered. The speed of sweeping with broadsword must be quick.

ACTION 2: Continuing from previous movement. Continue to sweep the broadsword to leftward, backward,turn the body to left 180 degrees, move the weight to the left leg, right leg bent and the heel of right foot raised, left palm pressing on the right hand. Eyes look forward(Fig.4-33).

Fig. 4-33

Key to the movement: keep the body upright, the shoulders relaxed and elbows lowered, the waist lowered and groin round and empty. Both arms remain the warding-off force. The"Qi"follows to the tips of body.

ACTION 3: Continuing from previous movement. Take a step forward passing to the inside of left foot with right foot. Following taking the step with right foot,turn the body leftward 90 degrees,both legs form a semi-horse stance,the weight is mainly on the left leg. Eyes look to forward-right (Fig.4-34).

Fig. 4-34

ACTION 4: Continuing from previous movement. Left foot inserts a step behind the right leg, both legs bent. At the same time, right hand rotates outward and swings broadsword leftward passing to the front of body to the outside of left shoulder, the edge of broadsword facing upward. Move the left palm to press on the right arm in the front of right shoulder. Eyes look to forward-right(Fig.4-35).

Fig. 4-35

Key to the movement: Forming the cross-legged resting stance, both hands crossed, the shoulders relaxed, both arms warding off outward, the "Qi" flowing downward.

ACTION 5: Continuing from previous movement. Continue to ward off both hands upward to the upside of head, the left palm pressing on the back of right hand, the edge of broadsword facing upward. Eyes look forward(Fig.4-36).

Fig. 4-36

Key to the movement: Lowering the body, both arms are raised to ward off,forming a circle form, to collect the energy for releasing.

ACTION 6: Continuing from previous movement. Right hand swings the broadsword upward, rightward passing to the upside of head and cut to downward-right, the edge of broadsword facing downward and tip of broad, sword pointing to upward-right. At the same time, press the left palm passing to the upside of head to the lower-left, it's lowered slightly than the shoulder. Eyes look to forward-right(Fig.4-37).

Fig. 4-37

Key to the movement: Cutting with the broadsword and pressing the palm must be coordinated. The body is lowered and the speed is quick.

Explanation: The previous 1-6 movements must be continuous.

Form 12 Dispel the Clouds and See the Sun

ACTION 1: Continuing from previous movement. Take a step rightward passing to the front of the left foot with the right foot, move the weight to left leg to form a left bow step. Right hand holds and swings the broadsword passing to the front of body in a lower arc to the left of body, the edge of broadsword facing upper-left, the left palm pressing on the back of broadsword. Following of sweeping the broadsword.Turn the body leftward 45 degrees. Eyes look to forward-right (Fig.4-38).

Fig. 4-38

Key to the movement: Footwork must be light, the waist lowered.

Usage: If the opponent attacking to my head, I should take a step backward and swing broadsword to support the weapon of opponent.

ACTION 2: Continuing from previous movement. Move the weight rightward, withdraw a half step backward with ball of right foot landing on the floor,the heel raised. At the same time, both hands support the broadsword upward to the upside of forehead, the left palm supporting the back of the broadsword. Eyes look forward(Fig.4-39).

Fig. 4-39

Key to the movement: Withdrawing the step backward and supporting with the broadsword must be coordinated, the legs bent and hips relaxed, the chest hold inward and waist relaxed, both hands warding off forming a circle.

Form 13 Beat Grass to Look for the Snake On the Left

ACTION 1: Continuing from previous movement. Take step to the forward-left with left foot, right foot inserts a step behind the left leg, both legs form a cross-legged sitting stance. At the same time,right hand holds and left hand press on the back of broadsword, both hands parry with the broadsword to the lower-left, tip of broadsword pointing upward. Turn the body leftward 45 degrees(Fig.4-40).

Fig. 4-40

Key to the movement: Footwork must be light and natural, the force is focused at the edge of broadsword.

Usage: If the opponent thrusting to my left leg with the spear, I can step sideward and squat down, and parry with broadsword and stick the spear, return according to opponent's posture.

Form 14 Beat Grass to Look for the Snake on the Right

ACTION 1: Continuing from previous movement. Take a step to forward-right with right foot, left foot inserts a step behind the right leg ,both legs form a cross-legged sitting stance. At the same time, right hand holds and left hand press on the back of broadsword, both hands parry with the broadsword to the lower-right, tip of broadsword pointing downward. Turn the body rightward 45 degrees (Fig.4-41).

Fig. 4-41

Key to the movement: Taking the step rightward and inserting the left foot must be quick, the body lowered. Turn the body rightward and use the shaking-force to push the back of broadsword outward.

Usage: If the opponent thrusting to my right leg with the spear, I insert a step and squat downward quickly and parry outward with broadsword, return according to opponent's posture.

Form 15 Green Dragon Comes out of Water

ACTION 1: Continuing from previous movement. Lift the left leg with the knee bent to form an independent stance. At the same time, right hand swings the broadsword lefward and forward in an arc, the edge of broadsword facing leftward and tip of broadsword pointing forward, the left palm pressing on the back of broadsword. Following lifting left leg and swinging broadsword, turn the body leftward 90 degrees. Eyes look forward(Fig.4-42).

Key to the movement: Turning the body, lifting left leg and swinging broadsword must be completed,the upper and lower parts must be coordinated. The bodywork is natural and light.

Usage: Swinging the broadsword to parry the weapon of opponent.

Fig. 4-42

ACTION 2: Continuing from previous movement. Stamp downward with left foot and lift the right leg with knee bent. Turn the body leftward 40 degrees. Right hand raises the broadsword upward and withdraws it backward slightly to in the front of left side of chest, the left palm pressing on the back of broadsword, the back of broadsword near the chest, the tip of broadsword pointing rightward. Eyes look forward(Fig.4-43).

Key to the movement: Stamping downward with left foot, the whole body collecting the energy for releasing.

Usage: Swinging the broadsword leftward, the edge of broadsword facing outward to stick and close the sharp of the weapon of opponent.

Fig. 4-43

Fig. 4-44

ACTION 3: Continuing from previous movement. Take a big step with right foot, move the weight rightward to form a right bow step. At the same time, right hand holds and thrusts forward with the broadsword at the shoulder level, edge of broadsword facing forward. Push the left palm leftward in an arc at the shoulder level. Eyes look to forward-right(Fig.4-44).

Key to the movement: Thrusting forward with the broadsword and taking forward with right foot must be completed at the same time. The force is focused at the tip of broadsword.

Usage: Take a big step forward and swing broadsword along the butt of spear to thrust the opponent's chest or throat.

Form 16 The Wind Scattering the Broken Flowers

ACTION 1: Continuing from previous movement. Move the weight to the right leg, lift the left leg in the front of right knee. At the same time, right hand rotates outward and swings the broadsword backward, leftward and upward passing to the back of body to upside of forehead. Withdraw the left palm to in the front of chest(Fig.4-45).

Key to the movement:lifting the left leg and swinging the broadsword passing to the back of body, the hips relaxed, the footwork is light.

Fig. 4-45

Fig. 4-46

Usage: The form is wrap-head broadsword, is used to guard the head.

ACTION 2: Continuing from previous movement. Drop the left foot to the outside of right foot. And then take a step rightward with right foot, move the weight rightward to form a right bow step. At the same time, right hand holds and swings the broadsword passing to the front of chest to cut horizontally rightward at the shoulder level, the edge of broadsword facing rightward and tip of broadsword pointing forward. Push the left palm leftward at the shoulder level. Eyes look to forward-right(Fig.4-46).

Key to the movement: Cutting horizontally with broadsword and pushing the left palm, pay attention to that the waist serves as an axis to release force, flowing through the shoulder and elbow, and ultimately concentrated at the edge of broadsword. The body must be upright and lower section must be steady.

Usage: Swing the broadsword to cut opponent's waist.

Form 17 The Wild Goose Inserts Golden Wings

ACTION 1: Continuing from previous movement. Right hand holds and cuts the broadsword upward, leftward and downward in an arc.Move the left palm to under the right armpit, fingers of palm pointing upward. Following the cutting with the broadsword, move weight leftward to form a left bow step,turn the body leftward 90 degrees. Eyes look forward(Fig.4-47).

Fig. 4-47

Key to the movement: Cutting to downward-left with broadsword, moving the weight must be combined with force of waist and groin, the force is focused at the edge of broadsword.

Usage: Swing the broadsword to cut the opponent coming from the left.

ACTION 2: Continuing from previous movement. Move the weight onto the left leg and lift the right leg with knee bent. At the same time, right hand rotates inward, continue to swing the broadsword downward, backward to in the outside of left leg, edge of broadsword facing forward, tip of broadsword pointing downward. Move the left palm to in the front of chest.Eyes look at the back of broadsword(Fig.4-48).

Fig. 4-48

Key to the movement: Standing on the left leg must be steady, the knee bent and hips relaxed. The upper and lower parts of body must be combined. The force is focused at the back of broadsword.

Usage: It's the technique of windmill and parry with broadsword, the force is focused at the back of broadsword to neutralize opponent's weapon.

ACTION 3: Continuing from previous movement. Stamp to the inside of left foot with right foot and lift the left leg with knee bent to form an independent stance. At the same time, raise the broadsword to in the front of chest, push the left palm to lower-left. Eyes look to the lower-left(Fig.4-49).

Fig. 4-49

Key to the movement: The upper and lower parts of body must be combined, the right leg must be steady, the left leg bent and hips relaxed.

Usage: Raising the broadsword up to parry the weapon of opponent. Lifting the left leg can kick to the lower section of the opponent.

ACTION 2: Continuing from previous movement. Bend the right leg and lower the weight. Take a step to forward left with left foot, the inside of the left heel, tiptoes hooked and turned inward(Fig.4-50).

Key to the movement: The weight is on main the right leg. Taking the left step, use the inside of

Fig. 4-50

left heel sliding along the floor. Raising the broadsword up and pushing the left palm must be remained the open force.

ACTION 3: Continuing from previous movement. Move the weight to the left leg and lift right leg with knee bent. Turn the body leftward 15 degrees. At the same time, right hand holds and swings the broadsword rightward, downward and upward in an arc to the outside of left shoulder, the edge of broadsword facing leftward and tip of broadsword pointing upward. Eyes look to forward-right(Fig.4-51).

Key to the movement: The body is upright, the leg bent slightly and hips relaxed, the right knee closed inward. The broadsword is hided in the left side of the body. The force is focused at the tip of

Fig. 4-51

Fig. 4-52

broadsword.

Usage: Hiding the broadsword and covering the head, attack dwells in defense.

Form 18 Yecha Searches the Sea

ACTION 1: Continuing from previous movement. Stamp right foot to the inside of left foot, and then take a step forward-left with left foot. At the same time, swing the broadsword to in the left side of body, tip pointing forward and edge of broadsword facing downward. Lower the left palm to the front of chest. Eyes look forward(Fig.4-52).

Key to the movement: Following the stamping, the "Qi" settles down, the weight is on the right. The broadsword is hided in the rear-right of body. Taking a step forward with the left foot, the footwork must be light.

Usage: Swing the broadsword rightward to neutralize the opponent's attack, and then swing it to cut or thrust at the opponent.

ACTION 2: Continuing from previous movement. Move the weight leftward to form a left bow step. At the same time, press the left palm on the left side of waist with the thumb behind and the other fingers in front. The right hand swings the broadsword upward, leftward and thrust to the left,the tip of broadsword. Eyes look to the forward-left(Fig.4-53).

Key to the movement: Shifting the weight and thrusting the broadsword must be coordinated. Thrusting to the left with broadsword must be combined with the turning of waist and groin. The force is focused at the tip of broadsword.

Usage: Swing the broadsword to support the opponent's weapon and thrust to chest or abdomen of the opponent.

Form 19 Turn Over Body Leftward to Cut

ACTION 1: Continuing from previous movement. Move the weight to the left leg and lift the right leg,knee bent and hips relaxed. Following lifting the right leg, turn the body rightward 90 degrees. At the same time, swing the left palm to in the front of head. The right hand swings the broadsword to in the right side of body, the tip of broadsword pointing forward and edge of broadsword facing downward. Eyes look forward(Fig.4-54).

Key to the movement: Turning of body and lifting the right leg must be coordinated. Swinging the broadsword must be quick. The upper and lower parts must be combined.

Usage: If the opponent attacking me from the rear, I turn body quickly and swing the broadsword to parry the weapon of the opponent.

ACTION 2: Continuing from previous movement. Stamp downward with right foot and take a step forward with left foot, the weight remains on the right leg.Turn the body rightward 90 degrees. At the same time, raise the broadsword backward slightly with tip of broadsword pointing downward, the edge of broadsword facing the rear. Swing the left palm downward to the front of chest. Eyes look forward(Fig.4-55).

Fig. 4-55

Key to the movement: Stamping downward with right foot, the weight lowered, waist relaxed. Taking step forward with left foot, the footwork is light, the inside of heel sliding on the floor. The force is focused at the left palm.

Usage: Parry with the left palm, the right hand holding the broadsword to get ready for cutting forward.

ACTION 3: Continuing from previous movement. Land the ball of left foot on the floor and move the weight forward to form a left bow step. At the same time, swing the broadsword backward, upward and cut to the downward front. Support the left palm to upper-front of head. Turn the body leftward 90 degrees. Eyes look to downward-front(Fig.4-56).

Fig. 4-56

Key to the movement: When cutting with the broadsword, the waist and hips turning,the wrist is rotating and shoulders are turning, the force is focused at the edge of broadsword. The left and right hands must be coordinated.

Usage: If the opponent attacking you from the rear, you can turn body quickly and cut forward with the broadsword.

Form 20 Turn Over Body Rightward to Cut

ACTION 1: Continuing from previous movement. Move the weight onto the left leg and lift the right leg with the knee bent, turn the body rightward 90 degrees. At the same time, right hand turns the wrist outward and raises the broadsword to the upper of forehead,the edge of broadsword facing upward. The left palm is pressed to lower-left of the body. Eyes look forward (Fig.4-57).

Fig. 4-57

Key to the movement: Right hand rotating the wrist and turning the body must be combined, the knee bent and hips relaxed.

Usage: If the opponent attacking to me, I turn body quickly and swing the broadsword to parry the weapon of opponent.

ACTION 2: Continuing from previous movement. Turn the body rightward 180 degrees. Stamp downward with right foot, the knee bent and hips relaxed. And then take a step to forward-left with left foot. At the same time, right hand holds and swings the broadsword to the right side of body, the tip of broadsword pointing to the downward front and the edge of broadsword facing downward. Push the left palm rightward in an arc to the front of chest at shoulder level.Eyeslookforward-left(Fig.4-58).

Fig. 4-58

Key to the movement: Keep the body upright, footwork light and steady. The force is focused at the left palm and the edge of broadsword. Get ready at all the time to cut forward with the broadsword.

ACTION 3: Continuing from previous movement. Move the weight to the left leg to form a left bow step. At the same time, swing the left palm to upper-left of head. Right hand holds and swings the broadsword downward, backward, upward, forward and cut to the lower-left. Following cutting of the broadsword,turn the body leftward 75 degrees. Eyes look to downward-front(Fig.4-59).

Fig. 4-59

Key to the movement: Parrying upward with left palm and cutting downward must be coordinated. Moving the weight forward must be combined with the tuning of waist. The force is focused at the edge of broadsword.

Usage: Cutting to the upper section of the opponent with broadsword.

Form 21 White Snake Spits Out Its Tongue

ACTION 1: Continuing from previous movement. Turn the tiptoes of left foot outward, move the weight onto the left leg and lift the right leg with knee bent. Turn the body leftward 35 degrees. At the same time, right hand rotates the wrist and swings the broadsword to in the front of chest, tip of broadsword pointing rightward and edge of broadsword facing forward. Press the left palm downward on the back of broadsword. Eyes look to forward-right(Fig.4-60).

Fig. 4-60

Key to the movement : Turn the toes of left foot outward, the heel serving as an axis .Moving the weight, lifting the right leg, rotating wrist and withdrawing the broadsword must be coordinate.

ACTION 2: Continuing from previous movement. Take a step rightward with right foot, move weight to the right leg to form a right bow step. At the same time, thrust the broadsword to the right at the shoulder level, the tip of broadsword pointing right and edge of broadsword facing forward. Push the left palm in an arc to the left at the shoulder level. Eyes look to forward-right(Fig.4-61).

Fig. 4-61

Key to the movement: Taking the right step, thrusting with broadsword and pushing left palm must be coordinated. Thrusting with the broadsword, the force is the shaking power.

Usage: Parry off the weapon of opponent, take a step forward and thrust to the opponent's chest or ribs with the broadsword.

Form 22 Holding the Moon in the Arms

ACTION 1: Continuing from previous movement. Take a step backward behind the left leg to the rear-left with right foot, ball of the right foot landing on the floor. Turn the body rightward 90 degrees. At the same time, bend and lower the right elbow so the broadsword standing obliquity, tip of broadsword pointing upward and edge of broadsword facing forward. Swing the left palm to the front of chest, to press on the right wrist. Eyes look to forward-right(Fig.4-62).

Fig. 4-62

Key to the movement: After moving weight onto the left leg, take the right step backward.

ACTION 2: Continuing from previous movement. Move the weight backward and turn the body right 70 degrees. Withdraw the broadsword rightward so the tip of broadsword pointing downward front and edge of broadsword facing downward. At the same time, push the left palm forward. Eyes look forward(Fig.4-63).

Fig. 4-63

Key to the movement: Taking the step backward and turning the body must be coordinated. Withdrawing the broadsword and cutting with the broadsword must be quick.

ACTION 3: Continuing from previous movement. Bend the right knee and turn the tiptoes of right foot outward. Turn the body rightward 20 degrees. Take a step to the forward-left with the ball of left foot landing on the floor. At the same time, swing the left palm in a downward arc to hold the guard of broadsword. Move the right hand in an upper arc to the front of chest so the back of broadsword touching on the left arm. Eyes look forward(Fig.4-64).

Fig. 4-64

Key to the movement: The three movements are decomposed movements of withdrawing the broadsword. They must be continuous and quick.

Form 23 Finishing Form

ACTION 1: Continuing from previous movement. Land the whole left foot on the floor. Separate both hands from the front to the respective side, the center of left hand facing forward and the part between the thumb and forefinger facing forward. Eyes look forward(Fig.4-65).

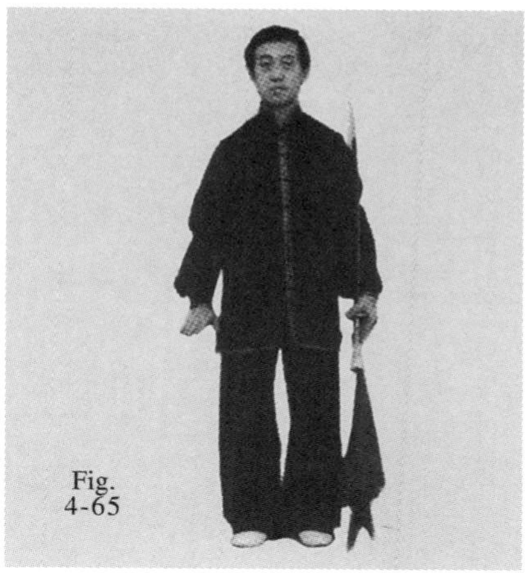
Fig. 4-65

Key to the movement: Take a little skipping step with left foot. Separate the both hands from the front of abdomen, the Qi flowing downward.

ACTION 2: Continuing from previous movement. Right foot is drawn to the inside of left foot so the feet are together. At the same time, swing both bands outward, upward, inward and downward, both arms rotating outward, the right palm is pressed in the right side of right leg, the center of palm facing downward. The left hand holding the broadsword is beside the outside of left leg. Eyes look forward(Fig.4-66).

Key to the movement: Standing upright with feet together, knees bent and hips relaxed. The whole body is relaxed.

Fig. 4-66

ACTION 3: Continuing from previous movement. Relax the right wrist so the center of right palm touching on the right leg. Eyes look forward(Fig.4-67).

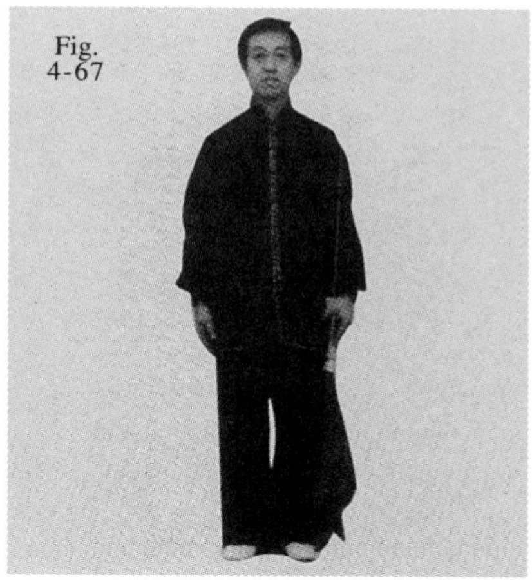
Fig. 4-67

Key to the movement: Stand upright with feet together, hang arms naturally down at sides of thighs. Keep the mind inward, the "Qi" flows to "Dantian".

Afterword

In the preceeding pages, Master Chen Zheng-Lei has faithfully outlined the fundamental practice of the first routine of Chen-style Taijiquan as it was handed down to him by his uncle, Chen Zhao-Pi. Master Chen has many years of experience, teaching countless numbers of students, and is a consummate educator.

That skill in Taijiquan is the result of long and hard hours of daily practice and is not due to any "magical" techniques is well illustrated in the following anecdote related by Master Chen. Chen Zhao-Kui had returned to his home village of Chenjiagou the year after Chen Zhao-Pi passed away. He took over the task of teaching the next generation of Chen family martial art instructors. He once told Chen Zheng-Lei:"If you have in mind the idea of your gongfu surpassing that of ordinary martial artists, then you have to practice gongfu harder than ordinary martial artists. If ordinary martial artists practice ten sets a day, then you practice thirty sets. If ordinary martial artists practice thirty sets a day, then you practice ninety or a hundred sets. Your gongfu will necessarily surpass that of ordinary martial artists when your effort is three times their effort. If you aren't mentally prepared for this, if you can't endure this kind of hardship, then you'd better change your career now before it is too late".

The relationship between teacher and student is an age-old institution in traditional Chinese culture and is the cornerstone of the Chenstyle Taijiquan transmission. Over the course of six generations, from the time of Chen Wang-Ting (c.1600-1680) to the time of Chen Chang-Xing (1771-1853), the Chen Family martial art was refined and fixed into it's current form. The old (or big) frame first routine that had been standardized by Chen Chang-Xing was first published by Chen Ji-Fu (Zhao-Pi) in 1935. This routine had 74 named forms and was apparently the same first routine taught by Chen Fa-Ke in Beijing from the early 1930's. At the same time that this basic routine was being presented to a wider public for the first time, there was an ongoing effort to preserve all of the complexity and nuance in these master practitioners' repertoire by naming every small movement. This can be seen in Chen Ji-Fu's "Old Chenjiagou Taijiquan" with 92 named forms. It was the version created by Chen Fa-Ke, however, with 83 named forms, that ultimately caught on. Largely due to the efforts of his son, Chen Zhao-Kui, it is widely practiced today alongside of the old frame first routine of Chenjiagou (which is presented here in English for the first time).

The other main line of transmission is that of the small frame which was first presented to a wider public in Chen Xin's posthumously published Illustrated Explanation of Chen-style Taijiquan (1933). Chen Xin was the first Chen family member to exhaustively commit to writing the inner principles (*li fa*) of Taijiquan that had previously been passed down only from teacher to student. In addition to recording and preserving, Chen Xin also created something new by fitting the Chen family martial art into a framework of Yi Jing (Book of Changes) philosophy. An example of this can be seen in his listing of the first routine with 64 named forms (coinciding with 64 hexagrams) and dividing these 64 small forms into 13 large forms. It seems more than likely that the references to Taijiquan as "13 Forms" in an early Chen family manual (Liangyi Tang Ben) of the small frame lineage were originally intended at least as an indirect reference to the "13 Chapters" or the Sun Zi (Sun Wu's Art of War).

Translation is at best an art and an inexact science. It has been a daunting task to bring the exhaustive Chinese text to life for the benefit of the growing numbers of Chenstyle Taijiquan enthusiasts worldwide. Inevitably, there will be errors in the translation; it is hoped that interested readers will find them and send in corrections to the publisher for the benefit of further editions. May this first modest effort serve as a starting point and a baseline for a whole new generation of texts - the Chenjiagou Taijiquan Series.

A Brief Biography of Chen Zheng-Lei

Chen-style Taijiquan's 19th Generation Heir

Chen Zheng-Lei was born May 1949 in the place of origin of Chen Style Taijiquan, Chenjiagou Village, in Wen County, Henan Province. In 1985 he graduated from Henan University with a degree in physical education.

From the age of eight, he studied Taijiquan under the tutelage of his two uncles, Chen Zhao-Pi, a famous instructor at the Nanjing Martial Arts Academy, and Chen Zhao-Kui, the son of Chen Fa-Ke. For over 30 years, he has practiced assiduously and achieved marvelous skill; because of this, he is known as an "Outstanding Master of Taijiquan" (Taiji Jingang) and enjoys a high reputation in China and abroad.

From 1974 to 1987, he won in succession over 10 gold medals at the Henan Province Martial Arts Competition, winning the competition on numerous occasions. He has also successfully defended his title as Grand Champion of Taijiquan at two successive National Taijiquan Competitions. In 1983, he was appointed as a coach at the Henan Province Martial Arts Academy. In 1987, he was appointed as a National Level - First Class Martial Arts Judge. At the 1988 China-Japan Taijiquan Competition, he came in first place. From 1988 to 1989, the team he coached won three team first places in the Taijiquan, Taiji Sword (jian), and push hands competitions at the Henan Province and National Martial Arts Meets. Individually, the competitors that he coached won 15 individual gold and 12 individual silver medals.

Putting his spare time to good use, Chen Zheng-Lei has written over 15 books, articles and reports, such as: Compendium of Taiji Boxing and Weapons (Chenshi Taijiquan Xie Huizong), "Discussion of Internal Energy in Taijiquan and Traditional Medical Theory" (Taijiquan Nei Qi Qiantan yu Jingluo Xueshuo). The first volume of the Compendium has already been published in Japan (in Japanese). In 1988, a Beijing publishing house, Gaodeng Jiaoyu Chubanshe, released a teaching videotape, "Transmission of the Art of Chenstyle Taijiquan" (Shi Chuan Chenshi Taijiquan Shu), that featured Chen Zheng-Lei performing Taijiquan and explaining its origin, contents, and practical applications.

In response to numerous invitations from Japan, France, Italy, Switzerland, Hong Kong, and the United States, Master Chen has gone abroad numerous times to teach Taijiquan. In China alone, he has taught thousands of visitors from more than 15 different countries and regions. Over twenty Chenstyle Taijiquan Associations and Chenstyle Taijiquan Research Societies have been established overseas.

Master Chen Zheng-Lei's students have gone on to matriculate at the Beijing and Wuhan Physical Education Institutes and he has trained over 15 of the coaches at those prestigious institutions. He has served as the Principal of Chenjiagou Taijiquan School (appointed 1987), established the Chenjiagou Taijiquan Promotion Center (1987) and served as its Head Coach, as Vice-Director and Head Coach of the Pingdingshan Martial Arts Research Institute (1988), and as Secretary and Standing Member of the Governing Committee of Henan Province (1985) and National Taijiquan Associations. In 1985, during a visit to Japan as a member of a high-level Chen-style delegation, he performed for the Emperor of Japan and was invited to the Imperial Palace as a guest. Master Chen also serves as the Taijiquan Advisor, Honorary Head, and Chairman of Japanese, American (San Francisco, 1990), French, and Italian Chen-style Taijiquan organizations.

In 1986, he was appointed to be a standing member of the Jiaozuo City Political Advisory Committee, and was selected as a Representative to the Henan Province People's Congress in 1988. In 1991, Master Chen was chosen by the editorial department of the China Biographical Yearbook (Zhongguo Renwu Nianjian) to be listed in the 1991 edition. In 1992, he was selected as a National Level High Grade Martial Arts Coach. In 1993, The Wen County Chen-style Taijiquan Research Association was established and Master Chen was selected as its head. In 1993, he was also invited by the Japanese "Chen-style Taijiquan Study Association" to be its advisor. In May of 1993, he went to French Polynesia to teach Taijiquan at the invitation of interested persons there. In July of the same year he went to Malaysia to teach. In December 1993, a written piece of his was selected for publication in Outstanding Individuals of Contemporary Reform (Dangdai Gaige Yingcai).

Master Chen visited the

United States in August 1996 to teach at the 1996 United States Wushu Association's Special Seminar and International Taijiquan Championship.

Brief Introduction to the Translators and Designer

Zhang Xin-Hu: Born in 1962, graduated from the English Department of Xinxiang Teachers College in 1982, several years later he graduated from the English Department of Henan College of Education. He was once a teacher of English in Wenxian No. 1 Senior High School, is now an interpreter in Wenxian, Henan Province China and a Senior Instructor of China Chenjiagou Taijiquan Popularization Center.

He has studied and practised Taijiquan for more than 20 years under the direct guidance of Grand Master Chen Zhenglei. Zhang Xinhu is well-reputed for his Taijiquan, taiji sword routine, Taijiquan teaching and Taijiquan exchange activities. He, at invitations, has taught Taijiquan in Europe for times in the passed few years. In September 2002, being a Senior Instructor, he received a TV interview on subject "Taijiquan" by China Central Television, the top TV station in China.

(Email: xinhzhang @hotrnail.com)

Gregory Bissell: Born in 1955, graduated from the Chinese Tutorial Institute in 1984 with a certificate in Chinese language studies. He began his study of martial arts in 1964 with Judo, and started to learn Chinese martial arts in 1975, studying Southern Shaolin. In 1981 he was introduced to Chen-style Taijiquan by Masters Feng Zhi-Qiang and Ge Chun-Yan of Beijing, China. In 1985, he continued his study of the Chen Style, studying the first routine and single straight-edged sword under Grand Master Chen Zheng-Lei in Wenxian, China. He studied further under Master Feng Zhi-Qiang when he resided in Beijing, China from 1986 to 1989. He is now the editor of the "Chen-style Journal"and lives in Honolulu, Hawaii.

Xu Hailiang: Born in Jilin Province of China, in March 1967. He graduated from Henan Pingdingshan City Taiji and Shaolin Wushu Academy and the Wushu Department of Wuhan physical Culture Institute. He has won numerious championships on Taijiquan, Taiji Swordplay and Shaolin Boxing at national and provincial level for 8 times. At present, he is the coach of Wushu in "Guangdong Province Wushu and Ballroom-dancingCollege".

He is the initiator of "Good Wushu Translation Studio", the main translator of *THE CHINESE WUSHU EXHIBITION SERIES.* What's more, he has translated over 20 pieces of Chinese Wushu Series VCD and several books about Wushu.

Dedication

The publisher would like to thank the following individuals and organizations:

Master Chen Zheng-Lei
Mr. Zhang Xin-Hu
Ms. Jeanne Bissell
Mr. Don Bissell
Ms. Sun Xiao-Yi
Mr. Herb Rich
Mr. Clarence Lu
Mr. J. Justin Meehan, Esq.
Ms. Marie Saulino-Lew
Mr. Rockne Tidd
Mr. Ronald Panunto
Mr. Francis Kemp
Mr. Anthony Arcuri
Mr. Richard Adkins
Mr. Dave Metz
Mr. Gary Sladek
Mr. Reed Brown
Dr. Greg Bantick
Mr. Sonny Garcia
Mr. Jimmy Lee
Mr. Dan Vencak
Mr & Mrs. George Ho
Prof. Douglas Wile
Mr. Stanley Henning
Mr. Michael DeMarco
The Traditional Wushu Association

图书在版编目(CIP)数据

陈氏太极拳剑刀/陈正雷主编;张新虎等译. —郑州:中州古籍出版社,2003.8
ISBN 7-5348-2321-8

Ⅰ.陈… Ⅱ.①陈…②张… Ⅲ.①太极拳,陈氏-基础知识-英文②剑术(武术),陈氏-基础知识-英文,③刀术(武术),陈氏-基础知识-英文 Ⅳ.G852

中国版本图书馆CIP数据核字(2003)第070511号

责任编辑:张 斌
责任核对:柳 明
出版社:中州古籍出版社
(地址:郑州市经五路66号 邮政编码:450002)
发行单位:新华书店
承印单位:河南第一新华印刷厂
开本:880mm × 1230mm 1/32
印张:11.75 **插页**:4
字数:291千字 **印数**:1—3000册
版次:2003年8月第1版 **印次**:2003年8月第1次印刷

书号:ISBN7-5348-2321-8/G · 500 **定价**:68.00元 $28/ £18